Wales and its Boxers

THE FIGHTING TRADITION

Wales and its Boxers

THE FIGHTING TRADITION

EDITED BY PETER STEAD AND GARETH WILLIAMS

UNIVERSITY OF WALES PRESS CARDIFF 2008

An observer is struck by boxing's intense preoccupation with its own history, its continuous homage to a gallery of heroes – or are they saints? . . . The boxing past exists in an uncannily real and vital relationship with the present. The dead are not dead, or not merely dead.

Joyce Carol Oates, *On Boxing* (1987)

www.uwp.co.uk

British Library Cataloguing-in-Publication Data
A catalogue record for this book is available from the British Library.

ISBN 978-0-7083-1915-4

Printed by Gutenberg Press, Tarxien, Malta

CONTENTS

CONTENTS

ACKNOWLEDGEMENTS

Each author has acknowledged in the text the help received from the many writers and commentators who have done so much to hone the great memories of fighters and their fights. Particular thanks are due to Lord Brooks of Tremorfa and Dai Corp of the British Boxing Board of Control, David Petersen, Caroline Jacob and Alan George of Merthyr Public Libraries, Lowri Jenkins and Dr Emma Lile of the National Museum of Wales, Roger Davies of Swansea University and Dr Elizabeth Stead. At the University of Wales Press Dr Dafydd Jones, Sarah Lewis and Siân Chapman were utterly professional and tolerant.

We have selected illustrations that are integral to the chapters that they accompany. We wish to thank the following for their help with the photographs:
National Museum of Wales for Jim Driscoll, Jimmy Wilde and Tom Thomas (shown with Driscoll and Welsh);
Merthyr Public Libraries for Howard Winstone and Eddie Thomas with Dowlais Amateur Boxing Club in the Penydarren gym in 1960;
Dr Glenn Jordan and the Butetown History and Arts Centre for Joe Erskine;
Jon Pountney for his photo of the 'Blacks v. Whites' poster;
Richard Shepherd for Ronnie James and Ike Williams at Ninian Park;
Media Wales Ltd. for Tommy Farr and Joe Calzaghe;
the photos of Freddie Welsh, Jack Petersen and 'Mac and his Boys' come from the private collections of Professor Dai Smith, David Petersen and Dr Stephen Williams respectively.

The editors would like to acknowledge the particular help given by Dai Smith.

PREFACE

There is no equal in sport to the transfixing drama of two men silently stalking each other in the ring, and it is this that lies at the heart of boxing. Nowhere else in the whole of sport is there so much happening, so much movement: fighters are never stationary; boxing is dedicated to perpetual motion. But it is also dedicated to inflicting injury. It is at once the most basic of sports and the most contentious, for it is difficult to be ambivalent about an activity that glorifies the primitive and glamorizes violence on the one hand, whilst highlighting the suppression of fear and the fusing of mind and body in a poetic tension on the other.

The contributors to this volume have all been captivated by the sheer theatre of boxing, whilst at the same time sharing a fascination with the ways in which the culture and aesthetic of the sport have been rooted in certain societies at various stages in their development. Wales has notably been one such society. Since even before the Industrial Revolution, the people of Wales have wanted either to participate in or watch organized fights. That is the background to these essays. In the foreground, however, we highlight the emergence, out of the everyday routine, of heroes who were admired not only for their bravery, strength and tenacity, but also for the grace of their movement and their instinctive understanding of the sheer science of controlled combat.

Initially, crowds of workmen had gathered on hilltops or at fairgrounds to watch local or itinerant fighters. In time, as heroes emerged, their supporters wanted them to prove that they were the best in the land or even in the world. As fame accrued, individual boxers found that, courtesy of the wireless, newsreels and press, they were fighting for a nation. The pressures to succeed in the public arena were greater for boxers than for any other athletes, greater perhaps than for anybody else in any walk of life. When success, or near success, came, the whole of Wales took pride in it quite simply because the qualities of bravery, style and excellence of the one man could now be seen by the world to be the product of a distinct nation.

PETER STEAD and GARETH WILLIAMS

CONTRIBUTORS

Desmond Barry is a Merthyr-born novelist and the author of *Cressida's Bed*, *The Chivalry of Crime* and *A Bloody Good Friday*. His shorter prose has appeared in the *New Yorker* and *Granta*. He teaches creative writing at the University of Glamorgan.

Hywel Teifi Edwards is an author, broadcaster and cultural historian, and was formerly professor in the Department of Welsh at Swansea University.

Martin Johnes teaches history at Swansea University. His previous publications include *A History of Sport in Wales* (2005) and *Soccer and Society: South Wales 1900–39* (2002). He is currently writing a book on the social history of Wales since 1939.

Paul O'Leary is senior lecturer in history and Welsh history at Aberystwyth University, and is the author of *Immigration and Integration: the Irish in Wales, 1798–1922* (2000).

Huw Richards is a freelance sports writer and historian. His most recent books include *A Game for Hooligans: The History of Rugby Union* (2007) and *Dragons and All Blacks: Wales v. New Zealand 1953* (2004).

Dai Smith was born in Tonypandy. He holds a research chair in the cultural history of Wales at Swansea University and has been chair of the Arts Council of Wales since 2006. His biography of Raymond Williams, *A Warrior's Tale*, appeared in 2008.

Peter Stead has lectured in history at universities in Swansea and the USA and is an External Professor at the University of Glamorgan. He writes and comments on Welsh political and popular culture, and is the author of *Acting Wales* (2002).

Daniel G. Williams is senior lecturer in English and Assistant Director of CREW (Centre of Research into the English literature and language of Wales), Swansea University. He is the author of *Ethnicity and Cultural Authority* (2006).

GARETH WILLIAMS is professor of history and director of the Centre for Modern and Contemporary Wales at the University of Glamorgan. He has written widely on the social history of Welsh sport and music, and his most recent book is *Sport: An Anthology* (2007) for the Library of Wales.

STEPHEN M. WILLIAMS lectures in sociology at the University of Glamorgan where his research interests include sport, masculinities and fatherhood. He is the son of the Cardiff-based boxing manager Mac Williams.

'A Brutal Passion'

BARE-KNUCKLE BRUISERS AND MOUNTAIN FIGHTERS

GARETH WILLIAMS

This is a land influenced by religion – a land of churches and chapels – a country beaming with professors of religion and abounding with men who vie with one another in winning their fellow creatures from the moral abyss to a firm, manly and upright footing in the world. Yet on the last Sabbath day, in the glow of an autumnal sun, amidst gorse golden and heather faded – amidst rocks that surpass the deluge in their antiquity and are clad with the hoar of ages – a crowd of men, young and old, assembled to take part in that brutalising practice – a prizefight! The scene was in a hollow on Cilsanws hill behind the Cefn – a secluded place often resorted to by lovers of dogfights, and as often echoing to better and higher occupations. We do not purpose to describe the scene on which an offended God looked down that Sabbath morn. Enough that for a long period these individuals, for we can scarcely call them men, with the ferocity of beasts, fought each other in endeavouring to win a paltry wager of a few shillings, until all recognition by their features was impossible. And, at length, after fighting about 10 rounds, the unfortunate man, David Thomas, became almost helpless; his eyes had a vacant stare, consciousness left him, yet goaded by a brutal mob, he fought for four more rounds. He was then struck so violently that he fell down, never to rise again. The mob then lifted him up and with the assistance of a few stakes, carried him back to that home from which he had issued, a few hours previously in the full vigour of health, a lifeless corpse – the victim of a brutal passion.

Merthyr Telegraph, 25 September 1858

The fighting instinct, especially among men, is as old as mankind, and only gradually did it move from the social reality it had always been to become an organized activity. It was the later seventeenth century before contests with the quarterstaff, sword or cudgel were replaced by fist-fighting; this was due partly to the English gentry's belated rediscovery of Classical accounts of boxing, and partly to the relaxed Restoration climate that followed the technical knockout inflicted on it by Puritanism during the Civil War. Soon formal rules would be drawn up, 'scientific' principles elaborated, championship matches arranged and, by the late eighteenth century even press coverage.

The first recognized English champion was James Figg in 1719, but not until Broughton's Rules of 1743 were strangling, kicking, wrestling and gouging outlawed. Named after the pugilist and trainer Jack Broughton, they stipulated that if a man was knocked down he was allowed thirty seconds to recover, by the end of which his assistants (seconds of another kind) needed to bring him up to the scratch-line in the middle of the ring for another round to begin and the fight to continue. The idea of timed rounds was still an alien concept so that when the champion of the Regency era Tom Cribb fought his first major contest in 1805 it lasted seventy-six rounds and over two hours, while the third William Thompson (Bendigo) fight with Ben Caunt in 1845 lasted ninety-three rounds. By that time the so-called London Prize Ring Rules, which had supplanted Broughton's Rules in 1838, had introduced a roped-off ring and a ten-second count, but their lax observance required the more thorough and longer-lasting revision by the famous Queensberry Rules of 1867, which, although they bore the name of an English aristocrat, were devised by a Welshman.

English prizefighting was at its peak between the 1780s and the 1820s, when it attracted royal patronage and large crowds. The handsome and skilful Whitechapel Jew, Daniel Mendoza (1765–1836), whose flashing eyes and aquiline features adorn contemporary prints, emerged as champion of all England, and he created great interest when he fought an exhibition bout at Neath in 1797. Swansea, too, dubbed an 'intelligent town' only a few years later, has always retained its affection for 'the fights'. In 1886 the 'Swaffham Gypsy' and former champion Jem Mace (d.1910) sparred before a large crowd at the town's Albert Hall, entertaining them with 'one of the finest pieces of boxing ever witnessed in Swansea, since Mace is as graceful as a gazelle and as agile as a chamois'. A hundred years later, as Huw Richards reminds us in a later essay, Swansea was producing champions of its own. One of Mendoza's keenest followers was the Prince of Wales, who attended many – and bet on all – of Mendoza's fights, and ensured that at his coronation as George IV in 1821 Mendoza and other 'brethren of the thudding fists', like

'Gentleman' John Jackson and John Gully, were invited as pageboys. They also doubled usefully as bouncers.

In this golden age when prizefighting had some claims to be England's national sport there would have been a generous sprinkling of Welshmen among the 30,000 who saw Tom Spring fight Jack Langan at Worcester racecourse in 1824. The ring had close associations with the turf, since race meetings were ideal boxing venues, with a wide social spectrum in attendance, as well as the local militia to police the assorted pickpockets, pimps and whores who patiently worked the crowds thronging the course and booths. According to Wetherby's *Racing Calendar*, favourite Welsh race venues were Brecon, Carmarthen, Knighton, Wrexham and Monmouth: the 4,000 who watched a quarryman called Parry beat Powell after 103 rounds at Monmouth in 1824 were there for the races, too. Some of them might also have witnessed the 'slashing contest' of an hour's duration at Brecon in 1835 and been among the 2,000 who saw a fight at Chepstow in 1851. On each occasion the 'Fancy', equally at home at the ringside and on the racecourse, were conspicuously present.

The 'Fancy' were in the Regency period an unholy alliance of the raffish aristocracy and the rough working class, whom the former patronized while the latter did the fighting, for it had been a lower-class sport woven into the fabric of wider society since the pre-industrial period. Prizefighters, jockeys and, in Wales especially, foot-runners – with such champions to the fore as Llanwynno's Griffith Morgan (Guto Nyth Brân) in the eighteenth century and Bryncethin's John Davies (*y Cyw Cloff*, the 'Lame Chick') in the next – were the first professional sportsmen to attain national celebrity. They were brought to a readership literate in English by publications like the *Sporting Magazine* (1792–1830), *Bell's Life in London and Sporting Chronicle* (1822–86), and the writings of the incomparable Pierce Egan, whose five volumes of *Boxiana* (1812–29) could more than a century later still inspire hardbitten journalists like the *New Yorker*'s legendary A. J. Liebling. The 'Fancy' are memorably captured by William Hazlitt in a famous essay of 1822. The question he posed then, 'Reader, have you ever seen a fight?', has lost none of its urgency today, and he depicts the raucous crowd as vividly as the contestants who are spitting blood, teeth and oaths. This apparent mixing of the social classes invites us to view prizefighting as a safety valve, a mechanism of class harmony; but in fact it had more to do with maintaining the authority of the elite by the ostentatious display of dress, reckless gambling, and patronage.

'I never saw anything more terrific than his aspect before he fell. All traces of life, of natural expression, were gone from him. His face was like a human skull, a death's head spouting blood' was Hazlitt's searing description of the defeated Tom Hickman. The victor at 'The Fight' in Hungerford in December 1821 was Bill Neate, a Bristol butcher, one of many 'knights of the cleaver' who were well known for their pugnacity and endurance, had learned bloodiness through the physical demands of their trade, and who personified, as Richard Holt has well expressed it, 'the age-old link between one form of slaughter and another'. There are abundant examples of fighters adopting stage names relating to their occupation, like Wood the Coachman, Hickman the Gasman, Hood the Weaver and Lyons the Waterman. The 'slashing carpenter' was how *Bell's Life* in 1834 described Hopkin Williams, who was ready to fight any man in Cardiff for anything from five to ten sovereigns. Welsh names – Posh Price, Tom Owens – are prominent in the early years of the ring, while Ned Turner (1791– 1826) was dubbed the 'pugilistic prince of Wales' by the *North Wales Gazette* in 1823. A southpaw and an asthmatic, bare-knuckled Ned, born in Southwark of Montgomeryshire parentage, was certainly a crowd-puller, witness the 30,000 who saw him fight Jack Scroggins at Hayes, Middlesex, in 1817.

While boxing's modern history indicates that its epicentre would be the inner city, its origins lay in the countryside, and interest in boxing was still passionate in rural Wales in the twentieth century. In a later essay Hywel Teifi Edwards recalls his youth in 'boxing-mad' Cardiganshire, a county with which middleweight champion Tom Thomas (d.1911) had close family links, and which produced Tommy Farr's trainer, Tom Evans. After all, in 1839 in mid Wales 3,000 had watched Price and Humphreys stalk each other for eighty-five gory rounds at Llanbadarn Fynydd, Radnorshire. Humphreys later died of his injuries.

Just as it required the densely populated environment of the Rhondda for Thomas, Evans and Farr to attain a later fame, it was the industrial uplands of Gwent and Glamorgan that were the first nurseries of the Welsh fighting class. Prizefighting, its chronicler in the Eastern Valley of Gwent, Brian Foster, tells us, preoccupied workers at the Blaenavon Iron and Coal Company, and centred on pugilists from the Pontypool district. Among the nine prizefights known for sure to have taken place in Blaenavon between 1854 and 1868 – only the tip of an iceberg – was the fifty-one-round pitched battle between local bruiser William Gullifer and John Morris of Brynmawr. In June 1863 a bloody encounter took place on Llanhilleth Mountain between the 'Sowhill Chicken' (Sowhill being an unsavoury district of Pontypool) and the 'Tredegar Infant' which was watched by a sizeable crowd, including a 'townie' element, some very probably from nearby Bristol, like London and Liverpool a major port with well-established traditions of dock-side fighting. Two months later they were back to see the 'Butcher Boy' fight 'Stitcher Bach' (the 'little tailor') near Pontypool.

They fought at dawn and in isolated or remote areas, for although bare-knuckle fighting could claim to be a national interest, it was illegal. No single piece of legislation proscribed it, but a shift in moral attitudes and a fear of assembled crowds made it increasingly vulnerable to prosecutions for unlawful assembly and public dis-order. Fights at secluded hillside locations beyond the clutches of authority, particularly in the summer months, became the order of the (early) day, but the law still managed to catch up with Smith Sage and John Tamplin in 1859 for fighting 'somewhere on the mountain between Blaenavon and Garndiffaith'. This bruising pair had been tipped off by a local constable the night before but had chosen to ignore his warning, unmindful that since the establishing of county police forces in mid century local custodians of the peace were less disposed to connive at these daybreak encounters, and better resourced to prevent them. The expressed hope of the Bench in 1859 that a financial penalty would be a deterrent to Sage and Tamplin's imitators was not realized. Ben Andrews and 'Dai Straw-hat', two Blaenavon Company employees, greeted the New Year in 1860 with a fistic ex-change that lasted two hours and twenty minutes, for a mere pound a side. In November 1865 the intense rivalry between Gwent's Eastern Valley and the Forest of Dean found typical and brutal expression in a contest between William Jones of Sowhill and John Morgan on the mountainside above the Glyn Pits on the Crumlin Road. In his recollections of the Sirhywi district, Myfyr Wyn (William Williams, d.1900) remembered the patches between Tredegar and Rhymney left saturated with blood on the first Monday of the month after pay-day – designated as Mabon's Day, after the miners' leader and Rhondda MP – when about a dozen men stripped to the waist and clouted one another 'till their own family could barely recognise them'.

With the number of rounds in these pre-Queensberry Rules days unlimited, encounters that evaded the arm of the law depended on the endurance of the fighters: Edwards fought Stevens on Rhymney Hill above Tredegar in 1860 for 127 rounds. Durability could have been the middle name of Pontypool's notorious Daniel Desmond, an habitual drunkard and law-breaker, regular lodger at Usk jail and rugged mountain fighter, whose encounter with Thomas Walsh of Pont-newynydd was halted after forty-six brutal rounds when, according to a press that saw themselves as moral custodians, the 'palm of black-guardism' was awarded to Desmond. For all their reputation for hard living and harder drinking, none of the hundreds of navvies working in the Eastern Valley laying the railway from Newport was a fighting match for Desmond, who in 1871 knocked one of them into a coma for a week.

A blackguard of even deeper dye could be found at a surprisingly later date a few valleys to the west, in the intimidating form of Redmond Coleman (1882–1927), the 'Iron Man of Iron Lane', Georgetown, Merthyr, who by 1922 was making his one hundred-and-twenty-seventh court appearance for drunkenness and unlawful affray. The ruffianly Coleman was a throwback to an earlier phase in the history of Wales's first industrial town. The collision of the pre-industrial era with technological modernity was encapsulated in the celebration of the arrival from Cardiff of the Taff Vale railway in Merthyr in 1841 by nothing less than a full-on prizefight between John Nash, champion of the Cyfarthfa works, and, from Penderyn, the 'emperor' of Merthyr's sordid 'China', Shoni Sguborfawr (John Jones), who was four years later transported on a convict ship to Van Diemen's Land for his role in the Rebecca Riots.

If such rites of violence seem poised uneasily between the pre-industrial and modern eras, they also acknowledge the grim reality that in places like Merthyr (especially Merthyr, with its foetid sewers, squalid cellars and crippling rate of industrial injury and death) working-class life was nasty, brutish and short. Fist fighting, as it always had done, and as modern boxing still does, exploited the underprivileged, celebrated violence and glamourized the primitive. As such, it was riven by the paradox that such an inhuman activity could also showcase the most human courage, conquest of fear and quest for excellence, for the confined space of the ring was for some an arena of liberation among the restrictions of the working-class environment. Constantly surrounded by a whiff of criminality, it was the last refuge of aristocratic scoundrels and the depressed poor alike, where, as Stephen Williams confirms for the present day, most of the money went to predatory promoters, managers and chisellers. Any inclination we might have to see it as merely exploitative, however, misleads: it was enjoyed by its protagonists, and the successful fighter, from James Figg to Tommy Farr and Joe Calzaghe, acquired status and esteem within his community and far beyond it. He gave symbolic expression to that community's values, and proclaimed the enduring appeal of attributes like courage and virility that were – still are – seen as the essence of manhood, a source of masculine pride and, often, female admiration.

We need not sentimentalize it, for all that. Bare-knuckles historian Dennis Brailsford is surely right to remind us that the older pugilism was harsh and brutal; it made only modest demands on science and skill, far heavier ones on strength and stamina. Prizefighting by the 1800s may have flown in the face of enlightenment values of progress and faith in human benevolence by which society laid such store, but the age was still one of coarseness and savagery where fighting cocks were fitted with vicious metal spurs, tethered bulls baited and dogs pitted against each other. It was an age of public floggings and hangings. As late as the mid nineteenth century public executions were still held in Cardiff, Swansea and Brecon, and it was noted that spectators from Merthyr were always well represented among the crowd of ten to fifteen thousand. In disease-ridden, industry-ravaged Penydarren and Dowlais the frightening rate of infant mortality meant that the average age at death in the 1840s was around 16. Fifty years later the average age at death of bare-knuckles fighters, according to Michael Isenberg, the biographer of John L. Sullivan, was 47, not untypical for working-class men but relatively low, considering that most prizefighters had survived childhood diseases to begin their careers as healthy young men. Bare-knuckle fighting was a violent sport and it thrived in a violent milieu.

But in the built environment it was becoming exposed to an increasingly intrusive constabulary. Driven underground, it became a cat-and-mouse game between magistrates, police and pugilists, acquiring some of the attributes of the chase that so attracted the criminal elements. In the south of England this fugitive aspect explains why many bouts took place near county boundaries where jurisdiction was often vague and policing intermittent. For that reason, Bendigo fought Ben Caunt in 1845 on the county perimeter at Newport Pagnell, and the famous Sayers–Heenan fight of 1860 took place at Farnborough on the boundary between Sussex and Hampshire. Tom Hickman – Hazlitt's 'Gasman' – fought Robinson in Monmouthshire in 1827 because they had been chased over the border by the magistrates of Herefordshire. To the *Merthyr Telegraph* in June 1862 'one of the most determined bulldog fights ever witnessed in the neighbourhood' – some 'hard pummelling' between Billo Bach and Jem Hundred for an hour and a quarter – confirmed the bad name of the area between Tafarnau Bach and Llangynidr, where the borders of Glamorgan, Monmouthshire and Breconshire met, as a 'complete nursery for would-be champions'.

Inevitably, there were occasions when the law triumphed. In April 1865, before the Regulation of Railways Act in 1868 banned special trips to prizefights, early-morning excursionists from Cardiff who had left at 4 a.m. to see a needle fight between Ned Llewellyn and John Williams (Jack Portobello) on Rumney Moors on the Glamorgan–Gwent boundary were met by the Monmouthshire police. At other generally better-policed times the law could still be ineffective: in 1884 a solitary constable arrived too late to prevent a fight on land between Tondu and Maesteg between John Davey, an engineer, and Thomas Davies, a miner. The two 20-year-olds fought twenty-eight rounds in forty minutes, an indication of a rapid knock-down rate, in front of an estimated 4,000, many of whom had travelled a long distance and compensated for the privations of the previous day's journey by forcing their way into a pub at Brynmenyn where they had caroused all night. On the other hand, a tip-off was valuable to Edmund Richards (aka Edmund Cabbage) of Pengam, who was due to fight William Lloyd of Tirphil in 1886. Whether or not Cabbage was so-named because of his horticultural interests, his ears or his intellectual limitations, on hearing that the police had got wind of the impending bout he at least had the sense to keep away, and the fixture was postponed.

Deferment, however, could be merely spatial rather than temporal when there was sufficient determination to see a contest completed. When a policeman approached the fight on Cefncilsanws Mountain above Merthyr in September 1858 which heads this essay, 'the crowd dispersed from that place, but assembled immediately after in a place a little further on and began to fight again', which resulted in the death of 30-year-old David Thomas and the committal for manslaughter of his apparently reluctant 18-year-old opponent Edward Lewis. In April 1862, before – like Bendigo earlier, and the revivalist Seth Joshua later – he renounced prizefighting for pentecostalism, Dan Thomas ('Dan Bach Pontypridd', d.1923) fought Joe Nolan of Birmingham for the British lightweight championship and £200-a-side near Reading, where the 'belligerents were surprised on three occasions and three rings were pitched in as many districts, the authorities being determined to prevent the fight taking place'. But it did, and was fought to a draw.

While ruffians like Pontypool's Desmond and Merthyr's Coleman were well known to the law, some fighters – or their backers – had the presence of mind to stage their operations in localities where their notorious reputations had yet to precede them. Evan Roberts (a 'well-known pugilist', not the evangelist) and John Richards, both of Maerdy, went over to Merthyr Mountain to slug it out for an hour and a quarter in 1885, and no quarter was given. Richards was 'possessed of only one eye, and his opponent, alive to the advantage to be gained by placing that solitary organ *hors de combat*, devoted all his energies toward that end'. The following year, two blacksmiths from Newcastle and Bristol – one of them, Finneghan, already sporting a black eye (the result, he claimed, of being hit by 'a piece of iron') – were summonsed for 'going to engage in a prizefight' in neutral Newport, where it was hoped they were less known to the authorities. Two Rhondda miners, Hutchins and Northey, were in 1891 similarly motivated to begin hostilities at the other end of the county from their own. They had already been bound over by Bridgend magistrates to keep the peace; at Cockett, Swansea, the police were deceived when their followers divided into two, and they eventually exhibited their art and sullen craft at Cwmdonkin Park, where Northey was banged so fiercely he failed to come up to scratch for the fifth round.

At least he was alive, since death was often bidden to the feast of Welsh prizefighting. The first Welsh champion, Ned Turner, spent two years in Newgate for killing a man in the ring, while Brown and Hollister were two butchers who fought literally to the finish at Swansea in 1831, when the latter was carried away unconscious and was 'considered past recovery'. In 1861 the occupations and the venue were different, but not the conclusion, when two colliers, David Mathews and Thomas Pugh, commenced operations near Cefn Mawr, Wrexham, at daybreak, and in round thirty-six Mathews was knocked down and broke his neck. In round thirty-nine blood gushed from his mouth and ears, indicating a haemorrhage and a manslaughter charge. In 1890 a similar judgement was brought against Cornelius Collins, after John Hughes, a haulier, died of his injuries in a fight on Llanwynno Mountain. Fittingly, it was in a converted slaughter-house in May 1894 that Aberaman's Twm Edwards, brother of later Glamorgan county councillor Wil Jon Edwards, saw his opponent die in the ring. They were fighting for £10 a side and with five-ounce gloves, though it was not a blow from Twm that killed David Rees but the force with which his head hit the floor; Twm was charged with man-slaughter and did time in the cells.

While the unfortunate Rees was, according to the doctor who examined him, 'a fairly nourished and fairly flabby well-developed man [who] had not the appearance of being well trained', the classic prizefighters, with their trademark rolling gait and squat, corpulent build, kept fighting-fit through skipping, jumping and running, despite an occasional physical disability. Just as the doubly handicapped James Bourke ('Deaf' Bourke) fought wearing a truss, Ewenny's George Heycock, 'The Bruiser' (c.1820s) had a deformed leg from a football injury. Legislation, regulation and increasing distaste for the brutality and criminal associations of the prize-ring, allied to the new expect-ations of spectators who still sought spectacle but within a safe and controlled environment, were by the mid nineteenth century marginal-izing old-style prizefighters. In so doing, they were attesting to their failure to attain the respectability of footballers, athletes, cricketers and even their one-time allies, jockeys, because they lacked a unified regulating agency to codify rules and oversee challenges and championships. That is what the 'civilizing' Queensberry Rules tried to do in 1867; though their impact was not immediate, they announced the beginning of the end for prizefighting, and it was no coincidence that the last public hanging took place the following year. In truth, the demise of the bare-knuckles prize-ring had been signalled in 1860 by the uproar which attended the Sayers–Heenan championship fight and Sayers's subsequent retirement. Prizefighting's defiance, as Dennis Brailsford portrays it, was symbolized at Sayers's funeral five years later, when the only dignity lent to the rough-house proceedings was the sight of his enormous mastiff sitting bolt upright and alone in the open carriage that followed the coffin.

While pugilists gravitated increasingly to travelling exhibitions and fairground booths, the irreconcilables made a separate peace. Toughened by their hard occupations in iron and coal they became an almost uniquely Welsh breed: mountain fighters, intimidating and frightening, like 'Dai'r Dychrynllyd' (Terrible Dai) from whom the physically imposing giant Watcyn Thomas, Wales's rugby captain between the two world wars, claimed descent. Such uncompromisingly rugged specimens supplemented their industrial-strength durability with raw meat and eggs, reckoned to give them ferocity and stamina, draughts of sour buttermilk (*llaeth enwyn*) and, during fights, swigs of something stronger. *How Green was My Valley*'s pugilistic duo Dai Bando and Cyfartha Lewis, 'rough but gentle men', are deceptively jolly; in reality, no one doubted mountain fighters' ferocity, and with their scarred faces, broken teeth and misshapen noses they were feared even in the fairgrounds.

The Queensberry Rules were drawn up in 1867 to replace the London Prize Ring Rules of 1838, meet spectator preference for displays of skill over savagery, and win back respectable, even royal, patronage. They took their name from John Sholto Douglas (1844–1900), the syphilitic Marquess of Queensberry, who had 'never known a degree be worth two pence to anybody'. Several times married, he was divorced by his second wife on the grounds of his 'frigidity, impotence and malformation of the parts of generation', but he still fathered four children, one of whom, Lord Alfred Douglas, would achieve notoriety as Oscar Wilde's 'Bosie'. The man who actually devised the rules that bore the noble lord's name could not himself boast such a lurid background: he came from Llanelli. John Graham Chambers (1843–83) went from Llanelly House to Eton and Cambridge, and spent his short life organizing sports events. The range of his interests and the energy he brought to promoting them was astonishing, and among the events he helped stage were the Boat Race, the first Cup Final and the first Amateur Athletic Club (later AAA) championships. He was champion walker of England, instituted championships for billiards, boxing and cycling, accompanied (in a boat) Captain Webb on his Channel swim and opened a Welsh shop in Chelsea. His brother Charles, less active, was nevertheless prominent in south Wales's sporting circles and became the first President of the Welsh Rugby Union. In 1867 J. G. Chambers persuaded the Marquess of Queensberry to dedicate a set of challenge cups for the AAC's first amateur boxing championships, and Chambers himself drew up the rules.

Hitherto the rounds in prizefighting continued until a man was felled, could last up to forty minutes, and were unlimited in number; under the old dispensation, too, even when contestants were knocked into unconsciousness, attendants (seconds) were allowed half a minute to bring them round before continuing. Where, in sum, there had been imprecision and even deliberate vagueness, the new rules were categorical, from the use of six-ounce padded gloves to the size of the ring (24 feet square), and from the length of a round (three minutes) to a specific ten seconds allowed for recovery from knock-down. Soon there would be weight categories too, so that blatant mismatches of size and weight – like Heenan's 195 lb, 6 ft 2 in. v. Sayers' 152 lb, 5 ft 8 in., in 1860 – were now ruled out. The new rules also prohibited the staging of fights on turf, paving the way for indoor arenas, the charging and regulating of admission fees, and therefore the control, if not exactly the civilizing, of the crowd. The Queensberry Rules, with their credibility underpinned by the aristocratic title that bestowed social status, brought prizefighting within the law. Boxing could now be better regulated and, it was hoped, a more rational, responsible and reputable business.

But the change did not come about overnight. The last English bare-knuckle championship was held in 1885, the last in the USA in

14

1889 between the bloated 'Boston Strongboy' John L. Sullivan and Jake Kilbrain. By then, Sullivan's fame had crossed the Atlantic, and when he visited Cardiff in January 1888 he was cheered by bigger crowds than had greeted Gladstone. His bout with 'Gentleman Jim' Corbett in front of 10,000 in a brightly illuminated arena in New Orleans in 1892 was the first gloved heavyweight championship, but if this was a turning point it was slow to turn. In Merthyr the young tearaway Redmond Coleman was, in 1892, only 10 years old. The blows that fatally floored David Rees in his 1894 fight with Twm Edwards came after forty-two rounds, with scarcely a policeman's helmet or Queensberry Rule in sight. Each round had ended not because a bell sounded to signal three minutes were up but because one of the men was exhausted. This was nine years after the *Aberdare Times* had in 1885 protested that:

> A more disgusting thing than prizefighting it is hardly possible to conceive . . . That it should happen in our midst is an outrage to decency, and the brutes who take part in it . . . should be punished severely. We cannot look upon such people as anything other than beasts.

In 1886 two Penygraig colliers, Powell and Foster, were charged with fighting on Cymmer Mountain. They had fought to a draw for two hours, at which stage the law arrived and the crowd dispersed, but the contestants were too drained to follow suit. Jack Northey was similarly left behind by the general stampede when the officers arrived to break up his fight with the Mountain Ash bruiser Nobby Wynne at Llantrisant in 1885; the hapless Northey was carted off to the local police station. The local constabulary concealed themselves in advance of a fight on Garth Mountain in 1890, waited for the crowd to assemble and the men to strip and begin fighting, then announced their presence. John Knifton, who had been trained by, and sparred with, the legendary Jem Mace, was in 1886 ambitiously hailed as 'champion of the world', or at least Merthyr, where he was well known for his fistic accomplishments. In 1887 he revealed an unexpectedly cultural side when he sent a sovereign to boost the funds of the Merthyr Orpheus Choral Society and even attended a rehearsal, for he was reckoned to be a 'man of great musical talent'. Were the old warriors getting soft? Hardly. In 1891 the *Merthyr Express* feared there was actually a revival of the good old cause. Those who thought prizefighting had finally been confined to the fairground booth on the fringes of the town, or consigned to the mountainside above it, had, it seemed, to think again. Horrified worshippers making for Bethania Chapel, Dowlais, one Sunday morning in 1892 were forced to skirt around an hour-long fight between two men 'literally covered with blood'.

The tide was turning, for all that. Generally speaking, mountain fighting was doomed as much by a widening humanitarianism as by its own illegality and brutishness, and it became obsolete as new criteria of fair and regulated competition condemned it to crackle away in its unreconstructed state on the margins of urban culture. It lingered on in the bloody spots above the valley townships, on the Thomastown Tips and in Graig Woods, an anachronism in a modern world.

What meaning could there have been to this mayhem? Was the prize-ring a forum for cultural conflict, an assertion of the atavistic as it strained against the stays of civilization? Are we, as sociologists claim, participants in an evolutionary progress which is gradually weaning us away from inflicting violence on each other to settling disputes by more rational means? World events and daily accounts of sickening interpersonal abuse suggest otherwise. Dog-fighting was officially prohibited in 1911 but it still takes place. Fist-fighting, viewed askance by the law since the eighteenth century, is likewise far from dead:

> Hundreds gathered to watch an illegal bareknuckle fight in Treforest at the weekend. Police were dispatched to the Top Tips at midday on Sunday, where a crowd of more than 200 from around south Wales had gathered to watch the unlicensed event. The arrival of the police prevented the fight from starting, but a makeshift boxing ring had already been erected . . .

This report could have appeared in any Welsh newspaper of the last hundred and fifty years. It is in fact taken from the *Pontypridd and Llantrisant Observer* of 6 April 2006.

'Peerless'

THE LIFE AND LEGEND OF JIM DRISCOLL

PAUL O'LEARY

The image is both casually familiar and startling at the same time. Two boxers circle each other warily in the ring, cautiously seeking out each other's defensive weaknesses. They jab and probe before attacking in earnest. Around them, in a penumbra of semi-darkness, a large crowd savours the spectacle of two men engaged in a controlled fighting contest. Their desire is to see one boxer break the deadlock and take the lead. Yet the thirst for a knockout that would bring the contest to a dramatic and definitive end is tempered by the wish to see the spectacle continue as long as possible.

The picture could be that of any professional boxing match during the twentieth century. What is startling about this familiar image is the pale and wiry, seemingly fragile, body of one of the contestants. For this is Jim Driscoll, and he is dressed only in gloves, boots and very brief trunks, while his opponent wears the more conventional longer shorts. The era is significant here. Before the First World War few male bodies were seen in such public semi-nudity, let alone filmed in that state. Jim Driscoll was a member of the first generation of sportspeople to have their sporting exploits recorded on film and shown in cinemas. In a generation when rugby and soccer players were so overdressed that they barely displayed their knees, let alone any other part of their anatomy, film ensured that Driscoll's was possibly the most widely viewed male body in Welsh history to that date.

A boxing match took place in an all-male environment, and the bodies pitted against each other in the ring were subjected to the gaze of other males only. Even so, the contrast with the audience in this film of a pre-war bout is striking. Among the spectators a grey-bearded man rises from his seat and makes his way to the ringside. He is top-hatted, wearing the black evening dress that marked him out to his contemporaries as a middle-class figure on public display. These two individuals – the scantily dressed boxer and the sumptuously dressed spectator – were the axis around which professional boxing turned before First World War. Jim Driscoll was a figure who bestrode that world.

Jim Driscoll was born in 1880 and grew up in Ellen Street, in a district of Cardiff known officially as Newtown and unofficially as 'Little Ireland'. Since the 1850s this part of the town had been the bane of the lives of local public health officials, who saw it as a cesspit of poor sanitation and unrespectable behaviour. The influences on the young Driscoll at this time would shape his future both as a boxer and as a man. Newtown was the closest Cardiff had to an Irish ghetto. It was bounded by a railway line to the north, a goods yard to the east, the dock feeder to the west and the docks themselves to the south. It was these physical boundaries that helped give the district its distinctive character. Crucially, it was not entirely separate from the rest of the city, nor were its inhabitants all Irish or of Irish descent, but the area did have a distinctive identity. For the Irish who lived there, this sense of who they were was partly rooted in the Catholic Church, which established a parish to cater for the district. St Paul's Church and Catholicism would play a key role in the upbringing and adult life of Jim Driscoll the combative sportsman.

Against a general background of basic living standards, the Driscoll family received a cruel early blow that reduced their circumstances even further. Less than a year after Jim was born, his father, Cornelius, was killed in a tragic accident in a goods yard near their home. This left his mother, Elizabeth, and a family of four children to fend for themselves in acute poverty (another sister had died a year before Jim was born). To be left without a husband in charge of young children in late Victorian Britain was one of the most vulnerable positions for a woman to be in. Elizabeth Driscoll was forced to accept parish relief, and the family had to move house in Ellen Street in order to adapt to their new circumstances – a reminder that a family's status often depended on which part of a street working people lived in, as much as on the neighbourhood. Soon Elizabeth Driscoll acquired the arduous and uncertain work of shovelling potatoes and fish from the holds of ships on the dockside. By 1891 – when Jim was 10 years old – the family was boarding at 3 Ellen Street in an overcrowded household of ten people. It was in this family environment of grinding poverty that Jim Driscoll grew up.

Another south Walian of Irish extraction, the working-class novelist Joseph Keating, wrote of his upbringing in the 1870s that 'boxing was a most admired accomplishment in our quarter'. Moreover, unlike the hostility that Nonconformist ministers displayed towards organized sport – and especially boxing, which was of dubious 'respectability' – Catholic priests embraced sport as a way of channelling the energies of young men into disciplined activities under the influence of the Church. A number of priests established boxing schools for youngsters in their parishes as a way of instilling in them self-discipline and diverting them from more dangerous activities on the streets. There was never a conflict between religion and boxing as far as Driscoll was concerned. Both piety and sport were essential ingredients in the distinctive popular culture that he inhabited in his youth and which, in turn, he helped shape as an adult.

The young Jim was just old enough to have seen at first hand the excited crowds thronging the streets of Cardiff in January 1888 to greet the Irish-American boxer John L. Sullivan on his visit to the town. Sullivan was already a well-known public figure, whose exploits in the ring were read about and discussed on both sides of the Atlantic. On his arrival in Cardiff members of the crowd unhitched the horses from his coach outside the railway station and pulled it through the streets of cheering crowds in a traditional symbol of respect. Even if the young Jim had not been present in person to witness these events, it was an occasion that would have been discussed and savoured among the Cardiff Irish community of which Driscoll and his family were members. Irishmen or women receiving public approbation in Welsh towns was a novel experience at this time, and it would have been a source of pride that 'one of their own' was fêted by the assembled throng. Boxing was a prized skill in Irish émigré communities on both sides of the Atlantic, and in the fullness of time Driscoll's own fighting career would come to exemplify that trans-Atlantic world.

Driscoll's working life began in the offices of the *Evening Express* in St Mary's Street, Cardiff, where he worked as a printer's devil. The boys who worked in the machine room formed their own boxing club, and wrapped waste newspapers around their fists in place of the gloves they could not afford to buy. Driscoll soon put this world behind him, however, and his boxing career began in earnest in the tough milieu of travelling fairground boxing booths. It was a testing apprentice-ship for such a slightly built teenager, but it taught him the virtues of agility and a sound defence against opponents of greater strength and bulk. By the age of 17 he was earning a sovereign a month for his efforts in the ring.

Those years exposed him to the harsh realities of aggressive and often violent masculinity in places like the booming coalfield settlements of the Rhondda Valleys. These raw townships were boisterous places with large populations of young males, mainly from rural areas in Wales and England, who had been attracted by the good wages to be had mining coal by pick and shovel in the pits. In these places, burly colliers enjoying their rare leisure hours and even rarer holidays fancied their chances against less well-built fairground boxers like Driscoll. As well as the boxing spectacle, the promoter often ensured that there would be betting on contests, thus introducing Driscoll to the sharp end of working-class betting on sport. He would retain a taste for gambling throughout his adult life, with a particular fondness for betting on horses.

This period of Driscoll's life is surrounded by folklore of the kind that sticks to successful sportspeople like barnacles to a ship. It is said that Jack Scarrott, who ran the booths, tied the young boxer's hands behind his back and offered a gold sovereign to anyone who could hit his boxer on the nose inside a minute. So adept was Driscoll at avoiding blows that Scarrott's sovereign remained in his pocket. Whether this actually happened or simply grew as part of the folklore surrounding Driscoll's early career is largely immaterial, because, as with most legendary tales, there was a kernel of truth at the heart of the story. The daunting experience of performing against all comers a number of times each day ensured that Jim's reflexes were sharpened and his defensive skills well honed. In the booths he gained valuable sparring practice and built up his stamina, a quality that would stand him in good stead in some of the very long bouts of his professional career that were then the norm.

Driscoll's professional boxing career spanned the years 1901–19, being interrupted by service in the army during the First World War. He fought a total of seventy-four professional bouts, winning fifty-six of them and drawing six, while nine were 'no decision' fights. Remarkably, he lost only three contests during these years. By the standards of his day he fought relatively few bouts. Other boxers endured punishing schedules, such as his near-contemporary, Jimmy Wilde, who fought 864 bouts in his career. Even so, during 1901 Driscoll took part in eleven contests and won them all. A major landmark occurred on Christmas Eve that year, when he beat Joe Ross to become Featherweight Champion of Wales. The following February he fought for the first time at the National Sporting Club (NSC) in London, a place that would become one of his favourite venues for both fighting and watching others compete. It was here that most of his title fights took place. On 28 May 1906 he beat Joe Bowker to take the British Featherweight title for the first time. A little under two years later he fought the Australian Charlie Griffin for the British Empire Featherweight title at the NSC, and won.

During the early years of his career, Driscoll trained assiduously, doing about seven miles of roadwork each morning, according to one source. But it was his skill and technique that set Driscoll apart. According to the boxing historian Fred Deakin, Driscoll was the 'complete scientific boxer'. Scientific boxing was based on defeating an opponent by speed and knowledge of an opponent's strengths and weaknesses, rather than by relying simply on brawn This style had been pioneered by the American fighter James J. Corbett, who had beaten John L. Sullivan in 1892, in the first championship fight under the Queensberry Rules. This was the first decisive move away from the dangerous, punishing and bloody world of the brawling prizefighter and a tentative step towards acceptance by the wider society.

Such precarious acceptance would always be imperilled by the close link that existed between betting on boxers and betting on horse racing, and although this was weaker by the early twentieth century it was a tradition that was continued by Jim Driscoll. His first trainer, Bob Downey, had been well known in the world of trotting. When Driscoll married Edith Wiltshire in June 1907 this connection with the world of horse racing was cemented further. His new father-in-law owned some of the best trotting horses in the country. Driscoll gambled on the horses and even took bets himself, and it is likely that a significant portion of his earnings was lost on the country's racecourses. Gambling was a central feature of male working-class culture, and was denigrated by middle-class reformers because it encouraged working men to expect something for nothing, but also because it meant living for the moment, rather than industriously saving for the future.

It was a formidable left hand that set Driscoll apart as a boxer. He used it to keep opponents at bay, preferring to hit but not get hit, before finishing a contest with a shattering right. This was a skill he demonstrated to great effect to an entirely new audience when he toured the United States between November 1908 and February 1909. Driscoll fought two six-round 'no decision' contests in New York and Philadelphia that greatly impressed sports journalists, with one describing him as having a 'rattle-snake strike'. In Boston he arranged a rematch with the Australian Charlie Griffin, whom he had beaten for the British Empire earlier that year. Griffin had been touring the United States, where he spread the story that he had been robbed of the decision against Driscoll at the NSC in London. Angered by this, Driscoll insisted on a rematch with the Australian before he returned to Britain: in the event, he won the bout and a great deal of satisfaction, earning nearly $3,500 in the process.

Driscoll breezed through several other fights before reaching the climax of his American tour, when he fought Abe Attell for the World Featherweight title on 19 February 1909. This was to be another 'no decision' contest over ten rounds, meaning that one of the boxers had to be knocked out for a decision to be given; winning on points would not be allowed. Driscoll failed to defeat Attell, but the verdict delivered the next day by sports writers who had been at the ringside was in the Welshman's favour. The consensus in the press was that Jim won at least seven rounds on points and was thus adjudged outright winner, but without a knockout Attell remained world champion. The usually fiercely partisan American press recognized that Driscoll was clearly the superior fighter and crowned him with the epithet 'Peerless', a tag that was to remain with him for the rest of his life.

It was after the bout with Abe Attell that Driscoll's legendary status as something more than just a gifted and successful boxer was sealed. The contest for the World Featherweight title had left the unsatisfactory state of affairs where Attell remained champion but his opponent was recognized as the winner of the fight. A return match with the world title at stake was offered, but Driscoll turned it down so that he could return to Wales to honour a commitment made before leaving for

America, to box in a charity bout for Nazareth House, a Catholic orphanage in Cardiff. The legend of 'Peerless' Jim Driscoll was now nearly complete. Not only had he risen from poverty to make his way in the uncompromising world of professional boxing, he had been deprived of recognition as world champion by a combination of the practices of American boxing and his commitment to the poor Catholic orphans of his home town. Striving, challenging, piety and sacrifice are all words that could sum up the transformation of the boxer Jim Driscoll into the legendary 'Peerless'.

The legend in motion was demonstrated by the reception at Cardiff on his return. He was greeted by crowds lining the streets, just as John L. Sullivan had been twenty-one years previously. This time the hero was home-grown, and he was carried on the shoulders of supporters back to his home in Newtown. As far as these supporters were concerned, the experience in America had made Driscoll in fact, if not by title, world champion, and he was now frequently billed as such before fights. His popularity enabled him to develop a popular music-hall sparring and punchball routine. His success and fame continued to grow when, in February 1910, he beat Seaman Hayes in a contest for the first Lonsdale belt at the NSC. This was a prelude to the most controversial fight of his career, when he met the other great Welsh fighter of the day, Freddie Welsh.

The two boxers had contrasting styles and attitudes to their sport, and this in turn produced polarized attitudes to them. The London establishment perspective of the National Sporting Club was supplied by Viscount Knebworth, author of the Lonsdale Library volume *Boxing: A Guide to Modern Methods*, in which he expressed his displeasure at the money-making activities and self-publicity of Freddie Welsh: 'This cold, callous attitude of making boxing not a grand fight so much as a paying proposition, if it is wise, is certainly not attractive', he opined. The nostalgic Knebworths of the boxing world wanted uncomplicated pugilism, a style they found in the upright stance of fighters like Jim Driscoll. Even so, the Viscount found it difficult to express unalloyed appreciation of this product of a Cardiff Irish background: 'Out of the ring Driscoll was erratic, quick tempered, excitable and generally Welsh', he wrote. Coming from this source and put in these terms, being 'generally Welsh' was clearly not intended to be a compliment.

This cutting assessment of Driscoll's personality and nationality positively dripped with English aristocratic condescension. It is likely that it stemmed from a bizarre incident at the NSC in 1913, when the popular British heavyweight 'Bombardier' Billy Wells was knocked out in seventy-three seconds by an unknown Frenchman, Georges Carpentier. An angry Driscoll jumped into the ring, calling Wells a coward, before bursting into tears and having to be led back to his seat by Lord Lonsdale. In spite of his Irish background, Driscoll shared the chauvinistic British nationalism of his day and could not bear to see a British boxer losing so quickly and ignominiously to an opponent from the Continent. Displays of emotion of the kind he demonstrated on that occasion were considered distinctly 'un-English'. By contrast, inside the ring Viscount Knebworth considered Driscoll to be 'as cool as ice'. It was this quality of icy coolness when faced with a formidable opponent that broke through the aristocrat's cultural prejudices and garnered his grudging admiration.

That legendary coolness broke down in the fight with Freddie Welsh. The preparations for the match did not augur well for a focused display of skill worthy of the two athletes. The two had been firm friends, but the pre-fight reports in newspapers and nit-picking over the terms of the contest were so intense and irritating that by the time the bout took place the friendship had evaporated. Moreover, instead of producing a feast of skill, the contrasting styles of fighting simply frustrated both fighters and spectators.

The fight took place at the American Roller Rink in Cardiff on 20 December 1910. Welsh dominated the opening rounds. His method of avoiding Driscoll's famous straight left was by clinching and throwing illegal kidney punches. By the sixth round both boxers were visibly irate by the way the fight was developing and it was clear to all that Driscoll was being prevented from displaying his superb style. He finally snapped in the tenth round, responding to Welsh's persistent foul play by head-butting him repeatedly under the chin, driving him back across the ring and forcing the referee to disqualify Driscoll.

There had been attempts to get the fight stopped, on the grounds that it prejudiced the morality of Cardiff. A petition signed by local citizens, including the Bishop of Llandaff and the President of the Cardiff Free Church Council, believed that the contest 'would have a degrading effect upon the people'. While many welcomed the opportunity to view the spectacle of the two most successful Welsh boxers of the day pitted against one another, others felt that the sight of two men seeking to knock each other out did little to add to the sum of human happiness. In spite of the sport's popularity, the legal status of boxing remained ambiguous in the years immediately preceding the war. A scheduled fight between Driscoll and the Birmingham boxer Owen Moran was banned in case it caused a breach of the peace. An appeal supported by Lord Lonsdale failed to overturn this decision, but the Crown eventually withdrew its objections and the fight went ahead in January 1913, ending in a disappointing draw. However, this fight was a legal turning point, because the law made no further interventions in an attempt to stop a boxing match.

The bout against Moran in January 1913 appeared to be the end of Driscoll's professional career. There were no more fights in the next eighteen months, and on the outbreak of war Driscoll quickly and enthusiastically joined the Welsh Horse, an example that prompted other local boxers to follow his lead and volunteer for service at the Front. After becoming Sergeant Driscoll, he used his unrivalled sporting experience and knowledge of physical fitness to train his fellow soldiers. The regiment quickly built up a reputation for boxing and won a number of titles, cups and medals. The pressure on Driscoll to train soldiers and to perform exhibitions along the line gradually told on his health, and this only improved once the war came to an end and he was relieved of his onerous duties.

Even apart from his time in the army Driscoll was a noted trainer and coach, who taught successful boxers like Jimmy Wilde a great deal. However, his influence on the sport went beyond personal advice and was disseminated through a variety of manuals designed to instruct others in the cultivation of perfect boxing technique. These included *Ringcraft*, first published in 1910, which went through three editions, *Out-fighting or Long-range Boxing*, which was published on the eve of the First World War and republished in 1921, and his *Text-book of Boxing*, which went through four editions. His manual on *The Straight Left and How to Cultivate It* was a popular publication in boxing circles and went through at least six editions; it continued to be republished several decades after he died.

These publications spanned the First World War, and so – unexpectedly – did Driscoll's boxing career. He was in his late thirties when he returned to the ring after leaving the army. After a gap of six years he was well past his best as a sportsman, as shown by the fact that of his last three bouts in 1919 one was a win, one a draw, and one he lost to a technical knockout. The comeback was motivated by financial need, and it was clear that he could still draw the paying crowds. When he fought Francis Rossi of Pontypridd over twenty rounds at Mountain Ash at the end of May 1919 he earned nearly £1,000 for his efforts.

Driscoll's last fight was against the French champion Charles Ledoux, the so-called 'Little Assassin', for the European Featherweight title, on 20 October 1919 at the NSC. It was an unfortunate anticlimax to a career that had seen such remarkable and consistent success before 1914. Driscoll had been unwell with severe stomach pains in the days leading up to the contest. To the shock of the spectators on the day of the fight, he appeared toothless and grey when he entered the ring and looked drawn and haggard. But in spite of this poor health, the decisive factor would turn out to be the length of the fight. The much younger Ledoux had insisted on a twenty-round bout, knowing that he would have the advantage over his older opponent in the later stages. For the first fifteen rounds Driscoll outclassed the Frenchman, drawing on his well-honed skills and the stamina he had built up over a long career. However, at the beginning of the sixteenth round Driscoll's corner realized that their man could continue no longer and, against his wishes, threw in the towel. It was an ignominious end to what had been such a distinguished career. A testimonial for Driscoll subsequently raised nearly £5,000. In the years that followed his retirement from the ring his health deteriorated until he died of pneumonia on 30 January 1925 at the age of 44.

If the building materials of the Driscoll legend were hewn out of the rugged landscape of his early life and subsequent successes of his sporting career, the coping-stone of that legend was put in place by his early death in relative poverty in his native Newtown in January 1925. His boxing career continued long enough, and his life ended young enough, for him to avoid the slow decline into old age and obscurity that has been the lot of many once-famous boxers. Just as film had spread images of Driscoll's sporting achievements to a wider audience than that of the spectators who were physically present to view his fights, so the same medium created and disseminated images of his funeral. In 1909 thousands of well wishers had greeted him ecstatically on his return from the United States as the boxer Europe recognized as the new Champion of the World. Now an estimated 100,000 lined the streets to bid him farewell. This was without doubt the largest funeral in Welsh history, and it was a mark of respect for the achievements of a professional fighter from an Irish-Welsh background.

Driscoll's obsequies bore all the hallmarks of a state funeral, and he died soon enough after the First World War for there to be a prominent military presence in the procession. That procession wound its way over two miles through the streets of Cardiff, from the church of St Paul's in Newtown to the cemetery in Cathays, with the soldiers of the Second Battalion of the Welch Regiment carrying their rifles reversed in honour of a dead comrade, marching to the sound of an army band. His coffin, draped with the Union flag, was carried on a gun carriage. Fellow boxers such as Owen Moran, Tiger Smith and Johnny Basham joined figures from public life in the ranks of mourners. Equally significant was the participation of orphans from Nazareth House, who carried flowers in honour of their most famous benefactor, accompanied by the nuns who taught and cared for them. Shops in Cardiff stopped business during the procession as a mark of respect for a popular hero.

In the light of this sketch of Jim Driscoll's life and career as a boxer it is inevitable that more general questions about sporting heroes and the role of boxing in working-class culture arise. Since the 1960s boxing has ceased to occupy the central position in the lives of working-class men that once it did. This form of combative masculinity is perhaps less suited to a world in which the ability to fight – even under the controlled conditions of a sporting contest – is no longer as prized an achievement as it was. Affluence and concern about the health risks of boxing have reduced the appeal of this form of masculine competition. In the light of these developments, it is worth noting Dai Smith's comment on the generation of fighters to which Jim Driscoll belonged. 'Their meteor-like careers', he writes, 'were obvious metaphors for a society where sudden death or misfortune, neither

29

rational nor harmless, was all too commonplace.' A later, more prosperous and risk-averse culture eyes such activities askance.

Some people have argued that Driscoll's distinctive ethnic and religious background meant that he could never become a truly repre-sentative or iconic sporting hero for a wider Welsh community. The response to his successes in the United States and the spontaneous and widespread grief that greeted his funeral belie this judgement. On his return from America, Driscoll was dubbed the 'prince of Wales', an epithet that demonstrated beyond doubt that his appeal extended well beyond the ethnic minority from which he sprang. The fact that Viscount Knebworth perceived Driscoll to be 'generally Welsh' is also of significance. Had Knebworth wished to denigrate Driscoll decisively in that period he would surely have drawn attention to Driscoll's Irish roots.

Against this background it is worth reassessing the legendary status that Jim Driscoll has acquired. In the decades since his death the legend of 'Peerless' Jim has grown apace. Artists in several media have been drawn to the life of this exponent of boxing. He has been memorialized, in the form of a statue, in a city that has become comfortable with remembering its successful citizens at the same time as it forges a new identity that distances itself from the past. Alexander Cordell wrote a novel based on the boxer's life, and the poet Grahame Davies has written a poem about him that eulogizes his devotion to the children of Nazareth House. Perhaps it is this facet of Driscoll's life – his ability to reach beyond the closed world of boxing and to connect with other human activities – that explains his attraction to a modern audience that is eager to shore up the legendary status of Jim Driscoll. His life spanned different social environments. Before the creation of the British Boxing Board of Control in 1929, boxing in Britain was dominated by the gentlemen of the NSC. This forced individuals like Jim Driscoll to negotiate their way between very different social worlds. Furthermore, his life forced him to move between the close social world of his Irish Catholic upbringing in Newtown and the wider culture of Cardiff; between the pious attach-ment to Nazareth House orphanage and the world of boxing, betting and horses; between competition in Britain and America; and between the requirements of peace-time sporting contests and war-time training.

Ultimately, the legend of 'Peerless' Jim Driscoll remains compelling because it is based on a life that refused to be limited or confined.

Freddie Welsh

WELSH AMERICAN

DAI SMITH

Freddie Welsh is our contemporary in a way no other boxer from the last century still manages to be. More than any other Welsh sportsman ever, his career in and out of the ring oozes the essence of post-modernism: iconic, playful, enigmatic, open to endless interpretation, an artefact that questions the virtual presence of what passes for reality and exposes the drear actuality of what we compress and represent as History. He was as complex and contradictory as the society which nurtured him and as tragic as the culture he helped to create with humanity's star-crossed needs in mind. To his story we need to restore consciousness of intent and of circumstance. His sporting life needs viewing in the context of his forming social identity and his desired relationship to the future society whose ideal lineaments he craved and described. The writer of history and the writer of fiction tell different truths in related ways but only now, perhaps, is Welsh cultural historiography beginning to reach the point from which the writer of fiction – which Freddie Welsh in graphic mode most certainly was – always jumps off. Freddie Welsh is a clue to a greater mystery we will not solve if we do not bravely allow opposites to remain in suspension, as he most certainly did.

Consider, then, Frederick Hall Thomas. He was born in 1886, the son of John Thomas, a Pontypridd auctioneer or buyer and seller of property, a man of wit and means, and of Elizabeth Hall, the daughter of a Merthyr hotelier when that iron town was still Wales's most populous centre. The family was, in terms of the overwhelmingly proletarian coalfield, middle class, prosperous and professional. Soon, Elizabeth ran her own hotel in Pontypridd, her first-born and eldest son went to local nursery and boarding schools before, after his father's early death and mother's remarriage, he was sent across the Severn to Long Ashton Public School, W. G. Grace's very own Alma Mater, in Clifton. Freddie rebelled against any academic or, rather, pedagogic discipline, and even against a subsequent apprentice-ship to a Rhondda boilermaker's firm as an engineer. In 1903, aged 16, with two friends of similar background and disposition, he swallowed the Canadian Pacific Railway's inducements to the Empire's youth to emigrate, and sailed for Montreal. He also went courtesy of the money supplied by his mother. Most of his Pontypridd contemporaries and future supporters, including Jimmy Wilde and later Tommy Farr, were only destined to migrate underground. Within a year he was back but, restless and again bankrolled by his mother, took off again, this time for three years, from Liverpool to New York City in 1904. The legend, and its embellishments away from actual witness, would grow thick and fast in later years, as Freddie learned to feed newspaper copy to the media which would tell his tale and sell his tickets: how, impoverished and desperate for a crust, he had stumbled into a department-store position as a physical instructor and had become, by chance, good at it, quickly graduating to prize-fighting in the numerous small venues and shabby halls of the eastern seaboard of the United States. He takes the name Freddie Welsh in case his mother hears of his deeds. Maybe. What is for sure is that he rode the rails as a hobo and toughened up enough to work for a fellow Welshman, another Thomas, as a strikebreaker for five dollars a day, three times the wages of Chicago's regular meat-packers locked out, 20,000 of them, for wanting more than twenty cents an hour and less than an unremitting pace of work in the city's huge stockyards. Freddie, and 2,000 other blacklegs, housed in the empty sheds now used as barracks, were protected by armed police and the private, ruthless Pinkertons. Bombs, gunshots, cracked heads and the occasional outright murder were indicative of the turbulent labour troubles of turn-of-the-century America, and close enough to what was happening in south Wales. The links would bring Big Bill Haywood, the syndicalist leader of the Industrial Workers of the World, from the States to greet the striking and rioting miners of Tonypandy in 1910. Frederick Hall Thomas could feel, almost, right at home.

When he returned home for 1907 Freddie had a fiancée, the New Yorker Fanny Weston née Weinstein, whose subsequent marriage to Freddie would stay under wraps for a number of years to ensure his ascetic image – physical training and non-indulgence in the 'vices' – would stay Baden Powell-pure for the Empire's Press, even as, in private, he lit up a cigarette and frequently relaxed by being 'lit up' himself. Disconcertingly, he now had an American style, of dress and accent, and notably of fighting – a defensive crouch rather than the classic upright stance of, say, Jim Driscoll – which did not endear him to the public, even a Welsh one, until he proceeded to knock out all and sundry and, with one rare loss of concentration, sweep away all before him as the lightweight champion – 9 st 9 lb – of Britain and the Empire, and as a constant transatlantic fighter, down to 1914, in pursuit of the world crown squirrelled away by successive American champions who, largely, learned to evade the canny Welshman.

One who did not, on his home soil in Cardiff, in December 1910 was 'Peerless' Jim Driscoll, acknowledged as the unofficial featherweight champion – 9 stone dead – of the world after he had comprehensively outboxed Abe Attell in New York earlier that year. Freddie weighed in, practically naked, at 9 st 6 lb and Driscoll, in sweater, trousers and boots, tipped the scales accordingly. But that was at 2 p.m. in the afternoon, and they fought late in the winter's night. Freddie's tactics, of holding, boring with his head, clinching to kidney punch and non-stop verbal taunting, finally enraged the classic stylist, who head-butted Freddie across the ring in a street brawl that promptly disqualified him. Gamesmanship, though, was always Freddie's game. It was why the dress-suited gentlemen of London's National Sporting Club only grudgingly admired him, and returned the same measure of resent-ment with which they adored gallant Jim Driscoll. Looking back from the 1940s the British boxing scribe, Norman Hurst, who knew both fighters well and thought Driscoll to be 'one of the greatest boxers and ring tacticians the world has ever known . . . fit model for an artist', sourly recalled Freddie as a

> ferret where business was concerned . . . Business man first, Fighter second, Business man third. That summed up the late Frederic [sic] Hall Thomas, known to fight followers the world over as Freddy [sic] Welsh. As a young man [he] had visions of making good as a big business man. America was forever luring him to her shores. In America he thought he could build up a fortune.

Freddie Welsh was a hustler. He organized a 'South Wales syndicate', which put up the purses and picked up the expenses – expecting a profit, of course – for his local contests and marketed 'their' fighter further afield. The coalfield society of the professional class from which he came was, after all, rich and thriving in the Edwardian era. Freddie staged ticketed open-air training events, to which women in particular were, and unusually so, made welcome; and he made them free, since it was publicity and advertising and public clamour which he wished to encourage. It was the long-term pound, not the short-term penny, which lay at the heart of his business plan. The population of south Wales saw its biggest decennial increase, largely through in-migration, from 1900, and Freddie cashed in by buying and renting out houses, all in his mother's name. He cultivated his public appearances outside the ring: a smile to flash his gold teeth from a railway carriage, a wave of his jewel-be-ringed hand, the glint of a diamond stick-pin. He mixed in the most affluent of companies, attracting in particular the support of D. A. Thomas, the millionaire owner of the Cambrian Combine in mid Rhondda, future Lord Rhondda and former Cambridge boxing half-blue. That tycoon – alongside other coal and land barons of the Welsh aristocracy of capitalism, and attended by the incipient Welsh bourgeoisie of doctors, lawyers, dentists, mine managers, engineers and shopkeepers – was at the ringside in Olympia, London, on 7 July 1914, the night Freddie became the first Welshman to become a world champion when he defeated the American Willie Ritchie over twenty rounds. The declaration of war with Germany early in the next month was almost an anticlimax after all that. It certainly was for Freddie. He had chased and cajoled Ritchie for a title fight across three years and two continents, and he had not been in it for the glory. To avoid the War and clean up as champ he had to return to America to undertake the series of 'no decision' contests in which he fought, with mind-numbing regularity, every conceivable challenger over ten rounds. Under the moralistic boxing laws of most states in America only a knockout could deprive the champion of his title, and no one was better equipped to fight stalemates than the boxer who now openly declared his loathing of the so-called sport in which he had long invested his human capital.

Freddie Welsh remained world lightweight champion until Benny Leonard, aka Benjamin Leiner, draped him over the ropes of the Manhattan Athletic Club, aka Casino, in May 1917. By then it was Freddie who was loathed. At home, occasional letters to the press accused him of being 'a slacker', as the slaughter on the Western Front bedecked the coalfield with black ribbons. In non-belligerent America he was increasingly depicted as the greatest pacifist ever to move backwards in the ring: cartoons drew him as a grand-daddy with safety in mind, but for three years as the champion he was gambling on his superior skill and filling, as the *National Police Gazette* put it, 'his coffers with gold'. For some Americans, bemused by the social circles he now sought to move in – politicians, bankers, industrialists, writers and theatrical producers – it was, patently, a case of the biter bit. Donald O'Brien of the *Los Angeles Times* choked with indignation even before 1914 was out:

Freddie Welsh is a young person who feels himself to be superior to his job. His manager . . . thoroughly despises boxing as a business. The result of which combination is that Mr Welsh is the worst failure of a lightweight champion who ever held the title.

Flattered by the society and companionship of these men [the rich and powerful] Freddie has but one idea, to be one of them. The world's championship means to him only the money and the increased glitter of fame that will make his position the surer among the men into whose circle of life he hopes to scramble.

In a few months, Freddie will make a face at the championship; poke his money in his pocket and the name of Fred Hall Thomas will go on the lists of some club and Freddie will begin the real fight of his life – to 'break in'.

In fact Freddie fought fifty three times between reaching his sporting summit in the summer of 1914 and falling off it in the summer of 1917. His last real triumph was in 1916, when, against all the odds and in the second of their three encounters, he somehow rejuvenated himself to bring ringcraft to his aid in utterly outboxing the younger, faster and all-American favourite, Benny Leonard, his nemesis within a year. Yet, for Freddie, the truth of his own views was now more important than the formerly circumspect notion of avoiding rubbing salt in the wounds of the boosters of the 'noble art', the 'sweet science' of fisticuffs.

With me fighting is a business, not a game: and certainly not a pleasure. I have forgotten the days when the glory of the title and the publicity it brought would have set my head swimming. Every businessman aspires to be the head of his particular business and it is the same in the prize-fighting art. I have craven the championship because it is the highest pinnacle of the business in which I was engaged. And now that I am there it is my business to stay there and make as much out of it as possible.

He was 31 when the 'staying there' stopped, and he was down and out and dead a decade later, aged 41. He had, once again, been netted by circumstances: America's entry into the War in 1917, which saw him, now an American citizen, enlist as Lieutenant in the US Army, based in Washington, to help retain and rehabilitate soldiers, and then, with age no longer his ally, missing out, despite a flurry of forlorn comebacks, on the post-war boxing boom that threw the sport, and the prize-money, wide open and catapulted fighters like his close friend Jack Dempsey to the heights of Roaring Twenties celebrity and wealth. Freddie would never be quite American enough. His American Dream had only one chance of staying afloat, but it was a major chance, or so it seemed, to those who attended the opening of his sumptuous Health Farm at Long Hill, near Summit, New Jersey, in 1917. This was his major investment: a plutocratic mansion on a hill, surrounded by fields, a river for fishing, a golf course, woods, orchards and sunken gardens, equipped with a gymnasium, squash court and two swimming pools, one outside and one inside, and where two dozen rooms were panelled in hardwood and an automobile could take you to New York City within an hour. Or you could stay indoors and read your way through Frederick Hall Thomas's well-stocked library; or maybe work your way through his well-stocked booze supply – for you could come here to train or to party. He had sunk the fortune earned in the ring in this venture. It was too grandiose, too intermittently used, too expensive to maintain, and a victim of the early Prohibition era that followed on the passage of the Volstead Act by Congress in 1919. When he finally could not keep up the payments and had to sell in 1926, he had already spiralled downwards into drink and depression. He died, apart from his family, in a seedy New York hotel in the sweltering heatwave of July 1927. The doctor said it was cardiovascular disease,

40

maybe aggravated by a beating he had recently taken in a speakeasy; the sceptical thought it was suicide from despair; the romantic that he had died from a broken heart; the historian might consider that they found the body of Frederick Hall Thomas, but that Freddie Welsh had long departed.

So now, we must consider this. Frederick Hall Thomas was born in Morgan Street, Pontypridd, just across the Taff, over the single-span bridge that was, in 1886, exactly 130 years old, and had been flanked since 1857 by the parallel road-bridge which effectively marked the end of any lingering sense of the market town as a mere confluence, signalling instead its full-blooded emergence by the 1880s as the urban gateway to the central valleys of the modern coalfield. The boy's roots, however, were in its earlier and even rougher origins: his paternal grandfather was Morgan Thomas, a monoglot Welshman and a champion bare-knuckle bruiser with plenty of backers to follow him, personally and financially, from one 'bloody spot' on the mountains to another for illegal fight-till-you-drop contests. His father John wore a new-found respectability along with his three-piece suits and watch fob, but he too was a 'sporting man', albeit confining himself to side bets and heavy wagers on anything from foot-racing to the fights in the itinerant boxing booths or behind the public houses he frequented and ran. In the first decade of his life young Fred lived in a town whose population quadrupled in size to over 30,000, and within a wider industrial cauldron which from the Rhondda Valleys down positively exploded in numbers to almost 200,000. There was a social riot of home-building, chaotic street lay-out, a pulsating migrant influx, entertainment in music halls and cinemas, colliery development, breweries and manufacture of goods, shops and markets, schools and chapels, pubs and accompanying police stations to allow a measure of control over a rowdy, young, largely male workforce who played as hard as they worked and drank to match. He would have seen and participated in a Welsh world overflowing its settled boundaries, so rapid and intense was the pace of social change. In Pontypridd, especially, English quickly became the lingua franca of the streets. Newspapers reflected, and often shuddered at, this shaken-up kaleidoscope of humanity. As in the American West, they were the harbingers of aspiration as well as the purveyors of sensation. With circulation in mind, they groaned gratefully over their journalistic duty to report serial accounts of the drunk and disorderly, debtors and bankrupts, the vicious and the murdered, cases of domestic rape and the nocturnal gangbangs that disgraced the Gateway to the Rhondda. They compensated by preening over the civic worthies who, with public parks and board schools and an army of policemen, tried to stem the Gadarene tide of cultural anarchy. The appeal to betterment came wrapped in the flag of local pride, with a trumpeting of patriotic fervour, both Welsh and Imperial. The boy Frederick Hall Thomas was, in every sense, at the centre of these things. He was its intimate. When he looked for a boxing soubriquet for himself, in a New York whose bustle would have come as a surprise only in scale, not kind, he first chose Fred Cymry or, in other words, we, us, ourselves, the tribe. Welsh was just a convenient and pronounceable translation.

He was sent away to public school because it could be afforded, but also because he was showing signs of a lack of decorum as marked as that of his grandfather. He scrapped in all the schools he attended, bringing to the disciplinarian traditions of Long Ashton the fist-fighting ferocity and bloody-minded rebelliousness he had discovered on the slopes of the Graig and in the stone-covered back lanes of his home town. Living near the old bridge in the Bridge House hotel and then at the Bunch of Grapes on the other side of the river, he joined the 'Bridge Gang', young ruffians intent on defending their patch from any one of the other 'Gangs of Pontypridd', a collectivity to place in the roll call of Victorian street armies from London's East End to the Gangs of New York themselves.

On his return as a professional fighter from America in 1907 and with a quick series of sensational victories to back up his claimed prowess, Freddie began the process that was his cultural destiny: to unite in himself the raw outlaw society of proletarian sport and the self-improving world of professional middle-class Wales. He became, literally, a bridge. He claimed to have studied the 'science' of physical culture and the 'art' of boxing, but he allied this to the school of hard knocks and brutal experience he had found on both sides of the Atlantic before he was 20. In an extraordinary way he personified unity within a south Wales that was riven, and would soon be so-marked for half a century, by irrepressible class division and social tension. He claimed that boxing – the padded gloves, the laws, the improved decorum – was fast establishing itself as a respectable pursuit, and he posed for photographs in evening dress on a bardic chair or in the country tweeds of an Edwardian gent. But he entered the boxing ring stripped for the primeval act of conflict in a sport that was no such thing, a tribal warrior, for sure, but one with an ambivalent identity and an ambiguous purpose. If Freddie had ever been born anew it was when, as a boy, he plunged into the Taff to rescue a drowning man, probably a worse-for-wear collier who had slipped from the bank into the fast waters of the Berw Pool, just above the old bridge and his mother's hotel. Freddie was a local hero at the age of 12 and a class act all his life, but it was the duality of his upbringing and of his personality which sealed his representative status for his pendulum society. There was never any doubt about where he had come from or for whom, beyond himself, he fought in the ring.

Before the Driscoll fight in 1910 he had trained in the Clarence Theatre in the centre of Pontypridd, and had charged a small fee for entrance to the always packed-out sessions. He donated the money to the new Pontypridd Cottage Hospital. A third of the 8,000 tickets for the fight, with the Cambrian Combine strike entering its third month, were reduced in price to accommodate some of his supporters. The cheap seats, 2,000 of them at 5s. a head, which he forced on the promoters of his 1914 world championship win at Olympia, guaranteed train-loads of 'Welsh toilers' disembarking at Paddington.

> . . . I have always had a soft place in my heart for the Welsh colliers, who have followed my career in all parts of the world, and have stuck true to me through thick and thin. I am very anxious to see a great crowd of my friends from the 'hills' at the fight at Olympia, and suggested to the promoters that they should provide an unusual number of low-priced seats in order to enable my collier friends to be present. The syndicate would not hear of my suggestion at the outset but I pegged at them and would not budge an inch, with the result that I won . . . [otherwise] it was not possible for my Welsh working-men friends who would . . . have to pay their railway fares as well if they wanted to see me fight.

43

Their voices dominated the arena when Freddie entered the ring late that night: 'Hen Wlad Fy Nhadau', in the full and choral repetitive version, with a blast of 'Sospan Fach' to keep the whole thing boiling. These were the men who booed D. A. Thomas, and his friends in their dinner jackets, after the victory, thinking them to be Willie Ritchie's American backers. One shouted, 'What do you American millionaires think of it now?' The reply was, apparently, 'Cymru am Byth', but, just perhaps, the jeerers were more astute than it may seem. After all, it was Thomas Jones, the quintessential professional Welshman of his day, who also thought that if 'Lloyd George is a Welshman, Lord Rhondda is an American'.

Now champion of the world – 'I was fighting for the honour of Wales' – the man who had become the great Freddie Welsh by beating an American champion returned home to lead one long triumphal procession in an open car from Cardiff up to Pontypridd, its streets thronged with admirers, and on, via the Bunch of Grapes, past the old bridge to the Taff's headwaters at Merthyr, his mother's home-town, where he boxed exhibition rounds for the crowd. This Wales was, with coal as its global fuel, already a world-renowned dynamo of modernity. Freddie Welsh was, by name and fame, proclaiming it so, and thereby imprinting Wales itself on a popular culture of sport that was world-wide, beyond the rugby football that had, in exactly this same span of time as his own life, become the Welsh 'National Game'. Frederick Hall Thomas emblazoned a red dragon on his silk dressing-robe, and took it off in the ring to reveal a sash around his trunks that was stitched with leeks and dragons. He had no qualms about the Union flag on his regalia either, but it was Wales he proclaimed to all who could hear, from Pontypridd to America, across an ocean one contemporary economist, surveying the argosies of coal-laden ships from Cardiff and Barry Docks, would soon astonishingly refer to as Wales's Atlantic lake. And here, in similar mode, is Freddie himself, in 1914, two weeks before the First World War ended all this cultural hubris:

> When I think of the size of . . . our little country, and then think again how small that portion of it is that we call South Wales, I am . . . filled with pride at the recollection of the things that have been done by the men of our race.

. . . A country where men can play rugby football as Welshmen play it – men who have beaten the best that the world can send against us – can, I am sure, produce boxers with the same qualities of handiwork and skill and courage which have made her rugby footballers famous and feared the world over . . .

I am looking forward to the time when we shall hold a straight flush from fly to heavy of British boxing championships. Even then the limits of ambition will not have been reached for there will be the world's titles to strive for.

Or, in his case, to flaunt and retain. That latter aim would soon sour his reputation in the America he adopted, but in his particular Wales his popularity never really waned, no matter what his tactics or his hard-headedness. Winning and surviving were indistinguishable in the ring for him, as they were, in life, for his working-class followers. Quite simply, Freddie did not play by the rules if he could break them. And, in a displaced sense, neither did they, if the rule of law was both oppressive and repressive. When he had faced up to the aesthetic superiority of Driscoll, the darling of the National Sporting Club, at Cardiff's American Roller Rink in 1910, it was only just over a month since crowds of miners and their womenfolk, thousands strong, had confronted mounted hussars and metropolitan police on the streets of Aberaman and Tonypandy. Their cries of rage were Freddie's ring-side jibes; their stone-throwing was Freddie's illegal kidney-punching; their un-British behaviour was his American-style fighting. Of course the fight ended in a brawl outside the Queensberry Rules, and naturally it cascaded into a free-for-all between the boxers' rival seconds and supporters, and then on through the crowd onto Cardiff's streets. For the striking miners, who had another twelve months of struggle to survive, but who did win a minimum-wage settlement in 1912, Freddie Welsh was one of them that night, and no matter who his opponent was, even the likeable Driscoll, he won for them. In the ring, in Britain at this time, Freddie Welsh was a revolutionary. That night he de-constructed the 'Beau Ideal' of British boxing. He had discarded the straight left and side-on posture of the classicist for the ducking, weaving, crouching, infuriating, ugly stance of a fighter who was not there to be hit but would suddenly unleash punches from every angle and at bewildering speed. He was coiled until his opponent's impatience served to become self-defeating.

Newspaperman James Butler saw and reported on the fight as being the only time Driscoll, in a brilliant career, had ever resorted to questionable tactics. This is how Butler remembered it:

This grim struggle took place . . . five days before Christmas of 1910. It captured the imagination of Wales. The Irish population of Cardiff was behind Driscoll, the rest rooted 100% for Welsh, who although born at Pontypridd, had begun his fighting in Philadelphia.

Welsh and Driscoll had never liked each other. As soon as Freddy ducked under the ropes he cast a contemptuous glance at his lighter opponent. It was deliberate tactics to rouse the Driscoll temper, because Welsh, a strong two-fisted American styled battler, realised he could not match the featherweight in skill, but in a rough-house scrap Welsh had few masters.

For four rounds it was all Driscoll. He gave the Pontypridd battler a lesson with his left hand, but Welsh was determined to get aside, and when he succeeded he opened up a vicious kidney attack which he learned in America . . . and also roused Driscoll's ire further by bringing up his head sharply in the clinches. Peerless Jim completely lost his head. He allowed Welsh to dictate the way the fight should be fought. It was the only time I saw Driscoll not in control of himself in the ring . . . So bitter was the hatred by the tenth round that the finest boxer this country has ever produced was rushing in red-eyed like a man gone berserk.

. . . It was now a street-corner fight, and not a pretty sight to watch, both men butting whenever the opportunity came. 'Peggy' Bettinson [the referee seated at ringside] was to blame. He had allowed Welsh to get away with 'murder' and the struggle had got out of his grip now . . . The infuriated Driscoll pulled his head back and, with a sickening thud, butted Welsh under the chin, and flung him halfway across the ring.

Freddy staggered and Driscoll, completely mad with temper now, went in for the kill, but the referee was roused at last, and climbed into the ring and dragged the crazy pair of combatants apart. He motioned Driscoll back to his corner, and awarded the decision to Welsh. But that was only a start. A more bitter fight than ever was now raging.

And that, of course, is the revolutionary's unconfinable intent. You do not play the game – you subvert it if you can. If you are Jack Dempsey, slugging the giant Jess Willard into the canvas with loaded gloves in 1919. Or Cassius Clay, suckering Sonny Liston into defeat by psychological trepidation. Or Muhammad Ali, absorbing and timing the power of George Foreman back against himself. Or Freddie Welsh, spoiling Jim Driscoll's party piece and self-discipline at the end of riotous 1910.

Trickery was an admirable trait in the minds of sports fanatics in south Wales. They applauded the feints and deceptions, all barely within the laws of a rugby football game, originally intended to define a middle-class English public school pursuit, which were elaborated by Dickie Owen at the base of working-class Welsh scrums. They delighted in the on-field circus japes of the half-back brothers, the Jameses of Swansea, who soon travelled north to play professional rugby, and in the wage demands made on behalf of professional football players by soccer supremo and strike-leader Billy Meredith, of Chirk, Manchester United and Manchester City. They saw nothing amiss in professional powderhall racing and in the ruses used – lead in the shoes, to be removed in later races – to obtain the best betting odds on their favourites. The burgeoning middle classes in Welsh rugby administration may have moved to ban Aberdare RFC in 1908 for the systematic bribery of opponents which allowed them to win the Glamorgan League, but the lifetime dismissal of Dai 'Tarw' Jones, the Rhondda rock of Welsh packs, including that of 1905 which defeated the All Blacks, would win him nothing but sympathy and no disgrace for the monetary offence. Freddie Welsh was a part of this Welsh mosaic too, and not only in his legitimate endeavour to make money from his business as a boxer.

The question that hovers over his career is the biggest of them all: was the victory over Ritchie in 1914 'a fix'? And if so, by whom? What is, generally, not thought to be in doubt is the superior boxing, overall, of Welsh against Ritchie. However, the American had only consented to the bout at all because, without precedent, Freddie was fighting for nothing. The entire purse, a 25,000-dollar guarantee, was to go to the champion, win or lose, with Welsh to receive half of any gate receipts left after all expenses were met. There were none. What is known is that the challenger had no such funds to guarantee Ritchie's prize money, or funds immediately to hand to pay back the guarantee. What is known, too, is that over half a million pounds in bets changed hands after the fight and that the rumours were of syndicates trying to get the 'fix' in, one way or the other. Freddie Welsh's explanation of how the fight came about at long last took refuge in the tribal lore with which he was selling his story to the world:

> It's natural with us Welshmen to sit the thing out. I'll never forget watching the men of my race squatting around, smoking their pipes. They're all miners. They're used to squatting down in the coalmines for hours at a time, with hardly room to move, picking away at the coal with short little backs. Then when they come up out of the mines after the day's work and want to rest they will sit quietly . . . I inherit that spirit and it was that alone that gave me the courage to wait patiently for my whirl as a world's champion.

Patience and, perhaps, the backing of a notorious New York gambler, Arnold Rothstein, who, by 1912, was the 29-year-old multi-millionaire kingpin of organized crime, later seen as the guiding intelligence behind the crime syndicates of the 1920s as Jewish advisory brain to the Italian Mafia. Rothstein, whose biggest coup was his involvement, or virtual involvement, with the fixing of the 1919 baseball World Series and consequent immortality as Meyer Wolfsheim in F. Scott Fitzgerald's 1926 masterpiece, *The Great Gatsby*, was mysteriously gunned down, aged 46, in a New York hotel room in 1928. He worked the race-track and politicians and the boxing game, all to his advantage, of course. He was, like Freddie, articulate and well read. No thug, just a businessman making money out of illegal activity. And employing armies of thugs – in loan-sharking and labour racketeering, as well as bootlegging and drugs – to allow him to do so. There is no doubt that he would know of, and maybe even personally know, the Welsh fighter as he would later know, certainly personally, his New

York Jewish compatriot, Benny Leonard. It was Arnold Rothstein, owner of judges and banker to politicians, who had arranged a boxing licence to allow Billy Gibson of the Bronx to promote fights in New York City. The grateful manager promptly assigned to Rothstein ten per cent of his fighter Benny Leonard's ring-earnings for life. Rothstein, in that sense, owned Leonard too and bet on him, before and after he took the Welshman's championship. Nor did it stop there with Rothstein. In 1922 Benny Leonard, challenging for the welterweight crown, deliberately threw the fight, on a foul, in order to be disqualified despite the fact that he had just been fouled himself. A.R., the 'Big Bankroll', cleaned up. Billy Gibson, notoriously shady in all his dealings, became the handler of another boxer from New York's East Side, the future heavyweight champion Gene Tunney, who overturned all the odds, to outpoint Jack Dempsey in Philadelphia in 1926. That was in Maxie 'Boo Boo' Hoff's Philadelphia, where the Jewish mobster's writ ran. Arnold Rothstein had rung his friend and accomplice to ensure it did. Hoff first paid off all Tunney's debts – 20,000 dollars' worth – and then claimed, in turn, twenty per cent of Tunney's future ring earnings. Gibson was certainly party to this, even if Tunney proved evasive later. Considering that Tunney went on to beat the infamous 'long count' against Dempsey in Al Capone's Chicago in 1927 Dempsey had politely declined Al's own influential help – those earnings, and hence those potential percentages, were considerable. Arnold Rothstein bet heavily on Gene Tunney both times. Arnold Rothstein claimed that he never 'bet on boxing'. Arnold Rothstein lied.

But back in 1914 Benny Leonard was just an 18-year-old starting out, and the big money was required elsewhere. According to Rothstein's latest biographer, the 25,000-dollar guarantee plus expenses that Willie Ritchie demanded to fight Freddie Welsh, and which was deposited in advance in a New York bank account, came courtesy of Arnold Rothstein. Did A.R. believe the betting odds against Ritchie would return his money if Welsh could be persuaded to throw that fight – as Freddie claimed a few years later he had been, lucratively, asked to do – or was it enough to let it be known he had bankrolled the fight and that the 'fix' was on, even if it was not? So, A.R. would bet with the odds, not against them, and take money from the suckers who thought he had fixed the fight for them. Or was the loan attached to Ritchie's future prospects? That seems most unlikely, since the fight was in London and Freddie the odds-on favourite. Besides, the money went to Ritchie only via Freddie and *his* backers, so it was, given the win, Freddie Welsh who was beholden; to someone, for sure. If to Arnold Rothstein, then, one way or the other, the gambler who never knowingly laid out money that would not come back would, one day, recoup from Freddie, too. Perhaps that day came in the Manhattan Casino in the summer of 1917, when a champion who was not counted out, merely retired by the referee, handed over the crown, and the percentage earnings that went with it. There are no ledgers to check, no accounts to be verified, no witnesses to call to the bar of history. Except maybe for the 'Little Hebe', featherweight champion of the world from 1901 to 1912 – with an unofficial loss to Driscoll in New York in 1909 and a loss to the heavier Welsh in 1908 – and Rothstein's 'bodyguard' and bagman on retirement. Abe Attell was always Rothstein's inside man in the boxing game; he was the layer of bets and double-crosses, for A.R. at the 1919 World Series; he coordinated and sat in on the meetings with Gibson, Tunney and 'Boo Boo' Hoff prior to Tunney's 1926 triumph; his memory of the two biggest gates in boxing history to that point, and until the 1960s, did not mention the fighters, Jack Dempsey and Gene Tunney, only the outside-the-ring gang lords of Philly and Chi: 'What you had was this: It was the Italians against the Jews. The Jews won!' Billy Gibson, Leonard and Tunney's so-called manager, was the 'William Gibson . . . of Fifth Avenue' who was named after Rothstein's murder as one of the gangster's closest and most trusted associates. So trusted he was a proxy for some of Rothstein's assets. And Freddie Welsh died in the Hotel Sidney, at 59 West 65th Street, a drinking joint and gambling den, or 'policy bank', where bets were cleared or, more to the point, cash collected from 'numbers runners' who worked the streets for criminals and gamblers like Arnold Rothstein, who held daily court, and dispensed personal loans at very high interest rates, from his Broadway restaurant HQ, Lindy's, on 50th Street, just a few blocks and a lifetime away. Damon Runyon immortalized the eating place in his Broadway vignettes as Mindy's and A.R. as 'The Brain'. This, too, was Freddie Welsh's world, as Ring Lardner, from personal knowledge, knew and Scott Fitzgerald, from genius, intuited. What we can, at the very least, say is that if Freddie Welsh, in his American persona, really does seem, from recent biographical digging, to be, in part anyway, the literal model for Fitzgerald's Jay Gatsby, as Rothstein was for his Meyer Wolfsheim, then, equally, we can imaginatively assume that by placing both of his fictional creations, Gatsby and Wolfsheim, in one telling frame he gives us another kind of fix on Freddie Welsh and Arnold Rothstein and the world championship of 1914.

The rite of passage towards becoming an American had, one way or the other, been completed by then. In a sense, his significant story was over, because both his twinned worlds, countries and identities, were about to diverge, even if it took a little while longer for him personally. In another sense such connection, real or imagined, as Freddie Welsh had seemingly forged brought him a different kind of longevity, a cultural role that American writers, though not Welsh or British ones, mined for creative insight. Before Dempsey lit up the minds of American poets and painters and writers, Freddie Welsh was moved centre-stage as a magnet to appreciation in Ring Lardner's stories. And if Ring Lardner's great friend F. Scott Fitzgerald, who allegedly boxed a few rounds with the retired Freddie, did indeed catch the traits of Freddie's remade, dream-like life in the eponymous hero of *The Great Gatsby*, then the case for his emblematic import-ance in the tableau of modern life that sport was revealing is crystal-line, even more than in the telling detail of a washed-up fighter who owns a health farm which Hemingway brilliantly evokes in his boxing-scam story, *Fifty Grand*, which reverses the Leonard fix of 1922 and adds a heavy dose of anti-Semitic rant to clinch its outrage. But all that is literary history, the sucking out of the bone marrow those vital juices which novelists need in place to enliven their fables with the meaning of individual lives. Cultural historians still need to see the panoramic picture of time as well as space, and so to exchange the camera's flashlight bulb for its wide-focus lens. Those great and insightful American writers, after all, knew the import of Freddie Welsh but little of Frederick Hall Thomas or of the society that requires him to have, then and now, meaning in and for itself.

Unlike James Gatz, who, as Jay Gatsby, stocked his library with real but uncut and unread volumes, Frederick Hall Thomas read, voraciously, as Freddie Welsh, and quoted his favourites to the world's press. He took his library with him in his cabin trunks wherever he went. The construct, complex and contradictory, that was Freddie Welsh is unimaginable in any other fragment of space and time. His sporting prowess was a means to an end, but that end was only in incidental terms a material outcome. He had a vision of himself that was a cultural dream which might translate, through individual attainment, a rooted and collective social being into an evolved and changeably flexible modern way of living. His Wales could then flourish as an America: his America could be infused by what had been the values of Wales.

War and Depression were the nightmare into which the dream turned. In America his lonely, impoverished death in 1927 antici- pated, for millions, the Wall Street Crash of 1929. In Wales the great strikes of 1919 and 1921 heralded the collective defeat of his 'collier friends' in 1926 and the social pit of the 1930s into which a generation fell. The latter knew that in 1937, in New York, Tonypandy's Tommy Farr was now, in truth, a cracked grace-note to the echo of the music Freddie Welsh had made for them as he crouched like a collier and battled like a street fighter. There was no way in which they would not have remembered how it was and how it had not, in the end, become; for if it was never, entirely, Freddie Welsh's Pontypridd, he, by virtue of the historical slipstream in which he had first found and then defined himself, was abidingly Pontypridd's Freddie Welsh.

Endnote

I first wrote about Freddie Welsh in 1990 in 'Focal heroes: a Welsh fighting class', an essay that attempted to elicit the social significance for our history of the private nature and public reception of the panoply of great Welsh boxers down to the Second World War. It was there that I drew an imaginative, and then wholly imaginary, link between *The Great Gatsby* and the most intriguing of all those Welsh boxers. It seems, from the exhaustive research undertaken by

Andrew Gallimore for his *Occupation: Prizefighter: The Freddie Welsh Story* (2006) that the fiction writer really did have aspects of the fighter in mind: real names and incidents echo from Freddie's life in Fitzgerald's novel. Fact eventually catches up with fiction. As with another detailed chronological account of the boxer, *Freddie Welsh: Pontypridd Legend* (2004), by Gareth Harris, I gratefully acknowledge both volumes for the sources of some of the quotations I use here about and directly from Freddie Welsh. Other material has come from the scrapbooks of the late Glyn Moses, a delightful man, compiler of Fistiana and self-confessed 'lifelong Freddie Welsh admirer'. I am not sure how much of my new interpretation would meet with his approval, but I thank him and cherish his memory as a fellow devotee of the 'enigma'. Amongst contemporary writers who found him so, and decidedly did not like him, were Norman Hurst, *Thrilling Fights* (n.d., 1940s), and James Butler (with his son Frank), *The Fight Game* (1954). My speculative conjectures about what Arnold Rothstein may or may not have done, with or without the knowledge of Freddie Welsh, largely derive from two biographical works: Leo Katcher, *The Big Bankroll: The Life and Times of Arnold Rothstein* (1959), and David Pietrusza, *Rothstein: The Life, Times and Murder of the Criminal Genius Who Fixed the 1919 World Series* (2003). The speculation is buttressed by the uncontested facts there uncovered, which I here re-position within Freddie Welsh's ambit to illuminate dark corners. Amongst Freddie's pall-bearers were Abe Attell and Benny Leonard, whose own wreath bore the single word: 'Sympathy'.

If my own imagination stretches too far in this essay, its reach can be attributed to an ambition to nurture cultural history as a more intellectually mature element within the exacting field of Welsh historiography, and to fulfil a private bet between this present writer and my late friend, Freddie's relative, Pontypridd's champion writer, Alun Richards, who knew full well why Freddie was both Welsh and American, and something else besides. He has won. So I have not lost.

Jimmy Wilde, the 'Tylorstown Terror'

GARETH WILLIAMS

One day in late October 1920 Mrs Maggie Wilde came out of a Caerphilly hotel, placed her hat on the windowsill, and went to fight Mary Bowen, who had left just ahead of her. Whether Maggie was in pursuit or whether Mary was waiting for her is unclear, but Mrs Wilde was knocked to the floor, broke her leg, and in a sitting position was thumped and kicked by Mary Bowen. Mrs Wilde's son Jimmy was at the time undisputed Flyweight Champion of the World, a title he held from 1916 to 1923.

William James Wilde, clearly, came from fighting stock. He came, too, from the Rhondda. Though he was born, on 12 May 1892, in Graig-berthlwyd, Quakers Yard, near Treharris, when he was a year old the family relocated to 8 Station Road, on the boundary of the townships of Pontygwaith and Tylorstown in the Rhondda Fach. So young Jimmy grew up in one of the two famous valleys whose astonishing increase of people (in) and coal (out) – 73.8 per cent of the workforce of Rhondda's 1911 population of 157,781 were miners, and by then he was one of them – would be mirrored in the rise and fall of his own career. When its population began to recede from its 1924 peak of 169,000, the once-explosive energies of the Rhondda subsided, along with those of Jimmy Wilde, who had lost his world title the previous year.

To that point, the coalfield's spectacular growth had produced champions as world class as its steam coal: record-breaking cyclists Jimmy Michael, Arthur and Tom Linton and George Burge sped out of the Cynon Valley to win from Bordeaux to Paris and New York; first-class rugby sides like Penygraig, Treorchy, Treherbert and Llwynypia provided the 'Rhondda forwards' – and more agile Rhondda backs – to carry the Welsh XV through its first golden era to the 'world's championship in rugby' (a contemporary Kiwi assessment) on a December afternoon in 1905. These sporting icons complemented the valleys' choral champions, who sang at the Crystal Palace, Windsor Castle, Chicago's World's Fair and the White House. Karl Marx was surely right to explain sporting and cultural 'superstructure' in terms of economic 'base'.

Its boxers proved that. If, at any time in the first thirty years of the twentieth century you had travelled up the few miles from Pontypridd to Porth – the gateway to the Rhondda, where the valley divides like the tines of a tuning fork – and then ventured up either one of them, you would have heard how that confined area had produced more boxing champions than anywhere else of comparable size in the world: Tom Thomas (Penygraig), Percy Jones and Llew Edwards (Porth), Freddie Welsh, Francis Rossi and the eight fighting Moody brothers (Frank and Glen the best of them) of Pontypridd, George Williams (Treherbert), Harold Jones (Ferndale), Billy Hughes (Dinas) and soon Tonypandy's Tommy Farr, nearly all of whom proceeded from the pit to the boxing booths of Jack Scarrott and on to Welsh and British championships. Percy Jones, like his contemporary Jim Driscoll, was unofficial world champion (the US did not recognize the fly-weight category until 1916), Freddie Welsh won an undisputed world title, and Tommy Farr, unforgettably, fought for one.

And we have yet to include the greatest of them all, Jimmy Wilde of Tylorstown. At 13 years of age, averse to discipline and schooling, he began work at the local Ferndale number 8 pit and was sent to the lower galleries, where he could insert his spindly frame into the 2 ft 6 in. seam, one of the south Wales coalfield's 'abnormal places' that de-manded the kind of twists and angles that would have baffled Euclid, let alone Wilde's later opponents. It was there the young Jimmy devel-oped the broad shoulders and reserves of strength and durability to survive an underground accident that nearly cost him his leg and left him with a permanent cavity below his right knee to remind him of it. But he was glad to be out of a home environment where there was little parental affection – his father is listed as a prisoner in Treharris police station in the 1891 census – and into one where his occupation offered the kind of opportunity he might have hoped for, but could not have anticipated.

In the colliery he found himself working alongside Dai Davies, whose broken face and damaged knuckles indelibly identified him as a mountain fighter, one whose two-hour, eighty-four-round bout with Ted 'Chops' Williams was still spoken of with awe in the Rhondda. 'Occasionally', Jimmy Wilde recalled, 'Dai would break off, lay down his pick, and crouching in the gloom with his face covered with coal

dust and his hands and body black, demonstrate this punch or that.'
Dai took Jimmy home for further tuition upstairs in his cramped
terraced house, where in the tiny bedroom he piled the few sticks of
furniture on to the bed and instilled in Jimmy economy of footwork
and body movement. In such a confined space there was little room for
manoeuvring – on his way to the world title, some of his most potent
shots would travel only a few inches   and he soon acquired the fast
reflexes with which to work rapidly and effectively at close quarters,
for he had no wish to be at the receiving end of one of Dai's hay-
makers. In 1914 a boxing correspondent thought that Wilde's secret
lay in his

> wonderful judgement of distance and almost uncannily clever footwork.
> You have seen those boxers who dance all over the ring, and you have
> heard them often described as artists in footwork . . . Wilde's footwork
> is of a different calibre. He never covers more ground than is necessary,
> and because of that he never tires himself. Always on top of his man, he
> shoots out that long left arm with exact precision . . . he never wastes
> a punch . . . Watch him as his opponent comes in with the idea of
> mixing [it] . . . Wilde sidesteps, but he does not move more than a few
> inches. In a few seconds before his opponent can recover himself Wilde
> is busy again with his piston-rod left hand . . .

He had an eye for an opening, and for Dai's daughter Elizabeth, whom
he married at 18. Lizabeth inherited from her chapel-going mother a
dislike of boxing, and Jimmy withheld from her as long as possible
that he was boxing in the booths, where he was undefeated in more
than a notional 700 fights between 1907 and 1913.

While they would continue to be features of the Welsh sporting
scene until mid-century, the boxing booths, with their naphtha flares
and sawdust, unscrupulous managers and primitive facilities, had by
the early 1900s broken the umbilical cord that had tied them to the
travelling fairs. They were still a hard school. A fighter received nothing
if he lost, only a modest sum if he won. Once, just over the mountain
at Aberdare, Scarrott, in whose booths Wilde fought for five years,
offered a pound to anyone who could last three rounds with this human
scarecrow, who proceeded to k.o. fifteen opponents, most of them

bigger than himself, in quick succession; the sixteenth, who won his pound, was nine inches taller and two stones heavier. On another occasion he knocked out seventeen opponents in a morning, and after a relaxing lunch of a bun and a cup of tea, another three in the afternoon – for 30s. (£1.50), not much less than a whole week's wages underground. The renowned referee Ike Powell, whose brothers Abe and Jack were Wilde's contemporaries in the same booth, remembered Jimmy knocking out every one of his twenty-two opponents one Bank Holiday Monday in Swansea.

He needed to fight to augment his income, for while he had scrimped enough to buy a house in Tylorstown it was soon filled when Lizabeth agreed to take in Jimmy's mother, three younger siblings and recover another sister from care; they would have two sons of their own, too. He had been fighting semi-professionally under Ted Lewis's management since 1910, but despite fighting on average three times a month he did not quit working underground until 1913,when, having just completed a seventy-two-hour shift, he travelled to Glasgow to meet the Scottish professional champion Billy Padden. It took the eighteen rounds before Billy tired under Wilde's relentless attack to persuade Jimmy finally to renounce the pit for a full-time professional career of his own. In the ring, an arena as restricting as the lower galleries of the colliery, Jimmy Wilde found freedom.

Photographs of the middle-aged Jimmy Wilde show a cherubic face wreathed in a seraphic smile. The young Jimmy Wilde did not have much to laugh at, nor in the ring was he exactly an angel. He began every bout with the pasty-faced solemnity of Buster Keaton, and audiences would chuckle at his puny seriousness. Scarrott laughed in his face the first time Wilde asked to join his troupe of booth fighters, and the crowd in the spacious upstairs room at Pontypridd's 'Welsh Harp' (now the Millfield) laughed again when he first appeared there, after walking down from Tylorstown to ask Ted Lewis for an opportunity on Boxing Day 1910. The hardened Cockneys of Blackfriars burst out laughing on Jimmy's first London appearance in 1912, but they soon stopped when he knocked his man out in the first round; and when later that year he made his first emaciated appearance at the National Sporting Club and the evening-dressed members retired smirking to the bar, they were soon laughing with him, not at him.

Coming from a Rhondda where entertainment was high on the social agenda, he liked to amuse the spectators by deliberately making his opponent miss before gliding away Ali-like without offering a punch. When he beat Georges Gloria at the NSC in May 1914, his superiority was so obvious that the Frenchman became totally exhausted and the referee stopped it in the ninth. *Sic transit Gloria*. According to one newspaper:

> Poor Gloria . . . The house laughed and kept on laughing but it wasn't laughing at him. The amusement was all at Wilde. His amazing insouciance, the uncanny ease with which he did everything he felt inclined to do and the calm air of superiority with which he refrained from hurting Gloria overmuch.

Jimmy was never cruel; sometimes defeated opponents collapsed against him with their arms outstretched, and he would gently lay them out like an undertaker and walk away – this 'was one of those things which you had to laugh at'. Even in winning the world title against the Young Zulu Kid in December 1916 he provoked mirth by the way he continually slipped his man.

This is what particularly endeared him to Welsh crowds, who valued no quality higher than insouciance, insolence and the reckless gesture, for boxing was still not accepted as a respectable activity among the social and intellectual leaders of pre-war Wales. Newspaper coverage of the sport was thin until the 1920s; until then it was precisely the challenge to accepted norms of respectable behaviour, as much as scorn for the lumbering or overconfident opponent, that working-class crowds from Wilde's earliest days in the booths irreverently savoured. Welsh boxers embodied the cultural confidence of their communities.

Although an American pressman thought the long-armed Wilde was 'constructed like a kangaroo', he didn't move like one; not, at least, if kangaroos hop. Film evidence confirms that Wilde never jumped around: rather, he slid or slithered. With his left foot nearest his opponent, his right on the ball of the foot and his head forward, he attacked from the bell, his arms low, his elbows at waist-level, his right forearm resting lightly on his hip, the left out at a right angle. He developed perfect leverage, so that after throwing one punch he was always in a position to hit again. With his skeletal physique he knew he would never win battles of attrition; he would have to knock his opponent out, and he couldn't get started quickly enough. Angered by the derision he received from the Cockney crowd when he met Matt Wells's Nipper at Blackfriars in 1912, he went straight to the centre of the ring to wait for his much heavier opponent to lead. When he did, Wilde beat him to the punch and they carried the Nipper to his corner; k.o. round one.

What he disliked was the crouch, so beloved of the Americanized Freddie Welsh with whom he sparred. He didn't believe, either, in covering up in order to conceal the head. Even his idol and frequent second, Jim Driscoll, who shared his belief in economy of footwork, was inclined to adopt this protective tactic, but Wilde always insisted on 'having a good view' of his man. The most frustrating opponent he ever met was the splendidly named Kid Nutter, at Tonypandy Pavilion in January 1914. The Kid hardly poked his face out from behind his gloves all night, a leather bulwark that Wilde found impossible to penetrate, forcing him to go the full fifteen rounds for a points decision.

He won four out of every five of his professional fights on a knockout, all except one of his fourteen fights by that method in world title year 1916, but he claimed never to go into the ring with the express intention of winning that way. To Jimmy Wilde the k.o. itself was only an incident in the wider canvas of the fight, and he delivered it when he chose to; by then, the groundwork had been so thoroughly laid that while the crowds may have been unaware of it, Wilde himself knew that his opponent was hardly able to defend himself. What a hundred years earlier Pierce Egan, the 'Herodotus of the London prize ring' (to borrow a favourite literary affectation of the great boxing writer A. J. Liebling), would have called a 'mill' was usually brought to its conclusion with a left feint and a wallop with the right. With the now-flustered opponent looking through a glass darkly, the air would fill with gloves as Wilde finished him off (to 'visit the boards', as Egan might have said) with a fusillade of rights and lefts.

Jimmy's stinging left was often compared to a piston rod or some reptilian tongue, but he himself saw it less as an end in itself than as preparation for destructive punishment with the right. This combination neutralized the many southpaws he encountered, which was why one of his regular sparring partners was Evan Williams of Pontygwaith, who said he thought his ribs would cave in after being hit by Wilde; he learnt from Evan that although southpaws were awkward in leading with the right, they often lacked a complementary strength in the other hand. Wilde could hit very hard and very fast with both. Not for nothing does *Ring* magazine rank him third in its list of the hundred greatest all-time punchers, behind only Joe Louis and Sam Langford. Though past his prime by the time he visited the USA in 1919–20, in Philadelphia in his second fight with Battling Murray a right to the jaw lifted Murray clean off his feet, and bounced him off the ropes back on to the canvas. 'There is strength in those lathy arms, make no mistake about that,' wrote the boxing correspondent 'Straight Left' in 1914, 'and when he hits, he hits.' Another seasoned critic put it equally pithily: 'Wilde is smaller than a split second and hits like Stanley Ketchel.'

It was former British bantamweight champion Pedlar Palmer who dubbed Wilde the 'ghost with a hammer in his hand', still one of the greatest epithets of sporting literature. Thanks to his mastery of timing, Wilde at under seven stone punched harder than most featherweights who were a stone heavier. 'No man', thought Palmer, 'can be taught how to punch. Either he can or he can't.' Wilde could. The rattle of Joe Conn's teeth after one of Jimmy Wilde's uppercuts could be heard around the ring in August 1918. Many of his bouts ended with his opponent virtually unconscious on his feet. This was literally true of Eugene Husson at the NSC in March 1914, while Wilde himself, after inflicting punishment on the Frenchman for six rounds, was breathing so regularly 'that if a mirror had been held up to his face, it would not have been blurred'. After being peppered by Jimmy's hot shots Husson's own face changed even as spectators watched. It was 'as though he had run into a nest of wild bees, or fallen victim to instantaneous mumps'. All Wilde's qualities were on show on 18 December 1916 when he fought the Young Zulu Kid for a World Flyweight title which the Americans would at last recognize. Their earlier failure to do so had cost Wilde's bosom friend Percy Jones of Porth his rightful recognition as world title-holder when he beat Eugene Criqui in Liverpool in 1914. But after Wilde's April 1916 k.o. of the USA's Johnny Rosner at the same Merseyside venue, he began to attract more attention in the home of the brave than any British fighter since Driscoll.

The view Stateside was that 'it would do the Americans good to see a real fighting champion go through his paces. We have had too much of [lightweight contenders] Johnny Kilbane, Freddie Welsh, and Al McCoy', so Wilde went up against Guiseppe di Melfi (Joe Demelfi), known because of his swarthy complexion as the Young Zulu Kid. In round two the Kid, several inches shorter than Wilde, felt the devastating impact of Wilde's favourite move of stepping inside a left lead and, as his opponent's head came up, hitting him with a right cross. With the 'Brooklyn Wop-American' bent over like two sides of a triangle searching for a third, a left hook followed by three rights to the jaw sent him to the canvas, but the Kid recovered to give Wilde stern opposition, and it was the eleventh round before Jimmy caught him with a left that nearly took his head off, a left–right combination signalling the end as three more rights put him away. A world title is not easily come by, and Wilde himself was sufficiently hurt to enter a nursing home for a few days to recover.

It was Wilde's size, or lack of it, that puzzled contemporaries, who were constantly bewildered that someone of such freakish proportions could go on to achieve a record of only four defeats in a hundred and forty professional bouts (and he reversed two of those in a rematch). With arms frequently compared to 3 in. gas pipes, reeds or drumsticks, a 12 in. waist, spidery legs and tubercular appearance, a fighting weight of 6 st 9 lb and a height of 5 ft. 2 in., the damage one so child-like in appearance could inflict was little short of miraculous. 'He ought to be in a museum', thought one American. A visitor to the NSC when Jimmy was among the ringside spectators couldn't see him for looking:

> It was not until [Bombardier] Billy Wells moved his right leg that we became aware that the limb was effectively screening so great a little man . . . At first we thought of asking [NSC manager] Mr Bettinson whether the LCC knew about the little chap being out so late.

He was, variously, a 'fistic ghost', the 'tetrarch of the ring', an 'atom of Rhondda rampancy' and the 'last word in fighting machinery', as well as the more familiar 'Indian Famine', 'mighty atom', 'human hairpin' and 'Tylorstown terror'. 'It is possible', observed referee Eugene Corri drily, 'that some of his 300-odd opponents had other names for him too.'

64

All of this further endeared him to his followers at home. He had blossomed in the hothouse of the south Wales valleys, in the temples not of the 'Fancy', like the NSC, but of the fistic faithful, where he had cut his and countless others' teeth in the less decorous surroundings of the Ferndale Pavilion, the Tonypandy Marquee, the Market Hall, Aberdare, and Merthyr's Drill Hall. It was upstairs in Tylorstown's 'Workies' (Workingmen's Club), under the watchful eye of his trainer Benny Williams, the former Porth sprinter, that he trained best, and where he could break off to play billiards or dominoes. It was to Tylorstown he returned whenever he could, to play golf at the Mid Rhondda Golf Club on Penrhys, and to the smallholding he shared with his father-in-law, with their hundred pigeons and other assorted feather-weights. It was to Tylorstown, naturally, that he returned after wresting the British title from Joe Symonds in February 1916, to be greeted by cheering crowds and a procession headed by the Ferndale Silver Band. For Jimmy was a son not just of the Rhondda but of the Rhondda Fach, and the townships of Tylorstown and Ferndale in particular were his 'good patch', whose boisterous workforce, caring little for censorious moral finger-waggers, still thrilled to the bare-knuckled encounters up on the 'bloody spots', where knockouts were never technical and the gleam of a policeman's spiked helmet could be seen for miles. Given contemporary high-minded disapproval, the strikingly sparse coverage of Jimmy Wilde's early career in the south Wales press becomes more explicable. It took some time for Pontypridd's respectable class to embrace Freddie Welsh as well.

For all its aping of high society there was a raffish quality, too, to the dinner-jacketed clientele of Covent Garden's National Sporting Club, which, since opening in 1892, retained something of the Regency world of swells, bucks and toffs. This was where Jimmy Wilde made most defences of his world title, and while he liked fighting there – he was not the first or last Welsh boxer to be seduced by the tinkling glasses of decanted port – the gentlemanly amateur spirit of 'playing the game' he sternly rejected. 'To play the game for the game's sake', he wrote in his *The Art of Boxing* (1923),

> is very admirable and should always be in the back of your mind, but I contend . . . that foremost in your mind should be to play this game for

yourself, in the best way that the rules will present . . . It is probably one of the greatest failures of present day sport in Britain that we are becoming too good at losing . . . we do not mind losing, and we do lose – in a blaze of glory. We are in this game to WIN, and all thought of loss is to be abolished. Losing is a shame . . .

In intention the NSC was a forum for working-class boys from areas of limited economic opportunity, like the East End, Liverpool, Glasgow and the Welsh valleys, to fight for the pleasure of its cigar-smoking, dress-shirted members. Sport was still carrying historical ideological baggage as part of a wider programme to civilize the inner city and urban ghetto, improve the health of the poor and keep young men off the streets and out of trouble. But the Welsh coalfield's working-class industrial communities were ribbed by a variety of their own social and recreational agencies – from miners' institutes to working-men's clubs, sports associations, choirs and cultural and religious societies – which meant that the south Wales that Jimmy Wilde was born into was not a feral world of vicious crime and violence, though they, and pockets of appalling destitution, certainly existed. These were communities with a strong work ethic, and any boxer would fail without it, for it called for strong self-motivation, monotonous dedication, and deference to the rules – and to royalty. 'I cannot let *him* down', Wilde is alleged to have said at the NSC when, against his better judgment, he finally agreed to overlook an error in the contracts to leave his changing-room and fight the heavier Pete Herman because the Prince of Wales was there that night in 1921. Such an attitude would have been readily understood by Jimmy's contemporaries in an imperial Wales that was patriotic and royalist.

Wilde, for all that, showed no haste to enlist in the wartime army, and like Jack Dempsey, who was similarly reluctant, incurred some disapproval as a result. In 1917 his reiterated appeal on the grounds that he was a coalminer supporting his family was refused and he was ordered to join the army gymnastic staff at Aldershot, where he trained as a physical instructor and soon joined his fellow Welshmen Sergeant-Instructors Jim Driscoll and Johnny Basham, friends from his Scarrott days. It was a common complaint that the army was more interested in sport than in the Germans, and Wilde was not prevented from defending his titles while in uniform. But whereas he had fought on average more than once a month throughout 1916, his relatively few bouts – four in 1917 – suggest not only the difficulty of finding new opponents at his unnatural weight, but also that, when reports from the Western Front were filling the newspapers with announcements of gallantry and death – when, as many contemporaries saw it, a greater Game was being fought elsewhere – it was not a good time to be defending sporting titles.

Given the dearth of flyweight opponents, Pontypridd's dapper, pince-nez'd Ted Lewis, who had been Wilde's long-term manager ever since their first meeting on Boxing Day 1910 (when Jimmy despatched the rated Tonypandy middleweight Les Williams to the canvas with almost the finality with which Les, a passenger on the *Titanic*, was consigned to the seabed in April 1912), could hardly be blamed for pitting his man against opponents often a stone heavier, for Jimmy, despite eating three meals a day and enough meat to empty an abattoir, rarely managed to exceed six stone ten. Wilde gave over a stone away to the rugged Tancy Lee, a 'pawky Scot', in January 1915, when Ted Lewis, much to Jimmy's annoyance, threw in the towel in the seventeenth, a defeat he reversed the following year. Joe Symonds too was only half a pound under eight stone when Wilde beat him for the British title early in 1916, forcing him to drop to one knee as if in supplication (or was it obeisance?) and raise his hand in surrender in the twelfth. Jimmy in his ghosted memoir *Fighting is my business* (1938) recalled

> grinning round as John Douglas lifted my arm, Johnny Basham darting into the ring and kissing me, Ted Lewis looking as though he had broken the bank at Monte Carlo, and the glorious realisation that the English flyweight championship and Lonsdale Belt were mine. Hosts of Welshmen were on their feet and singing 'Hen Wlad fy Nhadau,'

the same pugilistic patriots, we can assume, who had crowded into the pre-match weigh-in and shouted 'Cymru am Byth' all through it.

By 1918 there was already talk of Wilde retiring: he had been at his best before the War and after it never recaptured his former total mastery. He was reckoned to have been fortunate to have been given the decision over the Australian Digger Evans and lost to Pal Moore in the King's Boxing Tournament in December 1918. Jimmy's restraint in these bouts was attributed to his 'ice-cold brain' and resemblance to a 'circumspect tiger', but in truth his advancing years were catching up on him, and his second victory over the American bantam Joe Lynch in 1919 – in front of the Prince of Wales, whose visits to the NSC gave boxing the respectability it craved – was far from decisive. Though he returned undefeated and £23,000 richer from his 1919–20 tour of the US and Canada, North America did not see him at his best.

He should have announced his retirement then, but he hung on to fight Pete Herman in a no-title contest at the NSC in January 1921. On the night Herman was eight and a half stone, having put on weight even since the midday weigh-in. The crowd was restive after a scheduled fight between Battling Levinsky and Billy Wells had been called off, and this was the occasion when Jimmy ignored the significant weight difference so as not to keep the Prince of Wales waiting. But the hard-hitting New Yorker badly hurt Wilde and knocked him through the ropes three times in the seventeenth before referee Haley stopped it. 'Wilde is a great fighter', said Herman afterwards, adding 'and must have been a wonderful fighter years ago.' Jimmy won a large purse, but while he was spared the total blindness that eventually afflicted Herman, the true cost was severe headaches and memory loss.

Again ill-advisedly, for he had not fought for two and a half years, he chose, for the last time, to face that unique loneliness only the boxer knows when he is alone in the ring, and which he cannot escape until what Joyce Carol Oates has called the 'awful unfolding' has taken place. It unfolded for Jimmy Wilde with near fatal results on 16 June 1923 in the Polo Grounds, New York, when he lost his World Flyweight title to Francisco Guilledo, better known as Pancho Villa. Despite a slight advantage in height and reach, Wilde was ten years older than his opponent and had no answer as the Filipino remorselessly jabbed, cut, hooked and punched. The world champion was by now just a ghost; the hammer had gone. And Villa half-killed him.

Beforehand Wilde had relaxed at Freddie Welsh's health farm in upper New York State, where he had – lightly – sparred with Jack Dempsey. Villa's relentless attack in the fight itself must have convinced Jimmy that he had Jack back in the ring with him. The kind of controversy that often surrounded Dempsey himself arose at the end of the second round, when a blow from Villa caught Wilde on the back of the head as he turned away at the sound of the bell. Although the punch had already been unleashed it would have been disqualified in the UK, but it earned only a warning from the American referee. For his part Villa might have said, as Dempsey did in similar circumstance in his 1921 fight with Carpentier, 'What was I supposed to do, send him a postcard?' The fight ended in the seventh with Jimmy flat on his face on the canvas, and he was half way back across the Atlantic before he recovered full consciousness.

Having been paid £8,000 to fight Herman and £13,000 to fight Villa, he had the considerable sum of £70,000 banked when he finally retired after that deathless decider in New York, but he then squandered much of it in reckless investments in Rhondda cinemas, an unsuccessful starting-price business in Cardiff, and London West End musicals. The inter-war years were not kind to Jimmy Wilde, whose career trajectory, we can now see, corresponded so exactly with that of the Rhondda itself that they went into retirement together.

The master of his craft in the ring, Wilde was oddly accident-prone outside it. In 1922 he fell from his horse when out with the Pentyrch hounds. He suffered various car accidents, including one in Dinas Powys on his way to his home in Cadoxton in 1957, that accelerated his decline. By 1960 symptoms of Alzheimer's disease were apparent. Later that year he was attacked on Queen Street Station, Cardiff, while waiting for a train to Barry Island, where he ran a café. Had the 40-year-old Trethomas thug with a prison record tried it on twenty years earlier, he would have been atomized.

By 1965 Jimmy Wilde was a bedridden patient at Whitchurch psychiatric hospital, diabetic and in the grip of senile dementia. He was now living proof – though 'living' is hardly the word – that no sport compares with boxing in terms of the damage it does to the brain. We may think that thanks to the insistence on gloves boxing has progressed from the mountain-fighting days of Dai Davies. But a glove soaked in sweat and blood becomes a club: it might protect the fist; it certainly injures the brain. A knockout punch, medical experts tell us, can detach the skull from the brain within it, and damage the veins that connect the one to the other. Punch-drunkenness means the lessening of mental and physical capacities that results from the long-term effects of repeated blows to the head. The kind of permanent damage these can inflict is to be seen most poignantly in the twilight years of the magnificent Muhammad Ali. It didn't happen as publicly to the great Jimmy Wilde, but he paid the price, sure enough.

He died on 10 March 1969, without knowing that his wife and some-time sparring partner Lizabeth had predeceased him. At 76 he had outlived his world champion contemporaries Percy Jones (d.1922), Driscoll (d.1925, the same year as Villa) and Welsh (d.1927) by more than forty years. Only Herman (d.1973) outlived him. The 'story of his greatness', intoned his *Times* obituarist, 'may become so distorted that the young may believe it an exaggeration by those in love with the past. But he was perhaps the most talented man ever to slip on the gloves.'

Perhaps. Let the final tribute come from an unlikely source, the theatre and literary critic James Agate (d.1947). Agate suffered from obsessive-compulsive disorder, a condition which may have coloured his view. But he was quite clear that: 'Jimmy Wilde I still probably and fatuously regard as the greatest genius I ever set eyes on . . . a wistful human scarecrow with a yonderly expression that suggested a chorister in decline.' The Rhondda, not least Tylorstown, is still a choral crucible, but Jimmy Wilde was never a chorister, he was a soloist, and when he was on song the whole world heard him.

Endnote

Gareth Harris's *Jimmy Wilde* (2006) is an invaluable sourcebook. I am grateful also to Carolyn Jacob, John Jenkins, Wynford Jones and Chris Williams for answering various queries.

Hero of the Darkest Years

JACK PETERSEN

Best Wishes
Jack Petersen

PETER STEAD

Best Wishes
Jack Petersen

'Amazing scenes at Ninian Park', blared the *Western Mail* on the morning of 16 May 1933. Locals would have immediately appreciated that these scenes could not have involved Cardiff City AFC, who had already completed their home fixtures at the ground on 22 April in front of a miserable crowd of 7,000. On the evening of 15 May it was a boxing promotion that, according to early reports, had attracted some 53,000 to Ninian Park, believed to 'be the largest crowd ever to attend a boxing match in Europe'. In truth, there were only about 40,000 at Ninian Park that early summer evening, and they were to witness scenes that were as disorientating as they were amazing. It was, perhaps, only as people left the ground that the full import of the evening sunk in, for they had been present at what was soon being described as the 'greatest attraction in the history of boxing in Wales'.

Top of the bill that evening was the bout between Jack Petersen and Heine Muller of Germany. Petersen, Cardiff born and bred, was already a local hero. He was only 21 but he had won all of his twenty-two professional fights, including two fights in 1932 in which he had picked up the British Light-Heavyweight and Heavyweight Championships. Both those championship bouts had taken place in London, but Cardiffians had turned out in force to welcome home their first British champion since Jim Driscoll. As the new heavyweight champion he had been met at Cardiff station by a crowd of some 4,000, his open car had been driven through lined streets, and near his home on Whitchurch Common he had been greeted by a brass band. As he was 'cheered to the echo' observers commented on his remarkable appearance, for this 'spruce good-looking young man' had no discernible scratches or bruises and, but for his boxer's nose, it was felt that he could pass for an 'Oxford undergraduate'.

At Ninian Park Petersen, although generally thought to be the favourite, was up against a tough customer. Muller was a veteran of some 200 fights, many of them against leading European and American opponents; 'like all continental fighters', it was noted, he had trained 'for hardness'. He was given a warm Welsh welcome: never had he seen 'such sportsmanship'. Petersen, it was thought, would have to be careful against 'this clever boxer'. They were 'well-matched' in terms of height, physique and 'cool demeanour', and Petersen, it was said, would need 'to use his speed and punching power to box his way to a knockout victory'. Arrangements were being made for extra rail, bus and steamer services; German sailors would be coming up from the docks. Amidst all the speculation it was clear that Cardiff had been 'gripped by fight fever'.

'Petersen's Great Punch' was the *Times* headline that summed up a bout that was over before many spectators had been settled in their Ninian Park seats. After just two minutes and ten seconds of the first round, Petersen landed a short right to Muller's solar plexus that sent him to the canvas where, lying on his left side with his right arm draped over the rope, he remained momentarily immobile. The end had been triggered by a Muller right to Petersen's jaw: the Welshman remained cool and, spotting his opponent's unguarded body, 'found it possible to land a left to the ribs that was almost a feint', before 'in a flash positioning himself for a short right to the wind'. This punch, 'coming as it did on two well-balanced legs, with the full force of perfect timing behind it, scored the complete knock-out blow'. One reporter described this ending of the bout as 'magical'. Its immediate effect was to silence the crowd: they were simply stunned and perhaps initially felt cheated. They would need confirmation of what they had seen or, perhaps, missed if they had blinked. The experienced referee, Jack Smith, described it as 'one of the greatest punches he had ever seen landed, both in its delicacy and effect'. Muller himself was quoted as saying that 'I have never had a punch like it before'.

There was extensive post-fight analysis. Above all, the evening had been a triumph for the city of Cardiff, and a badly needed one at that. Cardiff's great Victorian and Edwardian coal-exporting bonanza was definitely over. In the mid 1930s the trade of Cardiff docks was but half of what it had been in 1913, and consequently over thirty-six per cent of the city's insured males were unemployed. Meanwhile, in those great valleys that constituted Cardiff's northern hinterland there were towns and villages where over seventy per cent of the labour-force were out of work. A striking feature of Jack Petersen's professional career was that it coincided with the worst years of the Depression that devastated south Wales. Invariably, readers could turn from the dramatic reports of their hero's victories to detailed accounts of Miners Federation conferences bemoaning the unemployment of over 200,000 British miners and the 'vile consequences' of means-testing. Furthermore, a stagnating Cardiff was becoming all too aware that economic slump could only mean cultural mediocrity.

It was the local football team that best indicated the nature of the crisis. Cardiff City had been one of the best teams in the Britain of the mid 1920s. Two weeks before Petersen knocked out Muller they had finished the season in nineteenth place in the Football League's lowest division. Worse was to follow, for a year later they finished bottom and had to seek re-election. With memories of their Cup success at Wembley fading, Ninian Park had well and truly ceased to be a focus of pride and enthusiasm for the people of Cardiff and the Valleys. Of course, there was always rugby but, at that time, Cardiff was not quite the unchallenged centre of the Welsh game that it subsequently became, and results could never be predicted. In the two seasons between 1931 and 1933 Wales played only one international in Cardiff, a defeat against Ireland. Meanwhile, it was undeniable that both amateur and professional boxing were all the rage throughout the whole region, and the press carried regular reports of successful weekly promotions at places such as Bargoed, Merthyr, Caerphilly and Llanelli, as well as Cardiff and Swansea. In 1933 there was growing speculation as to what this boxing mania could amount to. All of this contributed to the significance of the Petersen–Muller bout. For the first time there was the prospect that Cardiff could become something it had never been before, a major boxing venue to compare with London, Glasgow and Liverpool.

There was universal praise for the manner in which Cardiff staged the big fight and the way that the police, stewards and transport authorities had risen to the challenge. Boxing had decisively proved that it could handle 'rugby international and FA Cup size crowds', and, according to the *Times*, Ninian Park had 'proved to be admirably adopted to a great popular event'. Few doubted that a city not hitherto associated with boxing headlines would now inevitably stage British championship and even world title fights. The self-satisfied *Western Mail* predicted that the 'city's trade will increase by thousands of pounds'.

In the aftermath of the 'big punch' there was particular praise for the evening's promoter, the Newport racehorse-owner Jimmy Jones. It was Jones who had spotted the potential of Ninian Park, who had taken a chance on the weather (the day before, it had rained on Glamorgan's cricketers at the nearby Arms Park) and, above all, had gambled on low admission prices to bring in those masses for whom Petersen had become such a hero. The fact that amongst the 40,000 crowd there were some 15,000 customers who had paid only 1s. and 6d. as compared to a top price of 15s. was taken as evidence of Jones's entrepreneurial flair, especially as many of those paying that price would have been 'first-timers'. The Welsh promoter was using the Petersen phenomenon to create a new audience for the sport, and few would have begrudged him if he had taken title fights away from London, where it was felt that the 'charging of exorbitant prices had done much to ruin the boxing scene'.

Jimmy Jones had done well, but he was not the only south Wales businessman for whom the event at Ninian Park constituted a triumph. Indeed, Jack Petersen's whole career had thus far been a classic exemplar of how small local businessmen were using whatever assets were at hand to chisel their way out of the Depression. Recently, the boxing reporter Gareth Jones has slightly overstated things in arguing that Petersen was one of the first athletes to be openly promoted as a commodity, for, as Trevor Wignall firmly believed, 'professional boxers are tradesmen'. For Wignall, the leading British boxing correspondent of the 1950s, little had changed in the two hundred years of the sport: he saw fighters 'whirl their fists and (then) purchase expensive cars'. But Jones is right to highlight the streamlined nature of the Petersen plan. His career was throughout a brilliantly executed capitalist venture but one that at the same time takes us into a world of the same kind of personalities, deals, gambles, setbacks and sheer razzmatazz that have typically characterized all the most endearing and myth-making boxing cultures. To sustain such a culture every city has to become a little bit like the New York of that era.

The promising future that the Ninian Park fight had seemed to portend was above all a triumph for Jack T. Petersen, the father and trainer of the fighter, a businessman whose career represented a sparkling response to the opportunities that Cardiff presented and which would have required a Damon Runyon to do it justice. As the name suggests he was the son of a Norwegian, a ship's carpenter from Haugesund, a southern Norwegian port closely linked to Cardiff by the exchange of coal and timber. During his career Jack, the champion, was occasionally referred to as a 'Viking', but he was essentially a Celt, for his grandfather had gone first to Cork, where he had married an Irish girl. J.T. was born in Cork and had come to Cardiff with the family in the 1890s where in time he was to marry a local girl. Thus it was that his son, born in 1911, would have that potent mix of Irish and Welsh blood that has flowed through the veins of so many Welsh boxers.

In Cardiff Jack senior had almost inevitably been drawn into the boxing world of the docks area: he was by all accounts 'no mean performer', boxing in the Welsh amateur team and acquitting himself well in the ring against the great Jim Driscoll (gaining a draw, according to some tellers of the tale). Later, he ran a gym above a pub in the docks and then did some refereeing. He also studied medicine and the cult of fitness, travelling to Norway for ideas, and it was that background that finally allowed him in 1905 to purchase the Lynn Institute in St John's Square, in the heart of Cardiff's shopping district. From the outset the Institute was designed to be a pioneering venture that would provide a fashionable focus for both the city's sportsmen and businessmen. The Marquess of Bute would cross the road from his castle to enter the ring with Mr Petersen, and the Chief Constable was another who kept fit in this way.

The unique medical and social cachet of the Lynn Institute allowed masseur J. T. Petersen to cut a dash in Cardiff, and as the years went by he was to develop his image as both as a public personality and successful businessman. He became something of a dandy and ladies' man, wearing spats and bespoke suits from Evan Roberts. He liked to be referred to as either 'Doctor' or 'Professor', and he resided, not in the docks, but first in suburban Whitchurch and then in a cliff-top Barry property. Once, when he gave his new address as 'Porth-y-Castell', in actuality a leafy Barry avenue, a friend assumed that J.T.'s business acumen had set the family up in a castle. Eventually it was the emergence from the Lynn Institute of a champion boxer that brought J.T. affluence. What he could not have foreseen and what he would never have initially sanctioned was that his payload would come in the form of his son, one of three children resulting from an unsuccessful marriage to Malinda Rossiter.

J.T. had nurtured ambitious plans for the boy, who was christened John Charles Petersen. He wanted him to become a real doctor, and sent him to a private school in Hereford and then to St Illtyd's School in Cardiff, a reflection of the family's devout Catholicism. With his mother gone the young John was an unhappy and lonely child (a 'latch-key kid', suggests his own son, David), and inevitably the Lynn Institute became his real home. Bill Barrett has described how the young lad picked up pocket money there by cleaning and polishing, all the while listening to his Pa's tales of the great fighters of the past whom he had encountered in booths or on the docks. John started to train himself, and in time fought amateur bouts that were kept from Pa's attention with the connivance of two devoted sisters, who would hide him as his nose began to give the game away. Eventually Pa had to face the facts and, in so doing, he made it clear that his son's boxing career would have to be planned on his terms and his terms alone. Having won the ABA light-heavyweight championship in 1931 Jack Petersen became a professional, and one able to call on the whole medical and business resources of the Lynn Institute.

His father's medical expertise, fitness notions and training methods ensured that no professional boxer had been so scientifically prepared as Petersen. Perhaps even more remarkable was Pa's formula for the financing and marketing of his new product, the story of which has been told in detail in Bob Lonkhurst's biography of Petersen. Essentially, a syndicate emerged that brought together businessmen either known to Pa through the Lynn Institute or associated with the Stadium Club in London's Holborn. Remarkably, Petersen's first nine fights were all in London at the Stadium Club, and it was there that the package was honed and Pa's plans finalized. His son was cutting a dash in the metropolis, but it was clear that he was to remain a Cardiff-based fighter who returned home after winning his bouts. It was soon apparent that Jack had no great difficulty in over-coming bigger men. In truth he was essentially a light-heavyweight (he was usually under thirteen stone and often weighed in fully dressed), but from the outset Pa was aware that it was heavyweights that the public wanted and were prepared to pay big money to see. In his first professional fight at the Stadium Club Petersen took on Bill Partridge who was three stones heavier; the fight was stopped in the fourth round after the big man had been down twice. The tone of Petersen's career had been set. Back home, the clamour for their new hero to fight on home territory grew, and so it was that his eleventh fight took place at Cardiff's Greyfriars Hall, where a crowd of over 8,000 saw Petersen overcome Leo Bandies. All told, Petersen fought fifteen matches in his first eight months as a pro; he won them all and in doing so had emerged as a real crowd-pleaser, fully warranting the lucrative deals that Pa had negotiated. Here was a fighter, and a syndicate, in a hurry. Thus, within a fifty-day period in 1932, Petersen outpointed Harry Crossley at Holborn to win the British Light-Heavyweight title, and then at Wimbledon knocked out Reggie Meen in the second round to take the British Heavyweight title.

The boxing public had clearly taken to the young Welsh fighter, and even world-weary journalists were beginning to wonder whether something was happening that would breathe new life into the mediocre British heavyweight division, where both bouts and careers tend to 'end in bitter disappointment and, as often as not, in an atmosphere of derision'. As champion, Reggie Meen had been thought of as 'no better than many others before him'. Before the bout, the *Times* correspondent pointed out that Meen had no future as a possible opponent of leading Continental or American boxers, whereas Petersen clearly offered something more. Surely, he argued, Petersen would win, but what would be more crucial was the nature of that victory. What was needed was a decisive win, in which Petersen gave evidence of skill and ringcraft to complement his undoubted speed, courage and punching power. The general feeling was that Petersen was not quite yet the 'fully equipped fighter', not least because of his 'impetuosity'. However, the *Western Mail* reported that Pa had been working with him on a new method of delivering speedier punches that would offset his habit of taking 'outrageous chances'.

In the event Petersen knocked out the two-stone-heavier champ in the second round. He had totally outboxed Meen with fast straight lefts, right crosses to the jaw and a final right uppercut. Now the critical evaluations went up a notch. For the *Western Mail* this was 'as fine a display of fighting and boxing as has ever characterized a British title fight'. Even before the bout the *Times* had noted the comparisons that had been made between Petersen and Georges Carpentier, the handsome and stylish Frenchman who had been World Light-Heavyweight Champion and European Heavyweight Champion, and who had unsuccessfully taken on Jack Dempsey for the World Heavyweight title. Now the London paper was ready to go full out with the Carpentier angle: that final uppercut had been 'pure Carpentier', there could be 'no higher compliment'. The fight had ended in a manner 'that Carpentier, to whom Petersen bears a strong resemblance, could hardly have improved upon'. Interestingly, even as the *Times* congratulated Petersen on his Lonsdale belt, it reiterated its warning about that weakness he had shown in some of his earlier victories. For a moment, just before he had finished off Meen, Petersen had again 'thrown all science and thought to the wind' and there was just a fleeting chance that he might have 'lost his head'. Meen, however, was in no condition to take advantage, and Petersen had kept his cool.

When Jack Petersen went into the ring to take on Heine Muller, in 1933, he did so in the knowledge that the boxing masses were already on his side, and that the regular boxing insiders were just beginning to hope that some real class and promise had at last been injected into the British heavyweight scene. A defining moment had come in January, when Jack had defended his heavyweight title at London's Olympia: in round twelve he knocked out Jack Pettifer with a left hook: he had rendered unconscious a man six inches taller and four stones heavier. This was precisely the aggression and drama that British boxing was crying out for. By May, in the aftermath of the Muller bout, amidst all the praise for Ninian Park, the city of Cardiff and the promoter, there was now serious speculation as to what Petersen himself could achieve. For the *Times* man the great punch that did for Muller 'might have been landed by Robert Fitzsimmons', hitherto the only British world heavyweight champion. Recalling all the excitement of the 1890s, this correspondent suggested that Petersen's 'punch to the wind' would 'surely have dropped Corbett' or 'even Jeffries', the battering ram to whom Fitzsimmons had lost his title. Petersen's 'sensational' *coup de grâce* in Cardiff had considerably boosted the rhetoric and raised the stakes. Jimmy Jones could see fame and fortune beckoning. 'It is my ambition', he announced, 'to stage a world championship fight in Cardiff', and he was fully prepared 'to spend the money to convert Ninian Park into a first-class stadium'. He revealed that he had already cabled the New York promoter Jimmy Johnston, inviting him to bring over the current world champion, Jack Sharkey of Boston, 'providing that he beats Primo Carnera' (which, a few weeks later, he failed to do). If this approach failed, there was always the possibility of a European championship contest against the Basque Paolino Uzcudun, or a world light-heavyweight fight against Maxie Rosenbloom.

Those heady days of early summer 1933 were not to be the last in which Jack Petersen's talent was compared with that of previous world champions and his name associated with world title bouts. Bob Mee has suggested that 1934 'was Petersen's greatest year'. That year he won and defended the British Empire title, prompting *Ring* magazine to rate him sixth in its list of contenders for Max Baer's World Heavyweight title. The years between the defeat of Jack Dempsey in 1926 and the crowning of Joe Louis in 1937 formed a fascinating period of transition, in which there were six world champions of varying ability and in which the actual personnel of title bouts owed more to New York promoters' sense of box office than to boxing justice. In terms of pure talent Pa Petersen had no doubt that his boy could hold his own in the company of Sharkey, Carnera, Baer or Braddock, the successive champions between 1932 and 1937. His opinion was shared by none other than the great Jack Dempsey himself, who cabled Pa offering to manage Jack in any title fight against Baer. Pa Petersen lost no opportunity in letting the American (essentially the New York) boxing establishment know the worth of his boy. Bob Lonkhurst prints the exchanges between Pa and Nat Fleischer, who had suggested in *Ring* that Petersen was not a worthy contender. In a sentence that vividly evokes that whole world of 1930s New York, Fleischer commented that the Welshman had hitherto 'only beaten a series of bums dug up from the graveyard'. In truth both Pa and Fleischer (who within a few years was to praise Tommy Farr as the 'best British heavyweight for a quarter of a century') were aware that Depression America would only stage fights that would fill Yankee

Stadium. Even more to the point, Pa had no real interest in sending his boy to the States to fight for a pittance. Apart from anything else, he had no need to: Jack was able make far more money fighting at home.

And so it was that when Jack Petersen suddenly announced his retirement from the ring in April 1937 he had never fought for the World Light-Heavy or Heavyweight titles; indeed, he had never fought outside Britain. Still only 25, he brought an end to a six-year career in which he had been the chief box-office attraction in British boxing. Sir Arthur Elvin of Wembley once commented that the 'only time he made a profit was when Jack Petersen was on the bill'. From the early days at the Stadium Club, Pa had demanded top fees; once his career was launched Petersen never fought for less than £3,500, and for big fights he received even more. He drew some of the greatest crowds in British boxing history: 70,000 at White City, 60,000 at Wembley. Ninian Park had been left far behind. They came and they paid because they knew they would get value for money. He was, Stan Shipley was to argue, the 'most popular British boxer since Bombardier Billy Wells'. Jack's popularity was best explained by O. F. Snelling, who recalled that he was the 'most aggressive British heavyweight I ever saw'. The crowds came because he would be using both fists to end fights as dramatically as possible.

In those four years that followed the Muller triumph, Petersen registered some quick knockouts and great wins that thrilled British boxing fans and, not least, the thousands of Welsh enthusiasts who crowded the excursion trains that were laid on to take them to the great London venues (£1 return, including 'Lunch and Hot Supper'). However, there were also to be severe setbacks of a kind never experienced before the Muller fight. The first and most controversial setback came just two months later. Petersen's contest against the flamboyant former Irish Guardsman Jack Doyle attracted a huge crowd to the White City for a bout that classically displayed the power of money in professional boxing. Promoter Jeff Dickson guaranteed riches for all concerned, as he brought together two charismatic boxers who would be looking to finish things early (Doyle had seen off the giant Pettifer in only two rounds). In fact, this was essentially a mismatch, for Doyle was not really experienced enough for a crack at the title. He was taller than Petersen and had a longer reach, but initially the champion was able to score freely. Doyle responded with a series of wild punches, some of which were extremely dubious. Others, however, were effective, and after a right to Petersen's temple, the champion staggered; it seemed as if the title was about to change hands. Doyle was warned about his low punches, but took no heed, and when, early in the second, two more followed, the referee struggled to break up furious exchanges before disqualifying Doyle. The crowd were enraged: they had been denied anticipated scenes of carnage. The boxing establishment were even angrier at what some regarded as 'an unmitigated disaster'. Doyle's punishment was unprecedented: he was suspended for six months and his purse was withheld.

Petersen was still champion, but it could be argued that he was never quite the same fighter after that crazy night at the White City. His Barry doctor was shocked at his condition, and for years Jack would display the protector that one or more of Doyle's low punches had dented. Bob Lonkhurst has argued that the enforced rest that followed altered Petersen's schedule significantly, especially with regard to American opponents. When he returned to the ring in November 1933 it was to take on an older British fighter who was not only as popular but, remarkably, also smaller. The Cornishman Len Harvey, who in time was to hold the World Light-Heavyweight title that should have been Jack's, was a streetwise fighter well able to fight at close quarters and defend himself. At the Albert Hall Petersen had moments when he looked like a champion but, instead of relying on his reach, he fell into Harvey's trap, especially after his eye was cut in the eighth. After fifteen rounds, victory and the British Heavyweight title went to a fighter dubbed the 'octopus' and 'notorious' for his 'armlocks'. The decision was as controversial as it was surprising. At one point Petersen had been warned about a head-butt that he later claimed was an accidental elbow contact. The verdict left Petersen feeling cheated: he had experienced his first professional defeat.

Clearly, there was unfinished business here, and canny promoters matched the two men again in 1934 at the White City and 1936 at Wembley. Despite the hype neither fight was a classic: their contrasting styles tended to expose each other's weaknesses. In the first meeting Petersen regained his title by taking the fight to his opponent, closing his left eye in the fifth and stopping him in the twelfth. At Wembley Petersen out boxed an opponent who fought a spoiling game without landing many punches. Following his defeat in the first Harvey fight, Jack had to rebuild his career, and he did so with an impressive series of wins in 1934, in the process ending a brutal bout by stopping Larry Gains in the thirteenth to win the Empire title. The sheer and increasing physicality of Petersen's fights was, of course, exactly what the vast crowds wanted to see. And so it was that Jack was drawn into a series of disastrous bouts that ensured that, although he lost only five of his thirty-eight fights, he would 'be remembered', as his *Times* obituary would suggest, 'for the bouts he lost as much as for those he won'. His nemesis came in the person of Walter Neusel, the two-stone-heavier 'Blond Tiger' from Germany. The two men featured in a series of three uncompromisingly bloody battles, all of which ended with the towel being thrown in from Petersen's corner (in the eleventh, tenth and tenth rounds respectively). Terrific facial damage was inflicted in these bouts, the first two of which Neusel secured at the very moments when it looked as if he might lose. The third defeat by the German ended Petersen's career. Six months earlier he had lost both his titles to a giant South African, Ben Foord, defeat coming in the third after his eye had been badly cut. After the third Neusel fight the medical advice was unambiguous: fight again, and risk blindness.

There were clear medical reasons for Jack Petersen to retire at the age of 25 but there were other factors that had clouded the blue skies of the Muller days. The syndicate had long gone, and what is more, Jack was now his own manager. Family loyalty prevented any public dispute, but clearly there had been a falling-out over the Neusel arrangements. When Jack was married in October 1935 to Betty Williams, the daughter of a Cardiff auctioneer and greyhound enthusiast, there were huge crowds and a police cordon at Marshfield Church, but no sign of Pa. As reporters analysed the relative weaknesses displayed by Petersen in the last years of his career, it was noted that he often lacked good sparring partners and that he was never in the hands of a manager with true championship experience. These last days in the ring were also marred by friction with the up-and-coming Tommy Farr, who deeply resented the lack of 'common justice' that saw Petersen and the British Boxing Board of Control deny him a contest. Farr was only nineteen months younger than Jack but had progressed by a very different boxing and social route, in which the booths had played a large part. The very year that Jack retired, 1937, saw Farr win the British Heavyweight title and then ensure a legendary status in Wales by going the distance in a world title fight.

Tommy Farr's night at Yankee Stadium ensured that, in the slow process of recovery that characterized the next decades, the Welsh working class, and in particular his own mining valleys, had one defining achievement in which they could take pride. Meanwhile, there was never any doubt that the essentially suburban and bourgeois Jack Petersen had sufficient resources in his education, business background and wealth to launch a full and rewarding career in that part of Wales of which he was so much a product. 'Good Old Barry' had always been his response as he returned after every bout: its beaches and cliff steps had always played an important part in his preparation. In time, he was to take over a saddlery business in the main street and develop it as a pioneering sports shop. We local boys went in to buy tins of dubbin but really to ask for his autograph: the bespectacled, immaculately dressed and groomed giant always smilingly obliged.

After 1938 the Army had become a passion, and he took great pride in his eventual rank of Major; as a Staff Training Officer he had loved his work with cadets and of the part he played in grooming future champions, such as Joe Erskine, Dai Dower and Howard Winstone. He became one of the first ex-boxers to go into sports administration: the British Boxing Board of Control, of which he became President in 1986, named their London headquarters Jack Petersen House. As a member of the Welsh Sports Council, and eventual Chair, he became one of the most familiar and influential figures in Welsh public life. He moved to Cardiff, where briefly he served as a city councillor; later he was to live in Porthcawl. The Church was always important in his life: he served as warden, took the reading and to his children's embarrassment sang the hymns with a crooner's voice. He had become an Anglican at his marriage and, although resenting his banishment by the Catholic Church, much of his initial faith remained, and Catholicism was to remain an element in the family. The lonely childhood he had experienced ensured that his own family would always be his main concern: he gave his four children a good education and took considerable pride in their various careers in the army, business and the arts.

When Jack Petersen died in 1990 there were many tributes to his charm and to his half-century of public service: Lord Brooks spoke of how 'he had never refused an invitation'. Moving tributes took the form of reflections on a very distant era, when a very handsome young man, whose formal portraits could have served to illustrate Greek Classicism or German propaganda, became what Dan O'Neill described as a 'charismatic superstar long before the term was invented'. The *Times* suggested that he had been the 'most popular and certainly one of the most admired British boxers of his era'. The crowds had admired what O'Neill called his 'Corinthian' values and the *Times* his 'old-fashioned bearing'. In time the fans came to admire his terrific bravery and courage, but above all it was his commitment to non-stop action that had thrilled them most. Arthur Helliwell summed it up best when he spoke of Jack's 'tigerish fury' and 'reckless disregard for the punishment he might be taking'; it was 'his one fault, his fiery impetuosity' that had made him 'such a magnetic fighter'. At his death the remembrancers of the Welsh press stressed his Cardiff identity and how he 'had kept the city in his soul'. Contemporary accounts always gave a mention to the numbers of dockers and miners attending his fights. Newsreel images and his training routines had made him a familiar figure in the Valleys, and there, too, he was a hero. Bill Barrett reminded his readers that Jack had been 'sorely needed' in those dark days. At the funeral Stan Thomas of the Board of Control talked of how Jack had 'lifted the hearts of Welshmen everywhere' and of how 'as a nation of sportsmen we adored him': thanks to him, 'in those difficult early Thirties we stood ten feet tall'.

'Call me Tommy'

TOMMY FARR THE TONYPANDY KID

DAI SMITH

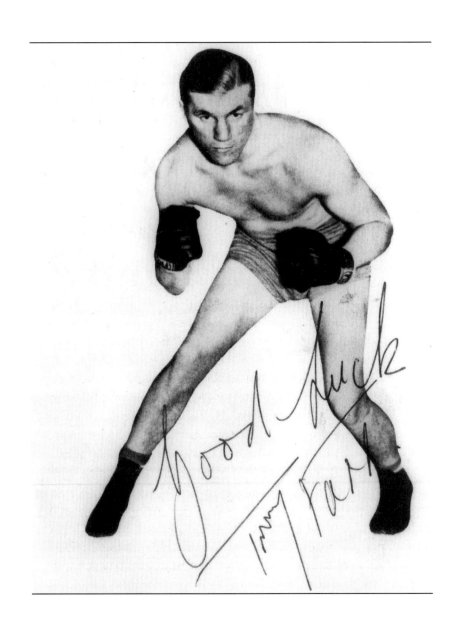

Good Luck
Tommy Farr

Tonypandy is one of those sites where public and private memories intersect. The industrial struggle around the Cambrian Combine strike which fanned out from Clydach Vale to spawn the social rebellion which was encapsulated by the destruction of the town's shops in late 1910 also tied the name of Winston Churchill irrevocably to Tonypandy. The then Home Secretary did send hussars and Metropolitan police to quell the revolt in mid Rhondda. It was remembered in Labour's crushing victory over the Churchill-led Conservatives in 1945 and nurtured as memory of its infamy in the subsequent elections of 1950 and 1951. But by then such public and collective notoriety for Tonypandy also mingled with an individual fame that was collectively cradled with a different kind of inextinguishable pride and which, with sweet irony, linked another Churchill to the township. That was the one-legged saddler from Penygraig, Job Churchill, mentor in and out of the ring to the boy who first fought for money at the age of 12 as the Tonypandy Kid and who, aged just 24, fought for the Heavyweight Championship of the World in New York City as Tommy Farr. From 1937 Tonypandy entered the public memory with a different kind of violent *éclat*.

The historical question is why a defeat could have such a resounding echo, and the cultural answer lies deep in the connection between Thomas George Farr, born into the large family of an immigrant miner from Cork in 1913, and the industrial urban complex made up of switchback streets and stone-strewn alleys that was Penygraig to the south, Clydach Vale and Llwynypia to the north, with Tonypandy itself bisected by the coal-fouled river Rhondda and defined, despite its thrown-together appearance, by the perpendicular and broad-shouldered bluff that was Trealaw Mountain to the east. All this, and its pubs and music halls and the gambling, street-fighting escapades of its workforce of over 12,000 miners employed in its still-beckoning pits – the Cambrian Combine in Clydach Vale, the Naval and the Anthony in Penygraig, the Glamorgan and Scotch collieries at Llwynypia – were the daily sights that young Tommy would take in as he stepped out from his first home, Railway Terrace in Clydach

Vale, to walk the couple of hundred yards to Tonypandy Square, from where the riots had exploded down Dunraven Street in November 1910. Then a favourite amongst the ransacked items of clothing were caps and mufflers – the uniform of the Edwardian working class – but when their Working Class Hero returned from his transatlantic expedition in 1937 the outfitters of Tonypandy displayed trilbies and ties – appurtenances of a Hollywood-enchanted generation – under the sales legend 'As worn by Tommy Farr'. Even the poverty which had entered the DNA of mid Rhondda in the inter-war years could not entirely close down the dream which he had brought back by breaking out. And none had tasted the bitterness of real poverty more than Kid Farr.

The crisis in the coal industry, which spiralled away in the immediate post-war years via national strikes and local lock-outs into full-blown economic depression, was compounded for the Farr family of four girls and four boys by the early death of their mother in 1922 and, soon thereafter, the permanent physical and psychological incapacity of their once-mighty father. Tommy was 10 years old. At home the older children cooked, cleaned and mended, and were dependent on the charity of their increasingly impoverished neighbours. On the streets Tommy pushed a handmade cart selling bits and pieces, from buttons and cotton to vinegar and white lime and soap. He doubled up as a delivery boy. School was soon left behind. His face and his fate were well known on the streets of Tonypandy. His destiny was inevitably seen as the pits and the brute apprenticeship of being a collier boy. He went underground in the Cambrian pit at the head of Clydach Vale, a cul-de-sac of a cwm shooting off for a few hill-entrenched miles at a right angle from Tonypandy Square.

It was the spring of 1927, and the season was the only hopeful thing in the sullen aftermath of the General Strike and lock-out of 1926. He worked at the coalface, an apprentice with a curling box to gather up the coal prised from the seams by skilled colliers, on call, up to his knees in icy water, to fill the drams with lump coal and help clear away the clod and stone, all to a price-list for piecemeal labour whose inadequacy had sparked the strike of 1910–11. The talk would have still been of that, and of the betrayals of 1921 and 1926, and the selective recall of men to work at the management's whim. Since 1923, until his victimization in 1929, the checkweigher, essentially the men's workplace representative at the colliery, had been Lewis Jones, Communist activist from Clydach Vale and, before his untimely death in 1939, author of those two sprawling epics of Rhondda life, the novels *Cwmardy* and *We Live*. From mid Rhondda alone twenty-two miners would within a decade volunteer as International Brigaders to fight in Spain. Three of them were from Clydach Vale, of whom Harry Dobson was killed at the Ebro offensive in 1938. The year before, Arthur Horner, Communist President of the South Wales Miners' Federation since 1936, had visited the volunteers, in July, in Spain. He reported back to his Executive that they quizzed him 'about the development in China, whether unemployment benefit had increased to accord with the cost of living, and many . . . wanted to know whether Tommy Farr would beat Joe Louis'. Neither they, nor the subject of their enquiry, would have found anything incongruous in the connected query. The Penygraig Labour Club, where Farr trained and fought from the late 1920s was refurbished and officially reopened in 1929 by Councillor Mark Harcombe of Tonypandy, the tsar of the Rhondda Labour Party for decades to come. When Farr trained and fought out of Slough in the mid 1930s he did so conscious that he was part of a surge of migration from the Rhondda to that light industry area and one whose connections were still on a two-way street, as he wrote openly to the Editor of the *South Wales Echo* to protest at the way his removal to Slough had apparently also removed him from the radar of Welsh journalists and promoters who claimed he had become, by the autumn of 1935, a mere try-out for better fighters:

> Just a line re. your remarks in last Saturday's article . . . You call me a punch bag. Ask [anyone who has fought him] . . . if I'm a punch bag. I am unlucky if anything but still undaunted. I haven't a scratch on me since I've been up in Slough. If I had the press behind me like Petersen . . . I would be having just as much money for my fights as they do, and fighting a lot more often. I am being pulled down, and you by making those remarks are not giving me a fair crack of the whip which is all I want. If anyone deserves to get on, it's me. I lead a clean life and do good by everybody . . . since I have been in Slough I have found work

for sixty-three Welsh unemployed, and if you would like me to write and confirm it let me know. Would any of the big noises do it?

He might have had no scratches since he arrived in salubrious Slough, but he already carried enough of them on his body, and attendant memories to mull over, before he got there. Most of them came from the colliery, not the boxing ring. There had been a minor explosion underground almost as soon as he had begun work, and shards of diamond-hard coal had splintered and pitted his face and body. It was these scars and the blue indentations of coal particles below the skin which caused Joe Louis to gasp, and perhaps for the first time to wonder how easy this Welsh miner would actually be, when they stripped for the weigh-in before their own epic began. Tommy Farr had no choice but to carry Tonypandy with him wherever he went. He always regarded fighting as child's play to anyone who had had to work underground, and readily said so. Exhausted and angry at a foreman's chivvying, he threw his shovel down for the last time when barely 16 and despite the desperate need for money to help support his siblings he never went back. And he never forgot.

He left, of course, to fight in the itinerant boxing booths of Joe Gess, and with mind-numbing regularity, often three and more times a month, on the undercard of the fight-nights which were stitched into the moth-eaten fabric of coalfield life. It was 1933 before he had his first fight outside the coalfield, very unsuccessfully, at Crystal Palace. He fled home to the known comfort of the scuffed and smoky small halls and pub gyms across south Wales. On fly-blown handbills and in the small newsprint of challenges issued and boasts strutted, his name flickers with a legion of others scrambling to make a mark in what Gwyn Thomas, born in Porth the same year as the fighter, would soon call the 'slaughterhouse of south Wales'. The phrase was shorthand for mass unemployment, mass migration and the euphemistically entitled 'material deprivation' which caused rickets in the womb. From 12 years old he fought, just out of the womb of any semblance of a protective society, as Young Tommy Farr or 'Kid' Farr or Battling 'Kid' Farr or Young 'Kid' Farr, against a host of other Young Battlers and Kid Scrappers going head-to-toe for six rounds and side bets. But Tommy, no immaculate natural genius of the canvas by any means, had two advantages the others never quite had: a genetic disinclination to take a backward step, and the opportunity to learn when and how to do exactly that.

The pits had given him a daily work ethic – though the phrase has an inappropriate ring to it – and, more brutally, in its below ground shadowing of the bloody spots that had once framed the slugfests of such as his father, a stage to frame his ferocity. Pit-fighting was often between matched pairs of colliers or their boys, the latter cajoled, or more likely bullied, into contests for amusement and bets when the miners gathered for their cold tea and cold snap breaks in the roadways off the coal headings. The sport was as brutally direct in name as in its nature. It was called 'in the holes', where holes about a foot or so apart were dug to the depth of a fighter's waist. The chosen contestants, maybe as many as four pairs facing off, climbed in and punched each other until one or other bloodied fighter was knocked senseless whilst still on his feet in his enclosing hole. They hit each other, Tommy Farr recalled, 'until they were virtually unconscious. I have never forgotten it.' He was, of course, good at it too:

> Those were fights [in the holes] amongst the hardest I ever had. It taught you to parry, to duck, and above all to take it. It may not have been a proper school but it did establish your courage. If you were good in the holes, you were good anywhere.

It was that 'anywhere' that he now ardently sought. He persuaded Joby Churchill, after endless nagging and persistence, to take his 'in the holes' courage to a level of ring knowledge where he could counter- attack after he had 'taken' it. He grew in height to just over six feet and in boxing size from cruiser weight to light-heavyweight by 1933, when he beat Randy Jones on points in Tonypandy to become champion of Wales at the age of 20. Joby Churchill could see he would never be a dynamite puncher or one able to dominate by sheer speed or intimidating bulk. His game would be to wear opponents down; to be first to engage and last to retreat. The classic Tommy Farr performance was one of non-stop left jabs and right-hand counters, delivered from a hard-to-hit crouch as inelegant as it was effective. He learned his trade piece by piece, until in 1934, emerging again from the Valleys, where he was chalking up victories on points in too-familiar places with all-too-familiar faces, he hit the rails once more and stumbled when he tried to move up the rankings. Londoner Eddie Phillips beat him in Holborn and in Wandsworth. That Farr was a hardworking and determined professional was clear, but his bitterness, and his chippy surliness, now grew, as he saw his career stall in the doldrums and older, more popular and more media-friendly boxers of good looks and fluid style, like the formerly amateur Cardiffian Jack Petersen, take the paper pounds, and seemingly, leave him with the penny coins. In the early winter of 1934 Tommy Farr fought in Llanelli for nothing, only his expenses. He gave the fee to the disaster fund set up for the 262 men and boys who had been killed in the Gresford mining disaster of September that year.

That year ended with another bang, as he knocked out his opponent in Trealaw in two rounds, and he opened 1935 with a one-round k.o. in the same place, but it would prove to be another frustrating year. In February he was defeated over fifteen rounds on points by his three-times nemesis Eddie Phillips, even though they fought at the Pavilion in Mountain Ash. There were reasons – notably an injured right hand – but no excuses, and he had to return to the task of building a solid, though scarcely dazzling, reputation. Meanwhile, to his intense frustration he had to watch Petersen hog the limelight, even though the lumbering German tank, Walter Neusel, defeated Jack twice. No justice for Tommy, thought and loudly protested Farr, who desperately wanted some, any, big pay nights. Then, after five straight wins, from October his fortunes perceptibly changed. First, in January 1936 he impressively outpointed the former light-heavyweight great, American Tommy Loughran, at the Albert Hall, and, undefeated that year, took the Welsh Heavyweight title in an eliminator for the British title when he knocked out Jim Wilde in Swansea in September. In every sense imaginable, though by no means foreseeable as the year ended, 1937 would be Tommy Farr's year of a lifetime.

He may have sensed it coming, however slowly, just as his own formative society had patently been on a cusp of advance after a decade of defeats. In 1934 there had been a slight upswing in the coal export trade and the first, small, wage increase for over a decade. The struggle against company unionism in certain pits reached a new dimension that heralded the fight back to dominance of the SWMF across the coalfield, and in 1935 dramatic stay-down strikes in south Wales made headline news across Britain, as did the truly total demonstrations of these stricken valleys, weekend after weekend in January and February 1935, when entire communities came out onto the streets against the government's proposed and vindictive Unemployment Assistance regulations. They were put on hold in the face of such gargantuan protests, and subsequently withdrawn: a common people's victory, and the first effective popular action since 1926. On the evening of 16 December 1935, Tommy, as a late substitute, fought and beat Rhenus de Boer in Bristol before a crowd of supporters who had travelled by train through the Severn Tunnel, and they were with him on the night of 21st December, five days later, in Cardiff, where a Welsh XV had that afternoon signalled the re-emergence of the national game by beating the All Blacks by 13 points to 12. Tommy duly knocked out, in round four, his very own former great hero, the veteran from Pontypridd, Frank Moody, who had in the 1920s single-handedly carried Welsh boxing's formerly strong reputation in the United States. That, too, had suffered. For a generation, it was becoming time to move on. Tommy's own time was coming. His luck changed. And then he made his own.

The ever-evasive Jack Petersen, intermittent British heavyweight champion since 1932, had been unexpectedly beaten by the ponderous South African Ben Foord for the British and Empire title in August 1936. Although Farr was still kept out in the cold by the promoters, with Petersen refusing to meet him before he had himself been rematched with Foord, even if in a non-title bout, fate intervened. Foord went down with influenza. Petersen took Neusel on instead, for the third and final time, and was, again, soundly beaten. He promptly retired. That was in February 1937, with Farr at the ringside. In March, also at Harringay, Tommy would be inside the ring with Foord to fight for the crown. It was the beginning of the six months that defined his life and established his legend. Like south Wales itself in the late 1930s, he would come through battered but intact.

He trained this time with Job Churchill back in Penygraig, running the mountains in the morning and ending up at the Cambrian pit when night shifts ended and talk could begin. His nights were spent yarning in pubs and working-men's clubs. Under the informal tutel-age of older miners Tommy Farr had been led to music and literature. Now that he could afford a gramophone and records, he had built up his collection of Verdi and the favoured Handel. His afternoons vibrated with their music. It was, anywhere other than in this south Wales at this time, an odd concatenation of cultures, but then, as Tommy frequently told puzzled newspapermen, he was just a faithful Sancho Panza to Joby Churchill's Don Quijote. When it came to tilting at windmills, though, quixotic is not the ready epithet. He was readied at his athletic peak of 14 st 7lb and he was meticulously prepared with a pragmatic fight-plan. If necessary, he would bore Foord to death. This was to be no blood and glory effort. It was a calculated retreat, maul and accumulate performance. At its end he was, at last, the Champion. Pay-day beckoned.

There was, before that, the obligatory return to Tonypandy to a civic reception, crowds in the streets, banners between houses in Clydach Vale – 'Welcome to our own hero' – and on the Square a word for the reporters, which he crafted with only one audience in mind, his own:

> These people know me for what I am and what I have been . . . Quite rightly, they expect me to be the same Tommy Farr in the sunshine as the one they helped in the shadows. There's a friendship here more priceless than a dozen championship belts.

He stopped his open-topped car outside a corner sweet-shop in Clydach Vale and, brandishing a white five pound note, itself a rare sighting in those streets, he entered like a latter-day Pied Piper surrounded by an army of children. One of them, the future actor Glyn Houston whose brother Donald would vie with Richard Burton and Stanley Baker for post-war fame, remembers him shouting over their heads, 'The sweets are on the Champ!' as he slapped the note on the counter. After he had beaten the dangerous and glamorous Max Baer the next month, he told these same Tonypandy kids: 'Call me Tommy and we shall be pals. Call me mister and we are going to have a few rounds.'

He had needed twelve to win on points in April against a bemused Baer. It took him only three to knock out, sensationally and in front of the Nazi ambassador von Ribbentrop, the conqueror of Petersen,

Walter Neusel, in June. It had taken him only three months, and eleven years of preparation, to become an overnight star. He revelled in the attention of newspapers and newsreels. Tonypandy was coupled with his name. In Britain in the late 1930s there was no doubt what that place-name signified from its past; or what it had struggled to bring about for the future. Tommy Farr was an early harbinger of the confident post-war Welfare State culture, with a Labour Cabinet and government that would positively bristle with ex-miners from south Wales: Nye Bevan, Jim Griffiths, Ness Edwards, George Hall, Arthur Jenkins, and Rhondda's Arthur Horner himself as General Secretary of the Miners' Federation of Great Britain. Tommy Farr knew this script, implicitly, and by heart. It is precisely, therefore, what he meant when he talked across the Atlantic directly to his own deep supporters, first and immediately so, after his defeat by Joe Louis over fifteen unforgettable rounds in New York in August of that turning-point year, 1937. They had sent him a cablegram to read as he entered the ring: 'We trust you Tommy. Win or lose our faith in you remains unshaken.' Trust. Faith. Not the words normally used to drive a fighter on. But then neither was the newspaper-reported statement from a mid Rhondda woman: 'Tommy has the spirit, we have hope.' His ring performance was, of course, his most profound and solo part in this act of communication between the fighter and his community. His crackling words were just an affirmative afterthought to that two-fisted soliloquy: 'Hello Tonypandy . . . I done my best . . . We, I, showed 'em I got plenty of guts. You know, the old Tommy Farr of old.'

We, I – as indeed they knew and exulted – had been given the unexpected chance to fight Joe Louis, the Brown Bomber from Detroit out of Alabama, only because the champion, having won earlier in 1937 his world title from the 'Cinderella Man', James Braddock, who had devastatingly beaten Max Baer in 1935, was advised by his canny handlers to avoid the former champion from 1932, the German Max Schmeling, who had knocked him out in a 1936 non-title bout that had derailed Louis's seemingly unstoppable run to the top. Schmeling would have to wait for a shot at the title until 1938, when he became yet another k.o. statistic victim in Louis's unbeaten twelve-year reign as World Heavyweight Champion. In 1937 Tommy Farr was considered easier pickings and, in turn, was easily persuaded to pull out of his own next, arranged fight with Max Schmeling. As it turned out they would never meet, as the Second World War interrupted all careers in every sense. Instead, Tommy Farr travelled in style aboard the *Queen Mary* to New York, the place Tonypandy itself only ever saw on the screens of its four cinemas.

Newsreel film of the encounter was showing across Britain within two weeks of the night of 30 August at Yankee Stadium. It was heavily and selectively edited to show the best of Farr. It seemed to confirm the sense of radio listeners that he had been robbed of the decision after carrying the fight to Louis. That was the impression of thousands, and especially those gathered around the radio transmission relayed in the early hours of the morning to homes, public halls and pubs in the Rhondda. The Canadian commentator Bob Bowman raised his orgasmic speech-levels in the fifteenth round to gasp how Tommy Farr was putting on a 'wonderful show'. Indeed he was, and indeed there were moments in the fight when his body-punching troubled Louis, but over the course of the fight there was only one winner and Farr knew it. He never claimed that he had beaten one of the greatest – *the* greatest, Tommy always claimed – champion the sport had ever produced. Nor, consummate showman as he became, did he ever disclaim it when others raised the issue. Neither was the brave non-stop rally by Farr in the very last round the vital three minutes, though, as the last and most thrilling round, it naturally lingered in the collective memory. The crucial and revelatory round, if we wish to read the fight closely as its narrative text unfolded, was the seventh, and its established context was entirely the individual story of the Welsh fighting underdog.

For this life-defining bout Tommy Farr oozed confidence. On his dressing-gown of yellow silk had been stitched a handkerchief-sized fiery red Welsh dragon which Freddie Welsh had worn on his trunks in 1914 when he became the world's lightweight champion. Now, at the end of a first round in which Tommy Farr had beaten Joe Louis to the punch and moved his left jab in and out of the champion's face, he had turned to Job Churchill and said 'Job, I can box better than Louis, and I'll take him places he's not been before.' Halfway through the contest it was Tommy Farr who was forced back to the places he had been before – the holes. Joe Louis opened the seventh with straight jabs and then unleashed his trademark left hooks, three in a row, to spin the Welshman around. The attack on a blood-spattered Farr, to face and body, big right hand piledrivers clustering in behind classic hooks, left the Kid from Tonypandy clutching the ropes to stop his legs buckling under him. When he ducked he was only ducking into more trouble. This is how Joe Louis's opponents invariably ended – bewildered, shell-shocked, toppling and then prostrate. Only Tommy Farr, squinting through cut-to-ribbon eyelids, did not fall. He found his corner. He had been in the holes again. And he came out, fast and grinning and aggressive, for the eighth. It had been decided. He would not go down.

Tommy Farr died, aged 72, on 1 March 1986, timing the significant moment to the end. After 1937 it is not the case that the rest of his life was without moment or significance. There were further pre-war fights, successfully in Britain, not so in America, and fame without end, along with a considerable fortune which, in the way of things with boxers, had a habit of disappearing. He had to make a comeback, after the war in which he had been found medically unfit to serve, to combat bankruptcy, and he worked, to some acclaim, as a big-fight reporter for mass-circulation papers. And Tommy – as his chronicler Bob Lonkhurst emphasizes in *Man of Courage* (1997), a useful supplement to Tommy's posthumously published but 1940s-written, *Thus Farr* (1990) – had the deserved luck to enjoy the clichéd, but true, long and happy marriage, living out his years in Sussex. None-theless, his significant achievement, and his cultural locus in the history of Wales, does pivot on 1937 and on all that had led up to it.

This is the burden of all the books and articles about him. This is what the doyen of American boxing writers, A. J. Liebling, suddenly recalled when he found himself sitting next to a hefty stranger on a flight from London to Dublin to report a contest in 1955: 'the hand-stitched face, with the high cheekbones, narrow eyes and Rock of Gibraltar chin came back to me out of the late thirties. He was Tommy Farr, the old Welsh heavyweight who went fifteen rounds with Joe Louis in 1937.' It is why a full-length documentary was made about him by the BBC sixty years after the fight in 1997. It is why, in the changing mythical Chronos of Rhondda's history, Gwyn Thomas (born 1913) wanted to write a biography of the miners' tribune,

A. J. Cook from Porth, but Ron Berry (born 1920) contemplated a life of the people's tribune from Tonypandy, Tommy Farr. No other boxer has had a musical play, *The Contender* (2007), written about him and performed in both New York and the Welsh capital. Tommy drew for the rest of his life on the cultural capital of 1937.

And so did all of us who lived in Tonypandy in the fallout from his fame. Tommy Farr, at a time of extreme deprivation, sucked the sweet lollipop that was Americana – crooning, swaggering and night-clubbing – but we, then and in the immediate post-war years, thereby tasted that sugar, even if at a distance. Earlier, Freddie Welsh had actively sought to create an 'American Wales'; he failed and became an American. Tommy Farr yearned to consume what was the flaunted popular culture of America; he succeeded, but did not materially change, and so, after 1945, he became hugely emblematic, for a gener-ation and more, of the meaning south Wales had come to have in the perception of the wider world. And at home it was of Tommy Farr my grandfather who had worked in Cambrian with him spoke to me, not of the riots which he had witnessed in 1910 or the communal marches of the sullenly defiant inter-war years. It was Tommy Farr we pretended to be when we scrapped on the coal tips above Tonypandy in the 1950s. He had never left us in spirit, and never could in reality after 1937. And then one day in 1986, shortly before he died, I was the last person to interview him on radio, and before the tape began, having mentioned Tonypandy and my grandfather, I said, 'Mr Farr, when we begin, may I call you Tommy?', and he half-smiled and half-snarled down the line from Brighton: 'Call me Tommy! If you don't I'll come down the line and knock you on your arse.'

His ashes were placed in his parents' grave in Trealaw cemetery. It faces back across the valley to Tonypandy. Abidingly so, as in the collective memory of Tommy Farr, the Tonypandy Kid.

'Boxing Mad' in Cardi-land

1945–1955

HYWEL TEIFI EDWARDS

My earliest memory of aroused interest takes me back to the summer of 1939 in the Cardiganshire seaside village of Llanddewi Aberarth. I was approaching my fifth birthday, living in 2 Water Street within a deacon's stride of Bethel Calvinistic Methodist chapel to the right of our house, and within a boxer's spat rinse of the cobbler's thatched workshop directly opposite. My inquisitiveness, not for the first time, had taken me to watch Dai Hughes at work on his last and to test his patience with incessant questioning.

A previous visit had implanted in my memory the strange name – Dixie Dean. The 'bois mowr' (big boys) competed in heading a ball over the central beam, with cries of 'Dixie Dean!' following every score. It was years later that I learnt of the 'aerial power' of Everton's fabled centre forward. But on this occasion, my attention had fastened on the many cigarette cards and newspaper cuttings tacked on to one of the walls, and in particular on a cutting showing a white man, in a threatening crouch, confronting an equally threatening, upright black man, inside a roped square.

A jabbing finger accentuating my curiosity, I asked: 'Who are these, Dai? What are they doing?' 'They're fighters, boi bach, boxers. The black man is Joe Louis, the World Heavyweight Champion – and that's Tommy Farr – TOMMY FARR – the Welshman who almost beat him in America. You eat an egg for breakfast every day and perhaps you'll grow up to be another Tommy Farr – a Tommy Farr from Aber-arth!'

Dai's Welsh cascaded over me and in no time he had pointed out other Welsh 'greats', shadow-boxing in exultation as he sang their praises – Tom Thomas, Jimmy Wilde, Jim Driscoll, Freddie Welsh, Frank Moody and Jack Petersen. Apart from Tom Thomas, a 'Cardi', men in Aber-arth didn't have such names. And they certainly didn't appear in public in their vests and long johns with a huge belt – a L-O-N-S-D-A-L-E belt as Dai slowly spelt it out – clamped around the waist. It would be some years yet before the celebrated photograph of Tom Thomas, Jim Driscoll and Freddie Welsh registered with me as a national icon. The proximity of Bethel's jealous God notwithstanding, I was to realize that there had also been gods to bow down before in our cobbler's workshop. Welsh boxing even had its trinity.

Even an ostrich's egg every morning would never have brought me within striking distance of Dai's pantheon, but I'm sure that my enduring fascination with boxing had its root there, in the cobbler's workshop, where Dai hammered leather in his own way under the primed fists of his pinned-up warriors. The old place has long since been demolished, but over the years I have never passed its site without hearing 'Dixie Dean!' shouted in triumph and the thud of punches given and taken to the accompaniment of the cobbler's exhortations. It is still there for me.

From 1945 to 1955, for one Aber-arth boy, the wireless set became a ticket to a ringside seat in the Royal Albert Hall, the White City Stadium, Earl's Court Arena, Harringay Arena, and even Madison Square Garden in New York. Oh! those battling wireless years that truly started for me on 23 February 1945, when the British Featherweight Champion, Nel Tarleton, the Liverpudlian 'Boxer with a Brain', withstood the challenge of Al Phillips, the 'Aldgate Tiger'. Tarleton, with one sound lung at 39 years of age, survived a pitiless tenth-round assault by the 25-year-old Phillips that still resounds in the memory.

What a force for atavistic engagement, for gladiatorial arousal, the wireless was, when W. Barrington Dalby's quivering appreciation of 'a *peach* of a right hook' could have you up on your toes, or prostrate, depending on whether your man had given or taken it. Sixty years later I hold it accountable for the fever in the blood that kept me from bed until 5 a.m. to watch the lethal Floyd Mayweather dispose of Ricky Hatton's challenge. And as expected, I heard those distant wireless voices in my inner ear again when I stayed up, on 19 April 2008, to watch 'our' invincible Joe Calzaghe account for Bernard Hopkins.

The year 1945 was an *annus mirabilis*. The end of the war was cause enough for celebration, but what highlighted that throbbing time for one 11-year-old was the weekly purchase of the *Boxing News* in Aberaeron. It cost 4d., and it started a successful quest for autographed photographs of the leading British boxers featured in it. The first to respond, by return of post, was Bruce Woodcock, soon to be, at 24 years of age, the British Heavyweight Champion, when

104

on 17 July, at Tottenham Hotspur's White Hart Lane ground, he knocked out Jack London in the sixth round before a crowd of 38,000.

How I willed his triumph every time he fought after that, exhorting him to greater effort as he gazed out at me from his russety photograph. His victories in 1946 against Freddie Mills and the redoubtable American, Gus Lesnevich, both of them world light-heavyweight champions in their day, were occasions for unbounded joy. His defeats against the Yankee sluggers, Tami Mauriello, who knocked him out at Madison Square Garden on 17 May 1946, and Joe Baksi, who stopped him in round seven after inflicting a severe beating at Harringay Arena, 15 April 1947, brought me close to heartbreak. I took a primitive delight in their subsequent battering by Joe Louis and when, in 1955, I first saw *On the Waterfront*, and spotted Mauriello as one of the 'heavies' beating Marlon Brando, playing a washed-up boxer, almost to death, I beamed on him a vicious resentment as enjoyable as it was irrational.

In rapid succession a number of contemporary British champions, some of whom were also Empire, European and even world champions, together with others who were leading contenders, followed Woodcock into my album of autographed photographs. I see them still, poised to do battle, each stance exhibiting a stylized menace, each look exuding self-belief. Freddie Mills, Vince Hawkins, Ernie Roderick, Ronnie Clayton, Jackie Paterson, Rinty Monaghan, Al Phillips, Ned Tarleton, Don Cockell, Peter Kane, Bunty Doran, the outstanding Randolph Turpin – they were all in my album, as were Jack Solomons, Britain's dominant promoter in the post-war period, his cigar jutting from his mouth like the jib of a crane, and Moss Deyong, his tuxedo worn, I'm sure, in recognition of what the 'Fancy' would have deemed worthy of the sport's then foremost referee.

Yes, I can still see them clearly, despite giving away my album when, as a 'fresher' in the University College of Wales, Aberystwyth, punch-drunk in the pursuit of a BA, I decided that it was not proper company for the poetry of Aneirin, Taliesin and Dafydd ap Gwilym, or the marvellous tales of the Mabinogion. In a life punctuated with follies, I've repented the rejection of my autographed warriors more than most. From time to time they haunt my dreams and, awoken by guilt, I could swear that I once heard 'Two-ton' Tony Galento mouthing his contempt for my betrayal of them in those immortal words he used to dismiss Joe Louis – 'I'll moider da bum!'

American boxers, of course, were 'too far away' for an Aber-arth boy to pester them for autographed photographs, but how I devoured accounts of the American 'fight scene' in the *Boxing News*. What a thunderous, blood-spattered decade 1945 to 1955 was in the history of American boxing. Joe Louis, Jersey Joe Walcott, Ezzard Charles and Rocky Marciano – the indestructible Marciano. I was drawn to Walcott, baptized Arnold Cream, because he had been one of Tommy Farr's sparring partners when he prepared to meet Louis in 1937. What's more, he read his Bible in the dressing-room before fighting and prayed in the ring afterwards. He was good for my Bethel-ridden conscience!

Was there ever a decade in the history of middleweight boxing to compare with 1945 to 1955 in America? Tony Zale, Rocky Graziano, Jake LaMotta, Sugar Ray Robinson, Carmen Basilio, Carl 'Bobo' Olson – and from France, Marcel Cerdan, and from Britain, Randolph Turpin. They were ring warriors of awesome power, hardness, merci-lessness and skill, seemingly constituted of mental and physical attributes on a different scale from those of other fighters, and of that constellation Sugar Ray's star shone, and still shines, brightest. To watch, again and again, such brilliant films as Stanley Kramer's *Champion* (1949), starring Kirk Douglas, Robert Wise's *Somebody Up There Likes Me* (1956), starring Paul Newman as Rocky Graziano, and Martin Scorsese's *Raging Bull* (1980), with Robert de Niro as Jake LaMotta, is to come as close as one can to the fighting spirit of those years in their intense, unremitting aggression, their terrifying dedication to the inflicting and suffering of pain, and their bravery in the pursuit of a consuming ambition – simply to be 'The Champ!' No matter how often I watch those films, it is always for me an adrenalin-soused experience.

Welsh boxers, yes, of course, they took pride of place in my album. Ronnie James, Eddie Thomas, Cliff Curvis, Johnny Williams, Dai Dower, Dick Richardson, Joe Erskine and Tommy Farr – the Tommy Farr whose ill-advised comeback was ended at the Nottingham Ice Stadium, 9 March 1953, when the referee stopped his fight against Don Cockell after seven rounds. Farr, as endurable as ever, protested against the stoppage, to no avail. He then took the microphone and led the singing of 'Hen Wlad Fy Nhadau', prompting the *Boxing News* reporter to say: 'For a man who had just gone through a gruelling half-hour, Tommy's singing was most clear and sweet.' Pathos reigned, with bathos close by. I wasn't tempted by Farr's 'second coming' to go and see him fight. I knew that he would bear no comparison with the man who had gone fifteen rounds with Joe Louis – the man on the wall in the cobbler's thatched workshop. I wanted to keep that image of him unimpaired.

If my own emotional involvement with Bruce Woodcock was exhausting, my investment of hope in Welsh boxers was doubly so. How I prayed for them to triumph each time they entered the ring. In Sunday School, any talk of David and Goliath would somehow veer in the direction of some Welsh boxer's prospects. An article in the *Boxing News* in May 1945, headed 'What's wrong with Wales?', was very troubling. Its author, E. A. Bayley, bewailed the fading of the 'old glory'. The famous photograph of Jim Driscoll, Tom Thomas and Freddie Welsh hung on the walls of homes and public places throughout the land, from where, looking down on present-day Welsh aspirants, the 'three seem to wear an aspect of reproach that the legacy of fame they handed down to their successors has been allowed to rust'. The 'three immortals' had long since died, but there had to be lads again to recapture past glories: 'The Welsh have ever been an instinctively combative people. They can be neat in execution, and have never been accused of being dull-witted. The soil is as fertile as it has ever been.'

What happened to Ronnie James, 'our one solitary rose' according to E. A. Bayley, when on 4 September 1946 he entered the ring at Ninian Park, Cardiff, to fight Ike Williams, the black American World Lightweight Champion, before a crowd of 45,000, did little for Welsh boxing's morale. Promoted by Jack Solomons, it was the first world title fight staged in Wales. James, the British Lightweight Champion, hadn't fought at 9 st 9 lb for two years, and he was weak from trying to make the weight. He was also almost ten years older than his 23-year-old opponent.

Listening to the wireless commentary and reading subsequent reports in the *Boxing News* was cause for lamentation. James had been boxing since 1932, and by 1946 had at least eighty fights behind him. Williams had started his professional career in 1940 as a 16-year-old, and had fought some seventy times. He was a devastating puncher at peak strength, and his speciality, his bolo punch, said to be a right uppercut under the heart, brought gasps and cries of pain from James according to the appreciative commentators. Knowledgeable critics in Aber-arth insisted that 'bolo' was simply the Welsh 'bola' (belly) misspelt, but stout-hearted Ronnie James could hardly have taken any physiological comfort from that. He was downed six times in all, and knocked out in the ninth round. In 1951 he emigrated to Australia, leaving behind him a well-earned reputation as a good boxer, full of pride and endeavour. A world title, however, most certainly exceeded his grasp. The 'three immortals' would have to wait a little longer.

Then along came Eddie Thomas, who, from the beginning of his triumphant amateur career in 1945 alongside Randolph Turpin, to the day he died, would be the epitome of Merthyr's boxing prowess and passion. What a striking character he was. After he outpointed Henry Hall at Harringay Arena in November 1949 to win the British and Empire Welterweight titles, he went on to defeat the Italian Michele Palermo for the European title at Carmarthen in February 1951. He was to lose that title the following June to the Frenchman Charles Humez, a defeat that cost him the opportunity to fight the formidable Cuban Kid Gavilan for the world title, and the following October, in his third championship fight within ten months, he lost his British and Empire titles to Wally Thom, a boxer of inferior talents. He ascribed the defeat to inadequate preparation, due to having to balance his boxing career with the cares of running a coal business. It was not an excuse, Eddie Thomas did not deal in excuses; it was a fact that as a professional he would sometimes go straight from his mine to fight. At his best he was, undoubtedly, made of the stuff of champions.

When he won the British and Empire titles against Henry Hall, he stood in the centre of the ring, microphone in hand, and in an arena long echoing with countless curses, and pungent with the smells of cigar smoke, perspiration, blood and who knows what variety of unguents and elixirs, sang 'Bless this House' with all the sincerity of a one-time Merthyr choirboy. Eddie Thomas was a 'winning' boxer in every sense as he gazed back at me from his favoured position in my album. I was an out-and-out fan of his, and I remain one.

Howard Winstone, Ken Buchanan – both of them world champions – and Colin Jones, 'The Punch', who came so close to making the pair a trinity in two world title fights with Milton McCrory, excelled under Thomas's tutelage and management. Steeped in boxing culture, nothing seemed to faze him. He could listen to Harry Carpenter expounding on Winstone's shortcomings in his dazzling encounters with the Mexican world champion, Vicente Saldivar, with a smile on his face. In him, and the admirable Winstone, something of the glory of the Jim Driscoll era was recaptured and Merthyr has no cause to fear the reproach of any of the world's boxing 'immortals', past or future, while Eddie Thomas, Howard Winstone and the heroic Johnny Owen are poised, in all weather, to bear witness to the old town's distinction as a powerhouse of Welsh boxing.

Cliff Curvis, in 1945 a 16-old Swansea-born southpaw, fought Eddie Thomas for the British and Empire titles at the Vetch Field in September 1950, and was outpointed by him at the end of fifteen rounds. Curvis, however, would avenge Thomas's loss of his titles by knocking out Wally Thom in the ninth round at Liverpool Stadium in July 1952. But his would be a brief reign and the abiding memory I have of his career is his defeat at the fists of Al Phillips in a final eliminator for the British Featherweight title, at the Royal Albert Hall, 2 December 1946. He was knocked out in the second round.

Listening to the commentary that bleak evening turned into another wireless 'appointment with fear'. Curvis was so young, so promising, so very easy for a schoolboy to relate to. With hindsight, I would see him as another Gododdin warrior, too brave too soon. At 12 years of age, the disappointment of losing international soccer and rugby matches was hard to bear, but when a Welsh boxer lost a significant fight, it was more grief than disappointment, owing to the intensity of hope concentrated on 'one of us' – that singular warrior who carried with him into the ring the fighting reputation of a whole nation. On the night he lost to Al Phillips, the youthful Curvis was fighting for the thirteenth time in 1946, and, given the age-old Welsh hankering after victimhood, I'm sure that not a few of his supporters suspected his defeat had been preordained by some malign fate. But in my album, Cliff Curvis was a fine boxer, and he remains an emotional tie between my boxing-mad boyhood and my almost-as-mad present. Ripeness is not all!

As for the Welsh heavyweights who fought between 1945 and the end of the 1950s, one can in retrospect only curse the damnable perversity of fate that gave us Joe Erskine, Johnny Williams, Dick Richardson and Tommy Farr (admittedly fighting from memory), when just one composite of their assorted strengths would surely have secured the world heavyweight championship for us. Erskine and Williams were skilful boxers, Erskine especially so, and they both of them won the British and Empire titles despite lacking punching power. Richardson punched hard enough to win the European title against Karl Mildenberger in 1962, but he was a crude pugilist, easily outpointed by Erskine in 1959, and demolished in 1963, as Erskine had been in 1959, by Henry Cooper's famed left hook. Johnny Williams lost to Jack Gardner in the 'fight of the year' at Leicester in July 1950, later took his British and Empire titles from him in 1952, and then succumbed to Don Cockell at Harringay Arena in 1953 after what the critics dismissed as a 'timid' performance. There seemed little on view to make American 'scribes' revise their seasoned opinion that most British heavyweights were rejected Bob Hope gags.

Whatever misfortune befell Welsh boxing, there was always the *Boxing News* to read and re-read, its weekly blow-by-blow accounts of all the main fights to digest, its insights into the pugilistic psyche to ponder, its perceptive reviews of so many boxers careers to appreciate. What a joy it was to read about Young Griffo, the Sydney-born feather-weight who died in the Bronx in 1927 and was said to have lost a mere 9 of 232 recorded fights, despite never entering the ring sober. He would often be dead drunk on the afternoon of a fight, taken to a Turkish bath 'and boiled till he showed some signs of consciousness', propped on his feet by his seconds when the bell rang and pushed into the centre of the ring: 'And Griffo, too drunk to move without toppling, would stand on a patch as large as a handkerchief for the whole round, and never once would his opponent succeed in hitting him. Wonderful, incredible Griffo!' Overcome with fumes, his opponents put a different complexion on punch-drunkenness.

When Tommy Farr was attempting a comeback, I learnt why his style was so well suited to fighting tough Americans. An old-timer described him as a 'turtle fighter', because when at close quarters with an opponent,

> [the] curve of his body from the small of his back, round the neck to the top of his head, did take the shape of a turtle's shell. It gave his punching muscles play, and enabled him to throw a short punch without telegraphing it.

All at once, the crouching boxer in the cutting pinned to the wall of the cobbler's workshop, became twice as dramatic, but I was to find it an impossible stance to maintain for more than a minute or so. The old-timer should have noted that Farr had a collier's musculature to power him, thanks to years spent crouched double underground, years which also, by the way, left him suffering from silicosis so that he was 'practically working on only one cylinder' when he fought Joe Louis. One read, and wondered. Tommy Farr 'AM BYTH'!

Yes, the *Boxing News*, with its photographs aplenty, set the imagination racing. Its literary idiom, if not matching America's boxing parlance, in its outrageous verbal inventiveness and combativeness, was attractively informative and to my mind *always* readable. I admit, it could rarely compete with a boxing culture that boasted such an incredible gallimaufry as America's, but it made up for it by providing its readers with quotations, tasters, that brought the American fight game to life in its brilliance and brutality, its humour and humbug, its graft and gore. You could savour them and suck on them for years. For example: Gene Tunney, in a press interview, remarking that Freddie (Red) Cochrane was the most articulate boxer he had met. To which a photographer replied: 'That's odd, he always speaks well of you.' And Joe Louis, on a punch to the ribs in his return fight with Max Schmeling: 'I just hit him, that's all. I hit him right in the ribs and I guess maybe it was a lucky punch but man, did he scream! I thought it was a lady in the ringside cryin'. He just screamed, that's all.'

In no time at all after becoming a regular reader of the *Boxing News*, I was into the 'fights that should have been' syndrome, for which, let it be clear, there is no known cure. A comprehensive defeat for a Welsh champion would inevitably have me summoning a Welsh 'great' to restore national pride. In 1957, Dai Dower, the British, Empire and European Flyweight title-holder, as delightful a 'floating butterfly' of a boxer as one could wish to see, challenged the Argentinian, Pascual Perez, in Buenos Aires for his World title. The 'Pocket Marciano', as Perez was known, shattered Dower in the first round, and Welsh ears were assailed, from afar, with what sounded suspiciously like derisory laughter. There was only one thing to do in the face of such a calamity – pit Perez against Jimmy Wilde. How would he have fared against 'The Mighty Atom'?

I remember a sense of wonder on first reading about the marvel that was Jimmy Wilde, reputed to have fought 864 times, losing a mere 4 contests. At the Polo Grounds in New York, 18 June 1923, he was knocked out in the seventh round by the Philipino Pancho Villa, who had badly hurt him with a punch delivered after the bell to end the second round. Wilde, then 31 years of age, not having fought for over two years, his right eye closed and cut underneath, refused to retire. For a purse of £13,000 he would fight to the end. Hailed as the greatest flyweight there had ever been, he left the ring a quintessential 'Champion', whose immaculate footwork, ensuring that he was never off-balance, accounted for his rare ability to knock out opponents considerably bigger than himself.

Jimmy Wilde held the World Flyweight title from 1916 to 1923, and, in the words of R. A. Haldane, was the 'greatest pugilist of any weight and any day since glove-fighting began, that this country ever produced'. For a Bethel-frequenting schoolboy, that was a tribute of Old Testament proportions. Baptized the 'ghost with a hammer in his hand' by Pedlar Palmer, the former World Bantamweight title-holder, this potent Rhondda-born sprite could have emerged from some Celtic netherworld to undo mere mortals, so extraordinary was the power his gamin physique could generate. It takes some believing that he could weigh in for a world flyweight contest at eight stones 'fully clothed, with overcoat and bowler hat on, and carrying his hand-case', and still make the weight comfortably. During the Great War (surely to the Kaiser's relief) he could not serve at the front 'because he weighed less than the regulation Army pack'.

Little wonder that I thought of Jimmy Wilde when Perez destroyed Dai Dower. Jim Driscoll said of him that 'he worked by some instinctive prod'. R. A. Haldane said that his blows came 'from the oddest and most unusual angles – sometimes from the neighbourhood of his knees'. Could it be that this was a fistic, Celtic shape-shifter? Unorthodox in style and uncanny in his ability to outmanoeuvre opponents, 'he did not just beat his men; he stunned them good and proper, with his little pipestem arms and his tiny fists'. Would Perez have held any fears for him? Never!

All boxing fans enjoy promoting 'fights that should have been'; it is an exercise that penetrates to the heart of the fascination boxing has for them. Jim Driscoll versus Howard Winstone? Joe Calzaghe versus Randolph Turpin, or any of the great American middleweights of the 1940s and 50s? If heaven be kind, perchance there will be a boxers' enclave where champions, unhindered by frontiers of time and space, will settle all the disputes about their relative greatness, that on earth have 'tired the sun with talking' on countless occasions. But on second thoughts, boxing fans would surely find heaven less than heavenly with their disputes resolved.

Before the final bell rings to silence this bout with the past, just one more 'fight that should have been'. When Tom Thomas, the Glynarthen-born, Rhondda-bound migrant, died in 1911 at the age of 31, 'Cardi-land' lost its one and only great fighter to date and Wales its first winner of a coveted Lonsdale belt. He won the British Middle-weight title in 1906, and his belt in 1909, and by the time of his death he was already a legend. From Carncelyn Farm in Penygraig he, too, hammered his way into prominence in the booths. It was said that he sparred with a bull – 'how?' is not a question to ask of a legend – and that he died in London of a rheumatic fever, probably brought on by his midwinter practice of breaking the ice and then plunging his body in the freezing water of a nearby pond. Sparta would have held no terrors for the iron-hard 'Cardi'. Who should have been his opponent? Without hesitation, I name the fearsome Polish-American, Stanley Ketchel, the 'Michigan Assassin', said to be 'made of pig iron' and hand-some to boot 'with frank blue eyes'. But, 'once inside the ring those soft eyes became the eyes of an assassin determined to get his victim. Then he was vicious, cruel, relentless, murderous, and well deserved his title.'

Ketchel lodged himself in my imagination as I read his 'fighting-life story', written by Wilfrid Diamond for *Boxing News* in 1953. I might as well admit the truth: he stirred the primitive in me more than any other fighter I had read about before, or have since. Of him, his manager, Dan Morgan, said: 'He was a savage . . . He couldn't get "enough" blood.' In an 'arranged' fight with the World Heavyweight champion, Jack Johnson, his killer instinct, ever scornful of prudence, drove him to knock the great man down – an impertinence that cost him the loss of four teeth in an immediate knockout. Ketchel was made to be written about and, praise be, he inspired Ernest Hemingway to write that unforgettable short story, 'The Light of the World'. As Daniel Williams shows in his essay in this book, boxers have always been good for literature.

In 1911, Tom Thomas was about to cross the Atlantic to fight the German-American Billy Papke, the 'Illinois Thunderbolt', for the World Middleweight title. Ketchel, the reigning champion, had been murdered in 1910 at the age of 24, and but for that he would surely have been awaiting Thomas's challenge. What better reason could there be for my wanting to match them in a 'fight that should have been'?

Billy Papke fought Ketchel four times in all, their second encounter at Los Angeles, 8 September 1908, depriving Ketchel of his title after a murderous foul blow incapacitated the champion early on, only for Ketchel to regain the title in their third encounter at San Francisco, 26 November 1908, and in their fourth clash again to reduce Papke to a bloody mess. They were, quite simply, terribly brutal fights: Papke's single victory secured in what was described as the 'bloodiest fight on record', and Ketchel's revenge that of a pugilist who 'wanted to chop his man to ribbons'. Papke is said to have been refused entry to his sister's house in San Francisco afterwards, she 'insisting that the pitifully battered, terrible human wreck was not her brother'.

Billy Papke would later on in his life shoot his wife and then commit suicide. Stanley Ketchel, would-be cowboy who loved guns and women, attracted the hatred of one Walter Dipley, a farmhand, who shot him with Ketchel's own rifle at Colonel Dickerson's ranch in Conway, Missouri. This most vicious of middleweights, the 'most relentless hitter ever to don a glove', was known to be outside the ring a man capable of much generosity and kindness, at whose funeral little girls from his old school at Belmont, dressed in white, strewed flowers before his coffin.

Oh! how Ketchel and Thomas should have fought. Tom Thomas, the Welsh-speaking 'Cardi', moulded to fight in the Rhondda, resplendent in his vest, long johns and Lonsdale belt on a cobbler's workshop wall a mere boxer's spit from the door of Bethel Calvinistic Methodist chapel in Llanddewi Aber-arth. He was predestined to win.

Black and White

WRITING ON FIGHTING IN WALES

DANIEL G. WILLIAMS

BLACKS v. WHITES

BOXING !

RIALTO STADIUM, MARKET PLACE
SUTTON-IN-ASHFIELD
TUESDAY, JAN. 8

Doors open 6·45 p.m.   COMMENCE 7·30 p.m. PROMPT.

Promoters : Messrs. J. COATES & Abe WOOD (Affiliated to the British Boxing Board of Control).   The only Licensed Promoters in Sutton-in-Ashfield.

STUPENDOUS 12 ROUNDS WELTER-WEIGHT CONTEST.

JACK McKNIGHT

(BELFAST).   Welter-weight Champion of Ireland.   Winner of over 200 contests, whose victims include Donald Key, Pat Haley, Northern Area Welter Champion, Herbie Frazer, Tom Bodell, Ted Kendall, Tiger Williams, Pop Newman, Bill Hardy, Tommy Connolly, Seaman Lawler, Chris Lovell, and a host of others.   V.

HERBIE NURSE

(CARDIFF).   The Coloured Welterweight, winner of over 150 contests, and has defeated such boys as Len Wickwar, Steve Hanley, Eddie Manning, Harry Evans, Donald Jones, Grif Lewis, Bryn Jones, Wallie Hutchings, Bob Parkin, Seaman Read, Gilbert Terry, etc.   Nurse has never taken the count in his career.

Special 6 rounds Feather-weight Contest.	Great 6 rounds Bantam-weight Contest.
RON PORTER V. JIM ASPREY	HERBERT BOOTH V. TOMMY AMMOTT
Nottingham. Both toe-to-toe fighters. Sutton.	Chesterfield. Two fast improving boxers. Hucknall.

GREAT 8 ROUNDS LIGHT-WEIGHT CONTEST.

BILLY STRANGE V. DENNIS RYAN

Stanton Hill.   Whose recent wins include Kid Staff, Jack Lindley, Art Rostork,   Ollerton. 9st. 9lb. Pitmans Champion of Notts.   Recently defeated Kid Staff
Billy Gibbons, etc.   (Who can forecast the winner).   at Nottingham.

SPECIAL 10 ROUNDS MIDDLE-WEIGHT CONTEST.

AL MILLER

(BIRMINGHAM) Coloured.   A tearaway fighter, known as the Black Tiger, winner of over 70 contests, whose recent wins include George Thornton, Butcher Stevens, Tom Bodell, Ted Husband, Tommy Allen, and recently fought a great contest with the Middle-weight Champion of Holland.   V.

BERT BARKER

(SCUNTHORPE).   Winner of 68 fights, whose record includes such boys as Pete Harricks, Ted Abbott, Donald Keys, Curly Wallace, Fred Oldfield, George Newton, Dennis Buckley twice, Pete Higgins Kid Seatt, Jim Crofton, etc.

REFEREE : Mr. FRED EASTBURN, Class "A" (Affiliated to the British Boxing Board of Control).

Timekeeper : Mr. Joe ORRIDGE, (Sutton)   Official Seconds : Ernest Heppenstall and Nobby Webber.   All Officials Licensed by B. B. B. C.

ADMISSION : (Including Tax) **1/-**   Outer Ringside reserved **2/-**   Ringside Reserved **3/-**

Seats may be booked at the King's Theatre, the Promoters, the Market Hotel, Market Place, Sutton-in-Ashfield, E. Coates, Gent's Outfitter, Station St., East Kirkby
Booked Seats to be claimed by 7-30   The Management reserve the right to refuse admission.   All Boxers contracted to appear.   Free Car Park on Market Place.

Photos of the Principals may be seen in Messrs. Hepworths' Window, Tailors, Low Street, Sutton-in-Ashfield.

"Reliance" Press, Peacock St., Mansfield.

In Owen Martell's acclaimed novel *Dyn yr Eiliad* (Man of the Moment) (2003), the main characters walk to

> hen dafarn y tu ol i City Road a mynd i eistedd mewn cornel yn y bar . . . Roedd gyda nhw luniau o boxers lleol ar y waliau ac un poster yn hysbysebu fight rhwng 'Whites and Blacks'.

> [an old pub behind City Road and sit in a corner in the bar . . .The walls were lined with photos of local boxers, with one poster advertising a fight between 'Whites and Blacks'].

Martell concentrates on the personal, individual, thoughts of his main characters, but suggestive references to Welsh history, culture and folk-lore appear between the novel's interior monologues. The narrator does not go on to explore the meaning and significance of the poster, but the reference is thought-provoking. The 'old pub' is the Tavistock Arms on Bedford Street, Cardiff, where the poster, dating from 1934, is still on the wall. The bout being described in stark racial terms is between Jack McKnight (Welterweight Champion of Ireland) and Herbie Nurse (Coloured Welterweight, Cardiff). The poster at once testifies to the crude racial terms in which boxing fights were described in the 1930s, while simultaneously alerting us to the complexities and contradictions inherent in the relationships between race, ethnicity and national identity in that period. For 'white v. black' on this poster also happens to involve, from another perspective, the white Irishman, McKnight, fighting the black Welshman, Nurse. This essay aims to explore the tensions and contradictions embodied in this poster, and does so by looking at the ways in which the 'black and white' of the boxing ring has often found itself reflected in the 'black and white' of the printed page.

From Mark Twain to Ernest Hemingway, Norman Mailer to Joyce Carol Oates, American writers in particular have been fascinated by the metaphorical and symbolic resonances of the boxing ring. Perhaps the most insightful American commentator on boxing, however, is the African-American novelist and essayist Ralph Ellison, whose seminal novel *Invisible Man* (1952) contains a number of allusions and references to prizefighting. A famous reference to boxing in the novel occurs when the narrator recalls seeing a 'prize fighter boxing a yokel'.

> The fighter was swift and amazingly scientific. His body was one violent flow of rapid rhythmic action. He hit the yokel a hundred times while the yokel held up his arms in stunned surprise. But suddenly the yokel, rolling about in the gale of boxing gloves, struck one blow and knocked science, speed and footwork as cold as a well-digger's posterior. The smart money hit the canvas. The long shot got the nod. The yokel had simply stepped inside his opponent's sense of time.

In his discussion of boxing and literature in *The Culture of Bruising*, the African-American critic Gerald Early uses this passage as a basis for exploring the uneasy relationship between white and black boxers in American culture. He notes that with the exception of Jack Dempsey and Gene Tunney, 'virtually every white champion has been, despite his style, a yokel: Sharkey, Braddock, Schmeling, Baer, Carnera, Marciano'. In contrast, black prizefighters have been regarded as 'Tricksters of style: Jack Johnson, Muhammad Ali, Sugar Ray Robinson, and Sugar Ray Leonard'. Against black opponents, states Early, 'white yokels were not even really fighters; they were more like preservers of the white public's need to see Tricksters pay the price for their disorder'.

The most well-known account of a white 'yokel' taking on a black 'trickster' is Sylvester Stallone's Oscar-winning movie *Rocky* (1976). Rocky Balboa, an inarticulate Italian-American, is plucked from obscurity to take on and defeat the quick-witted and agile African-American, Apollo Creed. Creed is clearly moulded on Muhammad Ali (even down to his rivalry with Joe Frazier). If Ali, in later life, would become an all-American hero lighting the Olympic torch at Atlanta in 1996, during the 1960s – when he embraced Islam, changed his name from Cassius Clay and resisted the draft – he was widely disliked, distrusted and vilified by many Americans. Thus, if the real Ali seemed invincible in the ring, the Hollywood dream factory could simulate his defeat at the hands of a white unknown. Balboa is improbably brought into fighting shape by Mickey, a weathered trainer played by an ageing Burgess Meredith. In advising his white protégé on how to deal with a threatening African-American, Meredith was actually repeating a role that he'd played – in a rather different context and for different ends – thirty years earlier.

A *Welcome to Britain* was a film made in 1943 by the British Ministry of Information with the support of the American Office of War Information. In it, Burgess Meredith is a GI guide who introduces American soldiers to some of the embarrassing situations that they might encounter while stationed in wartime Britain. A white GI is shown flirting with a barmaid, throwing his money around and making disparaging remarks about a Scotsman's kilt. Having outraged the locals he boards a train and gets into a compartment with an African-American GI. An elderly British lady invites them both back to her house for tea, and Burgess Meredith confides to the camera that while this sort of thing wouldn't happen at home in the United States, it's not unusual in Britain. The message is clearly directed primarily at white GIs, suggesting that they should adopt a veneer of ethnic tolerance – whether encountering kilted Scots or black members of their own nation – while in Britain.

Among the more notable GIs to have been stationed in Wales during the Second World War (apart from Rocky Marciano, who fought future Welsh rugby international Jack Matthews in a bout at St Athan) was the novelist Ralph Ellison himself. In his short story of 1944 'In a Strange Country', Ellison offers a fictional account of his time in Swansea and Morriston. It begins with the central character Parker, an African-American GI, sitting in a Welsh pub recalling events that have happened earlier that evening.

Coming ashore from the ship he had felt the excited expectancy of entering a strange land. Moving along the road in the dark he had planned to stay ashore all night, and in the morning he would see the country with fresh eyes . . . Someone had cried 'Jesus H. Christ,' and he had thought, He's from home, and grinned and apologized into the light they flashed in his eyes. He had felt the blow coming when they yelled, 'It's a goddamn nigger', but it struck him anyway. He was having a time of it when some of Mr Catti's countrymen stepped in and Mr Catti had guided him into the pub [. . .].

At first he had included them in his blind rage. But they had seemed so genuinely and uncondescendingly polite that he was disarmed. Now the anger and resentment had slowly ebbed, and he felt only a smouldering sense of self-hate and ineffectiveness. Why should he blame them when they had helped him? He had been the one so glad to hear an American voice. You can't take it out on them, they're a different breed; even from the English.

The passage traces a shift in Parker's perception of the Welsh, from initially including them in his 'blind rage' to his increasing awareness of their ethnic difference. Following an encounter with white GIs, Parker has a literal black eye that functions as a suggestive metaphor in a story preoccupied with issues of sight and self-perception. Upon entering the club with his Welsh hosts the light strikes Parker's injured eye – 'it was as though it were being peeled by an invisible hand' – and the story proceeds to explore the layers of identity that constitute the African-American self – the black 'I'.

In an earlier draft of a story based on his experiences in Wales, Ellison's main character tries to establish a sense of his identity by evoking the boxers whom he clearly admires. Sitting in an American Red Cross Club attached to Libanus Chapel in Morriston, he finds himself 'obsessed' by the first black heavyweight champion of the world, Jack Johnson:

They didn't praise him as they do Joe Louis, but what I like is that he went where he wanted to go and did what he wanted to do . . . Old Jack Johnson had something Joe Louis doesn't have. Have I? Dog beneath Joe's skin. All chained up inside. In the ring Joe's a controlled explosion. From containing himself. Joe's fight is a machine, Jack's was a dance. Those silent movies . . . Old Jack reached out for life . . . Fought them with his fists, fought them with his grin, fought them with his high-powered car.

While Ellison doesn't make the connection, it is of course somewhat appropriate that his central character should be thinking about

Johnson and Louis while stationed in Wales. For on 30 August 1937, Jack Johnson had a ringside seat at Yankee Stadium to watch Tommy Farr last the full fifteen rounds, only to lose on points to Joe Louis. Louis, despite his reputation as a heavy hitter, was really a stylist in Ellison's opinion, 'as elegant as the finest of ballet dancers'. Tommy Farr was thus another white 'yokel' defeated by a black stylist. From a Welsh perspective, however, that yokel's journey from Blaenclydach to Yankee Stadium embodied, as Dai Smith has argued, the cultural trajectory of industrial Wales itself.

The centrality of the Louis v. Farr fight in the Welsh imagination is captured in Selwyn Griffiths's sequence of poems *Arwyr* (Heroes), of 1989, in which the poet recalls being woken as a child to hear the fight 'yn clecian fel cesair / o berfedd y Philips' ('hitting like hailstones / from the innards of the Philips').

> Y gwyn a'r du
> yn colbio'i gilydd
> yn Saesneg,
>   a'r dyrfa'n genllysg o swn.
>
> [Black and white
> pummelling each other
> in English,
>   and the crowd a hailstorm of sound.]

The English being emitted from the radio is part of the unusual thrill of the fight for the Welsh-speaking child, and those who argue that the dominant Welsh experience of the twentieth century has only been captured in English might consider the fact that the most powerful literary account of the Farr v. Louis bout in Welsh literature, in either language, appears in this sequence of poems.

This is a fact that would also pose a challenge to those who, throughout much of the twentieth century, sought to defend a Welsh language and culture imagined to be rooted in organic rural communities against the encroachments of modern, mobile, 'industrial civilization'. In describing the *Culture and Civilization of Wales* to an English-speaking audience in 1927, T. Gwynn Jones illustrates his observation that 'among those brought up in a Welsh atmosphere, intellectual interest is general' by recalling 'a number of agricultural labourers discussing the subject of divine immanence, forming their own terminology with astonishing exactitude, and displaying wonderful originality of thought'. Even Flintshire miners, notes Jones, are able to discuss Welsh epigrams, 'appealing, as to an authority on the rules of alliteration, to a man whose name – Murphy – was not the only evidence of Irish extraction. This was some five miles from the English border, on the other side of which I hear discussions on boxing.' The point is blatantly clear; a valuable Welsh-language culture is sufficiently strong to even acculturate an Irishman into the ways of Welsh poetry, while the philistine English are the victims of a crass popular culture symbolized by that most exploitative and demeaning of sports, boxing. If T. Gwynn Jones saw a cultural distinction between Wales and England, for W. J. Gruffydd, ten years later, the cultural shift could be discerned in Wales itself, for while he could remember a time when 'who was the best preacher, who had won the chair, what choir had won' would be the questions exercising Welsh minds,

> today – in Glamorgan at least – what is of overriding significance for us as Welshmen are the prospects of Jack Petersen or Tommy Farr, or some other Englishman born in Wales to overcome with his fists an Englishman born in England or a black man from America.

Tommy Farr was in fact, like T. Gwynn Jones's 'Murphy', a Welshman of Irish extraction, and if he was unlikely to be caught discussing the Welsh bardic measures, Farr had some knowledge of the Welsh language. He recalls in his autobiography *Thus Farr* how his trainer Joby Churchill – 'a little Welsh-speaking man straight from the mountain' – would yell instructions in Welsh so that the opposing fighter and his team wouldn't understand him.

A character such as Joby Churchill is a reminder that Welsh-language culture has been far more diverse in its structures of feeling and forms of expression than the words of some of its culturally conservative spokespersons would wish. Boxing had already been portrayed in Welsh literature well before the 1930s. In his fourth novel, *Gwen Tomos* (1894), Daniel Owen, a sharp commentator on religious hypocrisy and Victorian mores, depicted a brutal fight between Harri'r Wernddu and Ernest y Plas (who has been trained to box at Oxford and is a representative of Anglican conservatism). And boxing reappears as theme and metaphor in what is perhaps the most celebrated Welsh-language novel of all, Caradog Prichard's *Un Nos Ola Leuad* (One Moonlit Night) (1961), where the Northwalian 'Now' (Owen) receives a battering from the experienced 'hwntw' Joni Sowth. There is, then, some appropriateness in the fact that the Farr v. Louis fight should be commemorated in the other language heard in the ring at Yankee Stadium in August 1937. If 'Arwyr' won Selwyn Griffiths the Crown at the 1989 Eisteddfod, he aspired as a child towards the culture of bruising rather than versifying, and in doing so offered a rather different account of the struggle, that had proved so disturbing for W. J. Gruffydd, between a Welshman and a 'black man from America':

> dan fy wyneb blac-led,
>   fi oedd Louis;
> a Huw Cefn Rhyd
> oedd yr arwr o Donypandy;
>   erys craith dan fy llygad hyd heddiw
> yn farc o fuddugoliaeth Farr.

> [under my blackleaded face
>   I was Louis
> while Huw Cefn Rhyd
> was the hero from Tonypandy;
>   a scar beneath my eye today
>   attests to Farr's victory.]

If Hollywood could concoct a white heavyweight champion in the shape of Sylvester Stallone in 1976, then the boys in the yard replay the fight while reversing the judges' decision. But the poet, significantly, is Louis: the blacklead transforms the white Welsh writer into a black American boxer. This connection between Welshmen and African-Americans recurs with a surprising regularity in Welsh literature on boxing, and calls for further analysis.

It is in the underrated writings of Jack Jones that we encounter the most sustained use of the tropes of whiteness and blackness in Welsh literature. Racial impersonation is central to both the form and content of Jones's suggestively titled *Black Parade* (1935), which attempts to offer a fictional account of the industrialization of his native Merthyr. During the course of the novel the central character, Saran (based on the author's mother), makes several visits to the theatre, and amongst the performances mentioned in the text we find *Uncle Tom's Cabin*, *The Octoroon* and, when the theatre is converted into a cinema, *The Singing Fool*. *Uncle Tom's Cabin* refers to the hugely popular stage production of Harriet Beecher Stowe's anti-slavery novel of 1852, *The Octoroon* was also an abolitionist work, written by Irish-American Dion Boucicault and first performed in the 1850s, while *The Singing Fool*, released in 1928 and the most successful talkie yet, was Al Jolson's sequel to *The Jazz Singer*. All these productions relied on 'blackface' performances, in which greasepaint or burnt cork was used to darken the skin, a tradition that can be traced back to early nineteenth-century American minstrelsy and that continued well into the twentieth century. In aiming to trace the cultural forms that industrialization bred in south Wales, Jones's fictional evocation of blackface performances offers a suggestive metaphor for the ethnic, linguistic and cultural changes occurring in Welsh society in the later decades of the nineteenth century and the opening decades of the twentieth century in which his panoramic novel is set.

The ways in which Jack Jones, influenced as he was by American novelists John Dos Passos and James T. Farrell, employed the racial imagery of American popular culture to comment obliquely on the changing ethnic composition of Welsh society can be usefully illustrated with reference to two boxing scenes that occur in *Black Parade*. The first presents the Welshman Harry plastering the Irishman Flannery's 'mug until the nose, moustache and lips were pounded into one piece of blood-soaked hairy flesh'. Glyn, the character from whose perspective we view the fight, is reduced to vomiting violently by the sight. The tone in which the other fight is described is rather different:

I'll knock that bloody smile off your chops,' muttered Harry as he went for the nigger bald-headed. But when he got to where the nigger had been a split second before the nigger wasn't there. But he soon learnt where he was when a stinging left came from somewhere to almost flatten his nose. 'Damn you,' he muttered, turning and charging in the direction the blow had come from, only to receive a stinger from another direction. And so it went on throughout the round, a round during which Harry saw but little of the coloured man who smiled . . . 'Science, that is,' murmured Billy Samuels proudly as the smiling un-touched negro returned to his corner at the end of the second round, by which time Harry was in a very bad way indeed . . . He was carried to his corner, where he was washed and brought to his senses, and after that was done Billy Samuels shook him by the hand and said that never had he seen a gamer chap than Harry had that night proved himself, and the negro boxer also shook Harry by the hand and said that he was the stiffest proposition he had met in any part of the United States of America or here in this country . . .

The black boxer is merely a 'nigger' when the fight begins, but is slowly elevated into the more respectable 'coloured man' and 'negro' in the face of the pounding that Harry receives. The African-American is introduced as Joe Wills before the fight, a name that implicitly evokes a widely covered American boxing controversy of the 1920s. The main challenger for the heavyweight championship, held by the white Jack Dempsey, was the African-American Harry Wills. A fight between the two men was never arranged, partly because Dempsey's promoter didn't believe in inter-racial fights, and partly due to a fear of race riots of the kind that had accompanied Jack Johnson's victories in the previous decade. Jack Jones splits Harry Wills's name between the Welshman Harry and the African-American Wills: a suggestive identification of both the Welshman and African-American with the boxer famously denied his chance to fight for the heavyweight title. The difference between the two fights in Jones's novel reflects a difference in the social, and fictional, status of the Irish and African Americans. Ethnic tensions between the Irish and Welsh, as Paul O'Leary has noted, were common in nineteenth-century south Wales, a reality reflected in the visceral violence of the bout between Harry and Flannery. African-Americans posed no such threat, and the way in which Jones depicts the scene seems to evoke – to adopt Gerald Early – a culture of clowning more than a 'culture of bruising'. Wills's perpetual smile and ability to disappear whenever Harry tries to land a punch is reminiscent of the trickster figure in African-American culture, and the clowning 'coon' of minstrel shows. The black boxer plays the kind of minstrel role that the grandfather describes in Ralph Ellison's *Invisible Man*: 'I want you to overcome 'em with yeses, undermine 'em with grins, agree 'em to death and destruction, let 'em swoller you till they vomit or bust wide open.' The minstrel mask is used to hide a submerged hatred, and the smiling boxer destroys Harry before patronizing him by claiming that he's never met stiffer opposition. This seems unlikely as, according to Jones's account, Harry never manages to land a punch during the whole fight. While Jones utilizes a heightened realism to depict Harry's bout with the Irishman Flannery, the fight with the African-American Wills seems to belong to the realm of symbol and metaphor rather than reality. Eric Lott, in his persuasive account of blackface minstrelsy, argues that to

> put on the cultural forms of 'blackness' was to engage in a complex affair of manly mimicry . . . To wear or even enjoy blackface was literally for a time, to become black, to inherit the cool, virility, humility, abandon . . . that were the prime components of white ideologies of black manhood.

In Jack Jones's *Black Parade* Joe Wills embodies the 'cool, virility' and 'abandon' described by Lott, and the ambivalence of Welsh responses to African-American masculinity is captured in the connection that Jones implies between the two fighters; the Welsh Harry and African-American Wills.

Returning to the terms of the Ralph Ellison passage quoted earlier, Harry in this scene is the 'yokel' taking on the black prizefighter, and while he fails to land the one devastating blow, he is arguably stepping into the prizefighter's 'sense of time' by getting into the ring in the first place. For the yokel to step into the boxing ring was to climb from rural provincialism into modernity. To be modern, as Marshall Berman argues,

> is to find ourselves in an environment that promises us adventure, power, joy, growth, transformation of ourselves and the world – and, at the same time, that threatens to destroy everything we have, everything

we know, everything we are. Modern environments and experiences cut across all boundaries of geography and ethnicity, of class and nationality, of religion and ideology: in this sense, modernity can be said to unite all mankind. But it is a paradoxical unity, a unity of disunity: it pours all into a maelstrom of perpetual disintegration and renewal, of struggle and contradiction, of ambiguity and anguish. To be modern is to be part of a universe in which, as Marx said, 'All that is solid melts into air'.

In Welsh literature the boxing ring represents this experience of modernity. The ring is a rapidly transforming society in microcosm, where, as in the industrial crucible of south Wales, 'yokels' are transformed into modern men. Between 1861 and 1911, as a result of the explosive growth of the coal industry, the population of the county of Glamorgan grew by 253 per cent, and in the decade preceding the First World War Wales was ranked second to the United States as a centre for immigration. Wales, a predominantly agricultural country of about 500,000 people in 1800, was transformed into an urban nation of 2,500,000 by 1911. In a society that saw major changes in the make-up of its ethnic composition the question of who was native and who was foreign, brother and other, became a question of some concern. Within this context, blackface, as Susan Gubar has noted, 'assures its audience that difference is visible, always encoded in the same way, skin deep'. While, as Kevin Gaines notes, minstrelsy in America reflected white anxieties over urbanizing trends amongst blacks, Susan Gubar further argues that race-changing conventions also 'enabled artists from manifold traditions to relate nuanced comparative stories about various modes and gradations of othering'.

Alexander Cordell contributes to one of those 'manifold traditions' by exploring 'modes and gradations of othering' in his typically vivid and sweeping historical fiction based on the life of Jim Driscoll, *Peerless Jim* (1984). Cordell makes it clear that the Cardiff boxer's Irish background makes him representative of the cultural melting-pot of early twentieth-century Cardiff.

Tiger Bay, formed between the canal and Bute Street, was an enclave that was neither Welsh nor Irish, but of its own; a melting-pot of every

129

nationality form Greece to China and Arabia to Spain . . . I walked slowly along the streets of Tiger Bay, savouring its humanity. For me these people were mine; neither English, Irish nor Welsh, yet identifiably of my blood. The rouged and powdered faces of the prostitutes, the slant-eyed Chinese, the stunted features of the starved and ill, of whatever creed or colour, these I counted as my own.

This early process of ethnic identification forms a basis for Driscoll's later identification with the African-American boxer Rastus. Described initially in stereotypical terms as the 'big black man' who speaks in a 'velvet, Negro spiritual voice', Rastus becomes Driscoll's trusted guide and companion when fighting in the United States. When Driscoll decides to leave America and return to his native land,

> [t]he only one who might have persuaded me to think again was Rastus, for there had been built between us, within an orbit of mutual pain, a masculine understanding, which comes from taking punches on the chin. And my pity for my new friend increased when I suspected that he was going blind. The culmination punching of two hundred fights had built tell-tale layers above his shaggy brows; the retinas of his eyeballs were intermediately displaced so that clear sight came and went, making oscillations of static objects: Rastus lived, I knew, in a kaleidoscopic world of phantom colours: sometimes, like me, he entered a dim, after-lit land where reigned nothingness.

Rastus is less a character here than an alter ego for Driscoll – as the phrase 'like me' suggests in the final sentence above. The African-American represents 'nothingness' and is a symbol of what Driscoll might become. The process of identification here connects symbolically with the earlier description of Tiger Bay which is itself 'a dim, after-lit land' in Cordell's description of it. In a society structured along the racial lines of black and white, binaries are broken and dissolved in the dim, after-lit land of the boxer's imagination.

The possibility, or indeed probability, of being maimed physically in the ring, present as a sub-theme in Cordell's nostalgically evocative story, is made central in Leslie Norris's writings on boxing. The brutality of the boxing ring is captured in his poem 'The Ballad of Billy Rose'

WRITING ON FIGHTING IN WALES

(1967), where an encounter with a beggar, whose name, Billy Rose, is painted on his 'blind man's tin', drives the narrator's memory back to the 'hub / Of Saturday violence' where he had witnessed the same Billy Rose being 'Ripped across both his eyes', ending a career in the ring and condemning the poem's subject to a life of penury. Maiming and brutality are also the key words in Norris's short story 'A Big Night' (1976), which has a racial subtext. Disturbed and apparently brutalized by having snuck in one Saturday to witness a professional fight between Cuthbert Fletcher and Ginger Thomas, the narrator, in the story's final scene, returns for Tuesday's session in the gym:

> Everything began to feel fine. It wasn't until I put the gloves on to spar with Charlie Nolan that I realised that something was wrong. I kept on seeing Ginger Thomas, destructive and graceful, his hands cocked, moving into Cuthbert, as he had on the Saturday night. I could see his face, relaxed and faintly curious, the sudden blur as he released three or four short punches before sliding away. I knew too that I was doing this to Charlie, but I couldn't stop. Charlie was bleeding from the mouth and nose and he was pawing away with his gloves open. I could tell he was frightened. Yet I kept on ripping punches at him, my hands suddenly hard and urgent and the huge, muffling gloves we used no longer clumsy.

We're told earlier that Cuthbert Fletcher (based on the real-life black Merthyr boxer Cuth Taylor) 'would have been featherweight champion of Wales except that he was coloured'. While the Welsh crowd cheer 'with relief and pride' when Cuthbert wins on points, it is the 'lack of emotion' as much as the 'precise fury and venom' of Ginger Thomas's attacks that captures the narrator's imagination. Norris does not explore the possible meanings of this identification as the fight is replayed in reverse, with Charlie Nolan / Cuthbert Fletcher receiving a pummelling at the hands of the narrator / Ginger Thomas. Having reduced Nolan to tears the narrator leaves the gym, never to return, just as Norris closes the door on the event, omitting any explanatory commentary and thus forcing his readers to consider the multiple meanings and significances of the two friends' repeat performance of an original contest between white and black.

The implicit connection that, as I hope to have demonstrated, so many writers make between black and white in Welsh boxing literature, becomes explicit in Jack Jones's dramatic narrative *The Black Welshman*, serialized in the *Empire News* in 1957. Jones writes in the first person as an African-American boxer who escapes to Wales, having killed a white assailant. Known as Tom Ross, but actually named Abraham Dowling, born free in Chicago to a father who had been a slave, the narrator becomes known as the 'black Welshman (*y Cymro Du*) because in time I spoke the language better than most Welsh people'. The erudite, racially conscious, African-American narrator recalls his early career in Chicago:

> I trained for my fights in a bit of a gym my employer had fixed up in a corner of the large warehouse in which I still worked as a packer. My trainer and seconds, all coloured men, also worked there. The work itself was good training for one who did not smoke or drink but I was not tied to my work now that I was making a name for myself in the ring. My trainer had for a time had the handling of Sam Langford, the coloured heavyweight whose lack of inches alone prevented him from going right to the top. I refused to be matched with a coloured man for the entertainment of crowds composed in the main of white men, few women watched fights in those days. White hopes I would take on at the rate of a couple per month but I would not use my fists on a black brother whatever the inducement offered. Later I did, but not until I landed in Wales.

Having evoked the conventions of black minstrelsy as a vehicle for exploring the social changes that he observed in his family's life in *Black Parade*, Jack Jones ultimately donned the black mask himself in portraying a Welsh-speaking, African-American ex-boxer who bears witness to the cultural shifts taking place in the Rhondda. The tale ends wistfully, with the black Welshman turning for solace to a bilingual Bible as he recalls the Rhondda of the past and the Welsh-speaking girl who was once the love of his life.

> Let's . . . leave my story just as it is, then I shall have more time for this Book of ours and all who are in it including our Saviour. But here am I talking to you when I should be reading, and fancy me, the black

Welshman, turning first to the English side. That's how it is, the Welsh language is on the wane here in Mid-Rhondda, where no-one ever spoke it so sweetly as you . . . Yes, a great change has come over the Rhondda in my time, it is now a Borough . . . The new Rhondda reads more than it boxes. I can't think of one professional boxer in the whole of the Rhondda these days, yet I remember when there were at least a dozen and another hundred trying to fight their way into the ranks of professionals.

Jones's black Welshman witnesses and offers a commentary on the industrialization of Wales, and sees the early effects of de-industrialization, manifested in the story by the fact that boxers are becoming a dying breed.

Neither Jack Jones nor his 'black Welshman' lived to see the Rhondda depicted in the most experimental and successful of all Welsh boxing novels, Ron Berry's *So Long Hector Bebb* (1970). The novel's landscape is quite literally postmodern: it is a world, as several characters testify, in which industrial mobility has become post-industrial stagnation.

'This Wales of ours is going to rack and ruin. I tell you, brawd, what's wanted is a bloody revolution. Wipe the slate clean, start all over again as if we'd just lost our bloody tails.'
'Back to the caves? He-he-he, not in our time, mister.'

The novel opens with Bebb planning a boxing comeback, having been banned for a year. He has already regained the British title by the time we get a third of the way through the novel, but things then take a turn for the worse when he kills a man for fondling his wife. In the crass, brutal, misogynistic, but at times linguistically dazzling world of the boxing fraternity Bebb gains some sympathy.

You had to cross Hector first to send him into one of his non-stop fits. What Millie Bebb does is fling her what's-it at him for Em to touch up her clout. Em sticks his hand there in open public! Like I say, God stone me cold, the man isn't born who'll take such. He was always on about Mel Carpenter's bad luck. Luck, by Christ. They reckon you could hear Emlyn's head smacking the counter from outside the Transport

Café. LUCK! Em's mouth spilling the old tomato juice. No wonder they took Millie away for a couple of weeks . . . Mind, speaking for myself I hope they don't find Hector. Never find him, that's what I hope.

While some characters compensate for material deprivation with linguistic bravura, Hector Bebb achieves a measure of freedom in leaving the ring to live a primitive life in the forests above the valley towns of Tosteg and Blaenddu. In Berry's novel the narrative trajectory from yokel provincialism to prizefighting modernity, embodied in the Ralph Ellison passage quoted at the beginning of this essay, is reversed. Rather than stepping into modernity, Hector Bebb steps out of modern time and returns to the mountains; the prizefighter becomes a yokel. The history of Wales as reflected in its boxing literature seems to have come full circle. But I will conclude this essay by noting that, in his return to primitive life, Bebb carries with him an image of his better self and an embodiment of the world that had given his life purpose and meaning: a copy of *Ring* magazine, where 'another shiny Negro posed on the cover'.

Endnote

Ralph Ellison is quoted with the permission of Professor John Callahan, Literary Executor of the Ralph Ellison estate. 'A Storm of Blizzard Proportions' is unpublished and exists in several drafts in the Ralph Ellison Papers, Library of Congress. The quotation relating to Jack Johnson and Joe Louis is from an early draft of the story. Leslie Norris is quoted with permission of Professor Meic Stephens, Literary Executor of the Leslie Norris Estate.

Entry of the Heavyweights

ERSKINE AND RICHARDSON

PETER STEAD

At Joe Erskine's funeral in February 1990 the Cardiff journalist Bill Barrett turned to Jack Petersen and commented: 'If only he had possessed your punch, Jack!' The smiling former champion replied, 'If only I could have had some of his skills!' Joe had died at the age of 56; sadly, Jack, twenty-three years his senior, would himself be dead before the year was out. The city of Cardiff's two holders of the British Heavyweight Championship had contrasting boxing and life styles, but they were to be forever joined together in the local pantheon of heroes.

Joe's title had been won thirty-four years after Jack's but, remarkably, only eight British heavyweight title fights had been held between Jack losing the title to Ben Foord in 1936 and Joe winning it from Johnny Williams in 1956. Williams was Welsh, of course, as was Tommy Farr, the champion in 1937–8. Wales was undoubtedly proud of its heavyweight champions, but had nonetheless shared in the general British boxing gloom in the post-war decade. Then, suddenly and remarkably, in the mid 1950s there was cause for hope; there appeared to be a new British heavyweight bonanza, with Wales well to the fore. Once again reporters were optimistically trotting out the old adage, 'as the heavyweights go, so goes boxing'. The big men were sure to inspire a new era for British boxing as a whole, and in the sports pages one could sense the anticipation.

In Wales the new era dawned at the unlikely and unromantic venue of the Maindy Stadium, a mile or so north of Cardiff's civic centre. Although the city had staged its first world title fight in 1946 (the lightweight contest between Ike Williams and Ronnie James), Ninian Park was not seen as a suitable setting for regular bouts, and attention switched to the municipally owned Maindy Stadium. Once a deep and dangerously flooded claypit, it had been filled in and reclaimed in the Depression and subsequently equipped for cycling and athletics events. Two bouts held at this intimate bowl in 1956 aroused the Welsh boxing public as nothing had since Tommy Farr's New York performance in 1937. They gave every indication of riches and pleasure to follow. In May Joe Erskine outpointed Dick Richardson of Newport to establish himself as the chief contender for Don Cockell's title. In August, with Cockell now retired, Joe's bout with the former champion Johnny Williams became a title bout. This was the first British heavyweight title fight to be held in Wales, and the locals were not to be disappointed. Wales was back in the big time.

The boxing public had been reminded regularly of the full significance of the Erskine–Richardson bout. 'There are huge issues at stake', argued Harold Mayes of the *Empire News*, for, given the crucial role of the heavyweight division, 'Britain's ring future for the next ten years may well rest on the broad shoulders of the man whose hand is raised on Monday week'. It was taken for granted that the winner on the night would go on to be the British champion, and already there was talk of the world title. 'It is a long time', reflected the *Boxing News*, 'since a bout between two young heavyweights captured the imagination as much as this one.' It reported that Wales seemed to be 'divided over its two young prospects'. The experts were divided too: it was clearly going to be a matter of Richardson's punch against Erskine's durability. Joe was 22 and unbeaten, with only one of his twenty-eight bouts drawn. His stamina had been amply proved in a worthy points win over the highly rated Henry Cooper. Dick was a little younger and, crucially, had displayed his power by stopping the Belgian Marcel Limage in the fifth, whilst the Erskine–Limage bout had gone the distance. It was thought that Richardson's best bet was to go for an early knockout. The quietly confident Erskine confided that he'd 'yet to see Richardson hit as hard as people say he does'.

The boxers did not disappoint. Promoter Sydney Evans ('Evans the Shrewd') had packed in some 25,000 or 30,000 (estimates varied greatly) and at a windy Maindy they were treated to what *Boxing News* branded as 'the finest heavyweight contest ever staged in Wales'. In 'ten rounds of slam-bang action' Erskine had outpointed his opponent in 'a stand-up fight that was a thriller from start to finish'. 'The speed of the fight' was thought to be remarkable, with 'both boys slamming into each other from the first bell'. As some had predicted, Joe was down for a count of nine in the fifth but a wink to his corner was reassuring. With blood flowing from an eye wound he fought on with style and stamina, keeping his opponent at bay with left jabs and rights to the head. It was a warmly greeted and convincing win, a win generally summed up as 'sparkling'.

The boxing world now opened up nicely for Joe. With the older generation of Cockell and Gardner standing down, and with his eye healed, he could after three months return to Maindy Stadium to fight for the title. He would be the favourite but not by much. Johnny Williams was a native of Barmouth (he was born on Christmas Day 1926) but his family had moved from the mouth of the Mawddach to the Rugby area when he was three and, as a boxer, he was always billed as 'the darling of the Midlands'. He was now 30, a veteran of many years in the booths and of over seventy fights, a career that had peaked when he outpointed Jack Gardner to take both British and Empire titles in 1952. Just over a year later, after fifteen 'epic' rounds, he had lost his titles to Don Cockell in what had been their third meeting. He was an admired boxer, like Joe essentially a stylist, but perhaps with a stronger punch. There were some who thought that he was lucky to have been given this second chance ahead of young prospects, such as Cooper and Richardson. In his column the great Jimmy Wilde wondered whether 'a slamming' received in a recent bout in the States had taken too much out of him. But in general promoter Syd Evans was thought worthy of a medal; 'all the ingredients are here', predicted the *Boxing News*.

'Epic' was again the favourite description of Erskine's fifteen-round triumph, his first bout at that championship distance. As in all the best lengthy duels, the plot took twists and turns, with Joe's corner performing miracles after one eye was cut in the fourth and the other in the ninth. Johnny gave his all, punching hard and doing well in the clinches, but Joe's left saw him home and at the bell his opponent beat the referee to the job of raising Joe's arm. The verdict was jubilantly acclaimed by a crowd who had endured rainfall that had amounted to a 'torrential drenching' in the final rounds. The *Times* man had thought that 'most of Cardiff seemed to be present' whilst *Boxing News* noted that the 'mackintoshed zealots' had remained 'rooted to their seats' in what they chose to describe as 'Cardiff's ill-starred municipal stadium'. Joe himself had found that victory had come more easily than expected. He gave thanks both to his cornermen and for the miracle that had seen his right eye reopen after being, for twenty seconds, 'shut as tight as an oyster'. At 22 he had won the title that had been his ambition 'from the first time I ever threw a punch': 'I've done everything which has been asked of me', he reflected, 'and I feel sure I can continue to do so'.

As the bout had ended and Joe's arm was raised, the *Boxing News* correspondent had noted how the new champion's 'calypso-chanting Tiger Bay admirers had swarmed all over the ring to mob their idol', and what followed was 'a demonstration of frenetic enthusiasm by hundreds of his dockland admirers'. Thus, it was conveyed to the public that Joe was a product of an immigrant community. His features were soon to be made familiar in newsreels and even more so in local television news bulletins, on which he regularly appeared, hooded and be-towelled, to report that 'he had been training hard in the hills'. Even so, reporters were careful with their words; Brian Glanville described him as 'a swarthy, amiable man'. Joe was on occasions more direct: 'my father was a West Indian, my mother a local girl. I am a half-caste, but in the Bay we are all one nation.'

'Tiger Bay', or more properly Butetown, was a small distinct district of a few streets in what was itself a clearly demarcated and isolated docklands community. Cardiffians were vaguely proud that their city could boast of such an exotic and cosmopolitan trophy of its great maritime past, and Shirley Bassey was always acclaimed as the jewel in its crown, but, in truth, they very rarely entered the world that existed under the railway bridges. Tiger Bay was a classic ghetto, and one that was looking distinctly shabby in the 1950s. On its own terms it had been a veritable melting-pot, with West Africans, Somalis, Yemenis, West Indians and Maltese making their contributions, many of the sailors marrying local Irish or Welsh wives. There had been very little integration outside the Bay, but in one respect, that of sport, the community had travelled well down the road of bridge-building. Over the decades Tiger Bay was to earn an honourable place in the annals of Welsh rugby by sustaining its own teams and by producing stars for first-class rugby union and league sides. Above all, there was Billy Boston, born on Angelina Street to an African father and Cardiff mother, and destined to be one of northern rugby league's greatest players. Joe Erskine was also an Angelina Street boy; he grew up just two doors away from Boston and as a schoolboy played with him in the same Cardiff Central and Wales team. Joe always boasted that he had played outside half for Wales and that it was only the breaking of an arm that led to the switch of sports. He often spoke of returning to play rugby 'for pleasure' when his boxing career was over.

Nevertheless, boxing was in his blood, and in many respects he can be seen as the last great product of the classic years of the boxing booths. His father, Johnny, was to become a familiar figure, wearing his fedora and shouting in his deep voice, 'Come on Joe' towards the end of every round his son fought. In his time Johnny, branded the 'Terror of Tiger Bay', was a popular booth-fighter, but in this regard he had to concede to his mother who, together with female relatives, had fought in the booths and had been known to knock out Valley inhabitants who entered the ring in order to make a few shillings. According to Geoff Rich, Nan was referred to as the 'boss woman of the fighting Erskine family'. She was known to have trained the great Jim Driscoll and to have sparred with Joe in his early days. She had brought up and trained Joe even as she ran her own furniture business from the Angelina Street home. She sent Joe out to fight saying: 'Get at him, and bring home the bacon.'

And for eight years Joe did just that. He retired in 1964, at a time when his opponents came from a new generation. In October of that year he was outpointed at Wembley by Billy Walker in a 'superbly exciting ten rounds'. The *Times* man was fascinated by the spectacle of a raw youngster actually learning boxing skills as he 'edged out the fading skills' of Joe, who had seemed to 'have had it wrapped up early on'. Walker's victory was popular and augured well, but the crowd also rose to salute the possibly unlucky loser, the 'old master of the British ring'. This appreciation of his skills had always been the basis of the British public's warm affection for Joe, but it was allied to an awareness of shortcomings that had imposed limits to what could be achieved. In truth, it was a frustrating career, in which bad losses were offset by great nights, after which there would again be talk of possible bouts at a higher level. In his first fight after beating Williams he was knocked out by the Cuban Nino Valdes, but in 1957 he seemed a new man when he impressively outpointed the heavier Joe Bygraves to win the Empire title: it was a polished performance in which he had 'punished the Jamaican with all the passionless efficiency of a headmaster dealing with an obstinate pupil'.

Reflecting on Joe's career, Paul Johnson recalled that 'he always seemed to be on the crest of a slump'. In January 1958 he travelled to Gothenburg in an attempt to divest Ingemar Johansson of his European title. Joe's trainer, Archie Rule, called a halt to proceedings after the thirteenth round. It was not a great fight, but it had been a compellingly gruelling one. The *Times* suggested it had proved that 'neither man could yet match the standard of world champion'. Yet in 1959 Johansson was sensationally to take the world title from Floyd Patterson. Erskine was never to aspire to that level, and perhaps it was during his nevertheless brave 'man of iron' performance against the Swede that his limitations became apparent. Worse was to follow, for within four months he was to lose both his titles when at White City he was knocked out in the eighth by Brian London, after being cut by a clash of heads in the seventh. He was never again to be champion, but in February 1959 at Wembley he outpointed the American Willie Pastrano, at that time rated sixth in the world and a future world light-heavyweight champion. Those who saw this bout counted themselves privileged; it had been a superb boxing exhibition, in which Joe's left had 'beaten a tattoo on the American's face'. The *Times* unofficially awarded Joe 'a world title', that of 'the cleverest heavyweight', but they were realistic enough to realize that the bout, 'rare experience' that it was, represented a 'literary backwater' in terms of the overall story of world boxing. The same could have been said of his victory over George Chuvalo. The Canadian, who some years later was to figure in two world title bids, was disqualified for head-butting in the fifth.

There were certainly some big names on the Erskine record, but the fact that he was British champion for less than two years in a ten-year professional career reminds us that he had been forced to share the various promotions and news coverage with a contemporary clutch of British heavyweights who, over a decade, provided their public with an almost relentless series of bouts in which boxing prowess and bravery had to share the stage with controversy, farce and not a little soap opera. It was a dreamtime for promoters, as each of the leading British heavyweights had developed their own passionate groups of supporters. There was also a potent ethnic dimension, as the two leading Welsh fighters seemed destined to clash with persistent Anglo-Saxon opponents. In the meantime, a year after having lost his titles to Brian London, Erskine had his second fight against his old Welsh rival, Dick Richardson. Staged at Porthcawl, the verdict was never in doubt. Richardson 'rarely laid a hurtful glance on Joe', who won on points. By the Newport fighter's standards this had been an unremarkable evening, for, although he had lost many big fights, what was termed 'his rough-house style' had won him a firm following, not least amongst promoters. In 1958 he had taken part in what was described as 'the most disappointing fight ever to be staged in this country'. He was declared the winner when former world champion Ezzard Charles was disqualified in the second for 'persistent holding'; in the opinion of *Boxing News*, Richardson had shown 'no great visible urge to break free'. At Porthcawl, in 1958 Richardson had been knocked out by Henry Cooper, but not before he had used his head to cut his opponent between the eyes. 'Dick was a dirty bastard' was Cooper's later comment, someone who had taken full advantage of the fact that referees rarely disqualified those who butted in early rounds. Cooper had known him in the army, when Richardson had 'terrorised Aldershot': on reflection, he suggested Dick had been 'a better fighter on the cobbles than he ever was in the ring'. He saw him as being 'as Welsh as they come', someone who fought as if he were 'still in the scrum'.

At every stage an attention-grabbing mix of success and controversy characterized Richardson's career. In March 1960 he went to Dortmund to win the European title against Hans Kalbfell, sparking a riot in the process. A few months later on a rain-sodden night at Porthcawl, he was disqualified for illegal use of the head in a bout with an American giant, Mike De John. The crowd had responded by throwing beer cans, chairs, newspapers and 'even an umbrella' into the ring, and it was only the prompt action of cornerman Dicky Dobbs that saved the referee from attack. Worse followed a month later, when Porthcawl entered the annals of boxing history as a place of shame. Memorably, Henry Cooper once described the arena that Sir Lesley Joseph had developed, between the candyfloss stalls, rides, slides and shows of his seaside fairground, as 'a dump'. It was a rough and ready place that saw boxing retreating to its own roots, and yet it could hold 12,000, a useful facility at a time when boxing had a newly recruited mass following in Wales. On a late August evening in 1960 Richardson was defending his European title against Brian London when, at the end of the seventh, the challenger was cut by what he manifestly thought was a butt. During the eighth the referee did well to break up the fighters. London was now shouting at his opponent, and all the while his eye was getting worse. At the end of the round, when the referee went to London's corner to stop the fight, his seconds complained bitterly: as the ring filled up, one of Dick's seconds was knocked to the canvas by an opposite number. What followed was described as 'a scene reminiscent of a Wild West saloon fight', and one in which spectators and seconds (including London's father) either exchanged punches or wrestled until the police (including, according to *Boxing News*, 'a good proportion of Welsh rugby second-row forwards') intervened. What made matters worse was that both BBC cameras and European boxing officials had been present on what was subsequently adjudged to be a 'bad night for British boxing'.

Brian London was fined £1,000 for his display of temper and never quite shrugged off the reputation that the frequently broadcast images of Porthcawl sustained, but the popular and hard-hitting fighter had a distinguished career, in which he outdid his Welsh rivals by going on to feature twice in world title bouts. Meanwhile, Richardson continued to be successful on the European stage. He twice successfully defended his title in Dortmund before losing it to Johansson in Gothenburg in 1962. Retirement came after Henry Cooper beat him in the fifth at Wembley in March 1963. Aged only 28, he had brought to an end a career in which he had lost fourteen of his forty-seven professional fights and yet done extremely well financially. In complete contrast to his 'rough-house' image that had so suited promoters, the so-called 'Maesglas Marciano' (he had grown up in Newport next door to the legendary former champion Johnny Basham), the one-time Teddy boy and London milkman invested his money well, ran a butcher's shop and enjoyed a long retirement. When he died, aged 65, in 1999 his obituarists enjoyed telling the story of Porthcawl, an incident that had actually resulted from the illegal use of the head, but at the same time they recalled a 'dashing colourful heavyweight who brought a touch of theatre to the dour British boxing scene' and who then in retirement had been a 'genial, affable, smiling presence' at the ringside.

In the early 1960s, as the British heavyweight game of musical chairs continued, it always seemed that either a Richardson or an Erskine bout was imminent. And everywhere the fans and Welsh heavyweights looked there was Henry Cooper. Erskine and Cooper first met when they fought in the ABA semi-finals in 1952 and all told they were to meet eight times as either amateurs or professionals; they featured together in four title fights. Joe, at the height of his powers, had out-pointed Henry in 1957: in 1959 the roles were reversed when Henry in the first defence of his title stopped Joe in the twelfth. Joe was given two more cracks at the title; in 1961 Henry won in the fifth, in 1962 in the ninth. By 1962 Cooper had been champion for three years, but the opinion was that he 'had slipped from grace' in beating Joe. The *Times* thought that he 'made hard work of it' and that he had fought in a 'tense and indecisive manner'. *Boxing News* reported that the crowd had booed the champion's 'lack-lustre' performance, and that all the cheers and appreciation had been for the 'plucky and polished Welshman', who had been denied a shock victory only by his bleeding eyes. In a note of nostalgia they recalled the 'confidence and competence' that had characterized Joe's period as champion just four years earlier. As they contemplated Cooper's 'lack of fire' and look of 'puzzlement' on that evening, they could have not have conceived of the full celebrity status awaiting the champion. At Wembley in 1963 his left hook almost gave him a victory over Cassius Clay and prepared the way for the former plasterer from Bellingham to go on, as 'our 'Enery', to be a star of television adverts and chat shows. For Thomas Hauser he became the 'patron saint of British heavyweights'.

In the years that followed Joe Erskine's retirement Henry Cooper was presented with many opportunities to make known his admiration for the opponent who he had known so well in the ring. There was no bad feeling between the fighters, although Cooper made it clear that he had no great liking for Joe's manager, the feisty and theatrical Benny Jacobs, who, in the adverts for his Custom House Street gym in Cardiff ('The Gym Where All the Champions Train'), billed himself as 'Britain's Premier Manager'. Jacobs had always maintained that in their 1961 bout Cooper had hit Joe after the bell. Talking to Brian Glanville, Henry commented that 'Joe's a silly boy. I mean, boxing; that's his long suit. Him and me's the best of friends, but I hate his manager.' In his autobiography Cooper highlighted Joe's impassivity, his poker face, the way he showed no emotion and his refusal to indicate whether a punch had hurt him. 'He was a hard man to box'; even when he seemed out of distance he could land a left, he always saw punches coming, and, swaying and rolling, with his head down, it was impossible to hit his chin. Cooper's conclusion was that 'I'd sooner have fought Brian London and Dick Richardson than Joe Erskine'.

The greatest contrast between Joe and Henry came in their later career patterns. While Joe fell on hard times, Henry was to host fund-raising evenings for his old friend, who had reputedly earned some £80,000 or even £100,000 in the ring. In 1990 he was to be present at Joe's funeral. The story of Joe's last twenty-five years does not make pleasant reading. He had tried wrestling, operating a gym and running a pub in Merthyr. Later, the Sunday newspapers were prepared to pay him for the details of his heavy drinking, his time as a Jehovah's Witness and, above all, the spectacular way in which he 'blew £70,000 on girls and gambling'. 'I was a mindless fool', he admitted, as he told how he had been addicted to the 'rattle of dice' since his early days in Angelina Street. His friend, the ex-fighter Dai Corp, remembered Joe as someone who would 'bet on two flies walking on a wall'. Eventually in 1990 the *South Wales Echo*, the paper which had always led the cheerleading, had to report his 'sad, sudden and lonely death' in an Adamsdown flat just a mile or so from Tiger Bay.

His funeral was almost as great an event as had been that of Jim Driscoll in 1925. After the service at St Mary's, the *Echo* reported on Joe's 'final trip around his beloved dockland'. The hearse travelled down Bute Street and then via Angelina Street and Loudon Square to Mountstuart Square, at the heart of Butetown. Dan O'Neill always remembered Joe as a man with no regrets or envy and someone with enormous pride in his community. 'In the Bay we are all one nation', Joe had explained. 'I remember Shirley Bassey before she was Shirley Bassey', he had boasted. He was a product of a once vibrant and thriving dockland, a community that had generated its own warmth and standards, but one that had been neglected and never fully embraced. His own decline only emphasized the extent to which his home patch was in need of a new vision. In retrospect we can see

Joe's career as a last blast of an old Tiger Bay and an old Cardiff. The images that one retains of Joe behind the bar in his Loudon Hotel and then later drinking in his beloved Old Arcade in the city centre remind us that in his last decades Tiger Bay and Cardiff's other dock-land communities were fading fast, and very much awaiting their role in the transformation involved in the Cardiff Bay Project and the wider programme of post-industrial regeneration.

In his prime, Joe had been a symbol of everything that was best about Tiger Bay, a one-nation or rainbow community that prided itself on supporting its youngsters and encouraging them to achieve excellence in their fields of endeavour. In 1955 a Cardiff journalist billing himself as 'Second' had identified the 22-year-old Erskine as a 'potential world heavyweight champion', not least because he pos-sessed a 'boxing brain'. At a training session the reporter had seen Joe working with the legendary Salaam Sullivan, once known as the fastest boxer in the world and someone who had sparred with Jim Driscoll. 'Second' saw distinct elements of Driscoll in Joe and had no doubt that now the 'Driscoll style, adopted correctly, will beat the world'. Sadly, that was not to be the case. Joe did not have a punch and, as the *Echo*'s Tom Lynn reflected, 'whoever heard of a heavy-weight without a knock-out punch?' On a visit to Britain in 1956 Nat Fleischer refused to rank Joe in the world's top ten (he did for a while make it to seventh), but the dissenting riposte of *Boxing News* was that 'non-punchers are always under-rated'. That may well be true, but it does not help if the non-puncher is, as Gilbert Odd noted, 'at 5ft 11ins, two inches too short for his own good' and has eyes that easily cut and bleed. So it was that Joe never had his chance at the top and was only briefly a champion. Perhaps Dan O'Neill was right to suggest that in a later age he would have fought as a cruiser-weight. What he bequeathed as a heavyweight, however, was the memory of a lovely boxer to watch, a true master of ringcraft: he was a boxer with a brain, as shrewd as he was brave. Paul Johnson asked for him to be remembered as the 'classiest heavyweight Britain has ever produced'. 'Watching some men in the ring is like being witness to a mugging', said Ken Jones, 'but Erskine's skill was a thing of beauty.' That is a judgement that should stand as Joe's memorial, and as a tribute to what was once Tiger Bay.

Boxing through the Shadows

HOWARD WINSTONE, EDDIE THOMAS AND JOHNNY OWEN

DESMOND BARRY

Is this a true memory or am I confusing one victory parade with another? Fourteen years old, January 1968, I stand among the crowd on the Merthyr High Street and strain over shoulders and heads to catch a look at two lads, who are much younger than me. Each one carries a boxing glove, the gloves used to win the World Feather-weight Boxing Championship. They wear matching woollen coats, short trousers, cropped hair. They catch the hand of their mam. Her blonde-highlighted hair is cut short, and she's wearing a fur coat. It's hard for me to see among the bodies. I'm a bit short of five feet tall at the time, not much more now. Wasn't Howard Winstone marching up the street, too? In the movie that runs in my mind, Winstone is out in front with Eddie Thomas, his trainer, and the civic dignitaries; and his family is behind. Or in this dream, am I younger? And is this is the victory parade to celebrate his winning a Lonsdale belt? Either way, it's a 1960s social realism movie like *Billy Liar* or *Saturday Night and Sunday Morning*.

In a special issue of the *Merthyr Express* to commemorate the fortieth anniversary of Winstone's world championship, an eyewitness account states that Winstone, 'wearing blazer and slacks' is taken into the Town Hall by a side door because the crowd is so thick in front of the building.

Does that make my memory movie a collage?

Now, I see Winstone come out onto the balcony where he's surrounded by councillors and the mayor in chains that glint in his reflected glory and I can't hear what the world champion says over the cheers. I don't remember any male voice choir, although the same *Merthyr Express* report says that the Dowlais Male Voice Choir sang 'We'll Keep a Welcome in the Hillsides'. The image of politicians on the balcony of a civic building seems Latin to me: Pancho Villa, Emiliano Zapata (played by Brando), Benito Mussolini . . .

But wasn't it raining?

After the three fights against Vicente Saldivar, which Winstone lost, the victory over Mitsunori Seki, where Winstone finally wins the title is an occasion for mixed emotions. Yes, he's finally won the world championship, but he's never beaten the great Saldivar. That is the fighter that Winstone – and Welsh fight fans who follow his career – wants to beat.

But after beating Seki, Winstone is undisputed world champion.

I remember my grandmother, from Ynysgau Street, her voice catching when she speaks of the two boys, each with one of their dad's boxing gloves, and her passing judgement on the Winstone divorce that comes so soon after Howard Winstone wins the title.

'She was from Trefechan, see', my gran says, as if that explains everything about the Winstone family's now notorious domestic conflicts.

And me, I'm fascinated by Benita, this maligned woman who divorces the town's world champion just after he wins the world title. There's some seductive darkness here that, at the age of 14, I can't begin to fathom, from which I am excluded. And I want in.

Boxing is the sport of gangsters. And gangsters' molls. How does Benita fit into that siren world? How could she split up with a world champion? Did she really stab him in the arm? Why?

And Eddie Thomas, former British, Empire and European champion, Howard's trainer, best cuts man in the world, after the fight is surrounded by these men in long black coats, who wear expensive suits, who like to smoke cigars.

Boxing – for me, the 14-year-old on Merthyr High Street – is Harry Levine, the Jewish promoter with the Cockney accent, in his dinner jacket and bow-tie. It's villains from the East End and Soho, drinking champagne and running books, and terrorizing grasses or dropping them in the Thames, feet encased in concrete overshoes. It's life in black and white behind the clean façade of *Sportsnight* with David Coleman; it's the BBC Sports Personality of the Year (Howard won the Welsh version in 1963 but didn't win the British version, even in 1968 when he was world champion). Boxing is Harry Carpenter reporting ringside. It's staying up late with my father to watch Cassius Clay fight Sonny Liston in the middle of the night; it's rooting for Liston the gangster against the loudmouth upstart from Louisville, Kentucky. And bitter disappointment. Liston refuses to fight in the seventh because of a hurt shoulder. And in the rematch, no longer Cassius Clay but the new-name Black Muslim, Muhammad Ali, drops Liston with a karate punch, for which we're sure, on the school playground, Ali's been getting secret training by a Japanese master.

Or maybe Liston took a dive.

This is the world of Brando on the waterfront.

And Howard Winstone connects us to this, not just a contender but finally a winner, a world champion. And behind all that innocence and Welsh good nature, the purse deals remain in the shadows. Where does the money go between the box office and the TV rights and the promoter and the manager? Someone makes money somewhere, but Winstone still walks on Merthyr High Street. And he doesn't drive around in any Rolls Royce. And who are these guys in the long black coats? Is there something dark and special about them?

Howard Winstone is twice my age when he becomes world champion. He's Buddy Holly and Elvis-style rock and roll. He's a sharp Italian suit with a single-button, narrow-lapel jacket. He's winklepicker shoes and narrow tie. He's slicked back hair and a comb in the back pocket. Eddie Thomas is his Welsh godfather, the Bill Haley quiff and knobbly cheeks, broken nose and cauliflower ears, big lips and heavy shoulders, Howard's minder. They're Station Café people, frothy coffee and fight pictures hanging on the walls. They walk our working-class streets as if they've just stepped down off a movie screen. That Merthyr should have a world boxing champion is as natural to me as listening to the Rolling Stones on the jukebox in the Arcade Café.

Merthyr's pubs and council-estate streets are full of hard men looking to build a reputation, but boxing moves Howard and Eddie into a parallel dimension, where fighting is abstract art, where a glass in the face is out of place, a sacrilege to the religion of refined violence, with its asceticism of roadwork and skipping rope, speedballs and heavy bags, head-guards and gum-shields, cuts men in the red corner. Boxers are untouchable, off-limits to pub brawlers. Boxers carry their – and our – violent myths from the streets to the pages of history. Our boxers mark the world. They put us on the map: British Champion, European Champion, Commonwealth and Empire Champion like Eddie Thomas, and with Howard Winstone, all of these . . . and World Champion, too, when he beat Mitsunori Seki of Japan.

When my memory flickers with its images of Howard Winstone's career, I can't remember the Japanese champion's name. The name that I don't have to look up is Vicente Saldivar. Merthyr's bloody boxing history is forged like a red-hot iron link to Mexico City's.

Back in the 1960s, Welsh working-class people are small of stature: undernourished genes after more than a century of industrial and rural exploitation, now getting fed on 60s' abundance, never short of mad courage and a love of violence. Winstone is a son of that brutal genetic. Saldivar is Mexico City mean streets: barrios and street gangs. Winstone fights Saldivar three times and each time the Mexican wears him down and beats him, the second bout's result disputed by every fight fan in Wales; by Winstone himself; and most definitely by Eddie Thomas. Is this referee Wally Thom's way of spiting Eddie Thomas? There's bad blood between the two of them from since they faced each other in the ring. From when Wally Thom took Eddie's British titles. And everyone knew Eddie was the better fighter.

The losses to Saldivar are agony for Winstone.

And they're agony for us on the streets of Merthyr.

Winstone embodies Welsh working-class winners. A capitalist bastard factory press can take off the tops of three fingers of his right hand, and he still has the grit to win over fifty professional fights before his first title shot, take Lonsdale belts and Empire Games gold medals. The second fight against Saldivar at Ninian Park has Winstone dominate for ten rounds, take brutal punishment in the fourteenth, and finish up with toe-to-toe slugging in the fifteenth. Saldivar is given the decision, the heartbreaking decision, by half a point. The third and last fight between them in Mexico City sees Saldivar stop Winstone in twelve.

Neither Winstone nor Saldivar can speak the other's language, but the extreme of corporeal risk they share and the pain of the violence they inflict upon each other has brought them together in a state of consciousness perhaps unique to men who have gone together to the farthest edges of physical and mental endurance, to an intimacy that was to continue outside the brutal temporal and spatial confines of the boxing ring.

Saldivar retires after the third fight with Winstone. The Mexican champion quits at the top. He has nothing left to prove. That leaves the featherweight crown open and the two boxers who have previously and unsuccessfully challenged Saldivar fight a bout for the vacant world championship. Winstone beats Seki in nine rounds, the referee stopping the fight because of a cut over Seki's eye. Winstone can finally claim the world champion's crown. He holds it for five months before he loses the title to the Spanish fighter Jose Legra. Saldivar makes a brief come-back two years later and regains his title in 1970. He can only hold it for five months before he's beaten by Kuniaki Shibata.

According to Winstone's sparring partner, Don James, in a BBC interview, Winstone's life would probably have taken a less troubled trajectory had the verdict gone for him against Saldivar.

The decision bothers Winstone long after the fight was over.

'He'd say, 'Why, Don, why didn't I have the verdict that night?'

Before I leave Merthyr in 1972, I still see Winstone around the streets, or in the bus station, where he runs a café called the Lonsdale Bar. It seems a difficult and unglamorous way to make a living after spending ten years as a fighter and a continuously fêted hero in the town. Years of sporting fame are no guarantee of continuing fortune, and I'm sure that an ex-athlete needs to find happiness in the ordinariness of every-day living when he finds there's little point in chasing the ever-receding mirage of public glory. Winstone marries again and raises a second family. If the remainder of his life brings its difficulties, it surely brings its private compensations, too, which his awed Merthyr public, quite rightly, can never share. It's alcohol that weakens his fighter's body; and it finally leads to his death at the age of 61.

Back in 1968, as Howard Winstone's boxing star is on the wane, another's is on the rise. The year after Winstone beats Mitsunori Seki, Johnny Owen becomes Welsh schoolboy featherweight champion. At the age of 20, a bantamweight now, Owen wins his first professional fight; and nine bouts later he's champion of Britain. In November 1978 he takes the Commonwealth title, and only fails to become European champion after a controversial decision against him in Almeria, Spain, against Juan Francisco Rodriguez on 3 March 1979. In the rematch, 28 February 1980, the judges make a unanimous decision in Owen's favour. In June of that year, he successfully defends his Commonwealth title, and in September he gets his chance for a shot at the world title against Lupe Pintor, another great fighter from Mexico City. Once more it's Merthyr Tydfil v. Mexico City. Just like Winstone v. Saldivar.

Because I leave Merthyr in 1972, I don't witness Owen's trajectory in the same way as I do with Winstone. A lot of my contemporaries leave Merthyr at that time, too. Not just to migrate to London or Southampton or other British cities, but a sizeable number of Merthyr boys – in their late teens and early twenties – head for the United States, where they form a small colony, west of Los Angeles, near the beaches of Santa Monica.

Inevitably, with the rise of a new sporting genius from the streets of Merthyr's housing estates where we exiles grew up, we keep close watch on the rise of Johnny Owen through the dark glass of our adopted cultures, mine in London, others in LA. We can watch the fights on TV. We can read about them in the newspapers. But we aren't on Merthyr High Street for any major homecoming victory parade after Owen wins a major title. We got out of Dodge but we know who we are when Owen steps into the ring. So when the world championship fight is set to take place in Los Angeles, the Merthyr boys on the hobble around the Pacific Ocean beaches are first in line at the Olympic Auditorium to get title-fight tickets for Johnny Owen v. Lupe Pintor.

Two old friends from Trefechan have tickets for the fight. They meet on the evening of 19 November 1980, in the Mucky Duck, a British exiles' pub in Santa Monica, a block from the Pacific Ocean beaches. The pub is packed. The Trefechan boys and a load of British fight fans, including a group of Scots, get well lubricated for the occasion. They pile into a coach and set off for the Olympic Auditorium. Coming down off the freeway ramp, they see the crowds in the parking lot among the low-riders and the chromed-up pick-up trucks, here and there gang colours, Latin Kings gold, East LA homeboys here to support Pintor.

From the parking lot a sympathetic security guard shepherds the Owen supporters into the auditorium and down to their seats. Inside, the atmosphere is hostile. A vast number of Pintor fans scream abuse at the British group. The boys from the Mucky Duck are showered with paper cups full of beer, then, cups of piss. Cherry bombs go off. Never ones to shy from a ruckus, still, the way they're outnumbered, there's nothing to do but take it. By the time that Owen and Pintor take the ring, the atmosphere between both sets of fans is poisonous.

When they see the two fighters in the ring, the American fight commentators cannot believe that someone as frail-looking as Owen, known as the Matchstick Man in Merthyr, has stepped into the ring with Lupe Pintor, hard-packed muscle and macho, El Indio, from Barrio La Colonia, Mexico City.

Owen is all ribs that show through the skin, ropy muscle and long bone. But the big features that reveal a lack of guile, and a terrifying innocence, outside the ring, transform within the ropes into ferocious focus.

Watching his previous fights, it seems to me that his style is like a windmill, whirling fists that flail his opponents into submission. Owen is all attack. He's tall and rangy and never stops punching. Pintor is a good deal shorter than Owen, but he's solid. He's a knockout artist, slower maybe, but all power. For the first seven rounds, Owen stifles Pintor and leaves him cut above and below both eyes. Pintor's corner needs to work out changes in the Mexican champion's ring strategy to counter the relentless attack of the Welshman. It's a credit to Pintor that he withstands that seven-round barrage. When he comes back into the fight he's working inside now with uppercuts and body blows that finally drop Owen in the ninth. Owen gets up but no way is he going to win this bout. Owen's mouth has such a deep gash that his whole lower lip has separated from the gum tissue. The referee wants to know from Owen's corner whether he should stop the fight. Dick Owen, Johnny's father and trainer, shakes his head. Johnny Owen is desperate to go on. This is his chance at the world title. It's the 'chink in Johnny's armour', as his father puts it, that is to prove fatal on that night of 19 September 1980, in the Olympic Auditorium, Los Angeles. Unknown to Owen or his father, the bone of Johnny's skull is so unusually thin that in the twelfth round, a savage uppercut to the chin causes the jawbone to shatter his skull and be driven up into his brain. It's a blow from which Johnny Owen will never recover. In these days of bone scans, Johnny Owen would never have been allowed to get into the ring. His body on the canvas, now in a deep coma, he will never regain consciousness.

And as the Mexican and Cholo fight fans chant 'Mexico! Mexico!' to celebrate Pintor's retention of his title by a knockout over Owen, the Welsh fans sense that something truly terrible has taken place in the ring: a sense of dread descends on them. They know that Owen's condition is far more serious than a simple ring knockdown, even if no one could anticipate the full extent of the physical damage at that moment. The victorious Mexican fans are frenzied. More piss and beer and cherry bombs rain down on the British fans. Everything is all too real and unreal at the same time. The British fans want out of the auditorium. Security guards step between the rival groups and usher Owen's supporters down the aisle steps and out through a side exit where their coach is already waiting for them in the parking lot. On the coach, the mood is black and anxious among the Merthyr crew. The Scots are riled up from the fight and the abuse from Pintor's fans.

'Let's go beat up some Mexicans.'

One of the Scots wants to exact some revenge.

One of the Trefechan boys stands up in the aisle of the coach.

'For God's sake, haven't you seen enough violence for one night?'

'Violence', the Scot says. 'I'll show you fucking violence. You haven't seen any violence yet, you Welsh prick.'

And as the bus pulls up outside the Mucky Duck and all the fight fans get off, the Scot attacks the Trefechan lad and the ruckus goes off. The Scots use carpet knives, too. And a lot of the Welsh boys end up in the emergency room of an LA hospital needing stitches for lacerations and plaster for broken bones.

In all the debates about whether it is ethical for two men to go into a ring in order to punch each other into submission, to risk death, what's mostly ignored is the inherent violence a boxing crowd is ready to unleash among rival supporters at any fight venue in the world. In an armchair in front of the television, the sight of two men hurting each other in the name of sport is sanitized, even if it stirs blood lust, excitement, passion. Live, the emotions are cranked up to frenzy levels. At Madison Square Garden in 1995, watching Oscar De La Hoya, another LA/Mexican great, fighting Jesse James Leija, I was prepared for the bodily adrenal rush catalysed by the roar of masculine voices urging their champion to violent excess, but awed by the shrill female voices screaming in the row behind me: 'Kill him! Kill him! Kill him!' It's as if the circumscribed violence within the ring evokes demons around it capable of leaving boxing fans possessed. What happened among the British fight fans on the night of Johnny Owen's fatal injury is in the realm of psychosis. But it's by no means unusual. Cardiff football fans taunt Swansea football fans at a Calzaghe fight: 'You Jack bastards, you Jack bastards!' It's looking to provoke a ruckus. What is it that keeps what happens in the ring clean and the mayhem outside it in the realm of evil? It doesn't take much to step over the line.

These questions are in my mind when I go up to Merthyr from Cardiff on a Valleys Line train for the unveiling of the statue of Johnny Owen. Owen's is the third statue of a boxer to be unveiled in Merthyr in recent years: Eddie Thomas and Howard Winstone are already cast in bronze in and around the town centre. Merthyr reveres these boxing alchemists who have refined the violence of the pubs and streets into pure art. These men are immortalized in bronze and literally put up on pedestals.

The train pulls into Merthyr railway station. The rain lashes down.

In the short distance from the station to Zoar Chapel, my clothes are soaked through. Before unveiling the flag there is to be a memorial service here. I make my way up the narrow wooden stairs to the gallery. TV cameras, lights and sound equipment are set up beside the brass pipes of the organ. The family of Johnny Owen come in to take their seats in the front pews. And with the family, dressed in a black leather jacket, with dark grey hair and moustache, is Lupe Pintor. Beside him is his beautiful wife, Virginia.

The pastor stands up and delivers a sermon about Johnny's austere dedication and how the young people of the town can learn from that. Sitting up in that gallery, I'm not a hundred per cent convinced. What goes through my mind is that this is all very strange: strangely Welsh, and strangely nonconformist, and terribly puritan. In all those years of training, Johnny Owen never had a girlfriend. Johnny Owen was unique. He made his decision, and it was that monastic dedication that took him all the way to the summit of his career. But when I think of other kids who grow up on Merthyr's housing estates, I think: dedication, yes; healthy living, yes; respect for others, yes. But I can't imagine Pintor denying himself a woman for all those years. And I couldn't imagine it for myself.

Coming out of the church for the unveiling ceremony, I follow the congregation to the town centre. We walk under the lashing rain. I stand behind three Merthyr hard cases, who stare poker-faced at the champion boxer who's travelled all the way from the bright storefront colours of Mexico City to this grey and wet shopping centre nestled in the dark green valleys. How are these hard men going to react? I'm worried they'll be looking for revenge.

Pintor reaches up and grips the sodden white, red and green Welsh flag. To cheers he pulls it down off the metal statue. Among all the cheers and the anthem singing, Pintor stands in the middle of this mob and the three hard cases in front of me push their way toward him. I'm waiting to see what happens. Then, one of them reaches out a hand to Pintor and says, 'Thank you . . . thank you for coming.' Everyone wants to shake Pintor's hand. He has a wide and delighted smile on his face.

I lose track of him then, of his wife, of the Owen family and the hard cases and the dignitaries. The Owen family and Lupe Pintor and his wife leave for some kind of reception. The committee, who organized the making of the statue, follows after them, diminutive men, grey-haired, in long black coats, men I might have seen in the parade that day when Howard Winstone brought home the world featherweight champion's crown, who would have looked much bigger to me back then, who intrigued me back then. The sculptor who made the statue has been given a verbal promise, in a meeting in the Rhondda, that among those who were raising money for the statue of Johnny Owen – perhaps among these very men in their long black coats – there were well-off patrons who would pay the remainder of the fee the sculptor was owed for delivering it on time, even if the public fund-raising fell short of the price agreed. Was the sculptor ever paid the balance owed to him for the statue?

I go back to the railway station to get a train back down the valley.

In recent years, by good fortune, I come to meet Geraldine L., from Argentina, who translated for Pintor while he was in Wales. A piece of the movie is missing for me. I want to know what happened at the reception.

'It was like something out of a story, almost unreal', she says.

I understood that some people in Johnny Owen's family had been angry with the father for bringing Lupe over to unveil the statue. We were at the reception and at first it was all very hostile from some of them. And I thought, 'Oh Lupe, he's South American, he's saying all these things

160

to make them happy but he probably doesn't mean them.' But then, suddenly everyone was crying and hugging each other and apologising to each other and thanking each other for coming and for the hospitality and I saw that Lupe meant it; he really did, and so did they, the family. Really, it was beautiful. After all this tension they were all in this really emotional moment together. You couldn't have invented a better end.

Big Mac and his Boys

THE PROFESSIONAL BOXING ENVIRONMENT IN SOUTH WALES
*c.*1960–1990

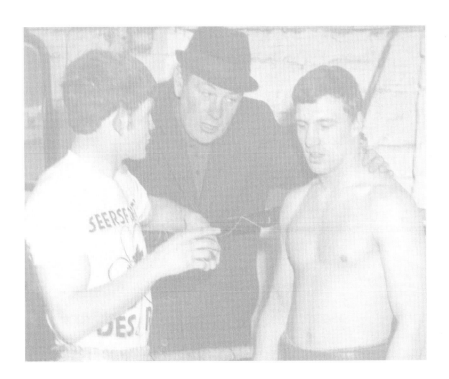

STEPHEN MALCOLM WILLIAMS

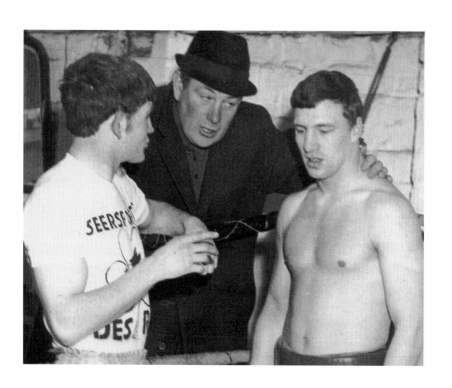

As a child in the 1970s, after being involved in a slight fracas in school, I was summoned to sit down with my father to discuss the matter; even today I remember the conversation. My father listened to the excuses for my behaviour and to be fair – my poor performance in the fight, and then told me something that has stuck in my head ever since. He announced, 'violence is the family business', and then proceeded to show me how to punch 'properly' so it would enable me to make a better scrap the next time around. This story will probably shock the politically correct lobby, who may jabber on about 'toxic parenting' or some other psychoanalytical theory, but this was not as sinister as it might appear and was part of the whole working-class masculine culture that I was brought up with. Indeed, my father, a Cardiff dock-worker, also had a passion for films, particularly gangster movies, so I am not sure even today whether he plagiarized this phrase from the cinema, but it certainly made an impression on me. The reason I did not just dismiss his comments and his very well-informed anecdotes on how to punch was that he also had another 'job', and that was as a professional boxing manager. My father was Mac Williams, the Cardiff boxing manager, who had, from humble beginnings in the early 1960s, built up a stable of professional boxers that by the mid 1970s was described by many media pundits at the time as probably the biggest 'pro' boxing stable in the UK. And most, if not all, of my early memories were coloured by that fact. I lived in a council house where we had professional boxers and other celebrities visiting virtually every day; it was not unusual for my mother to cook Sunday dinner for a large percentage of our 'extended family'. These men fascinated me, as they looked like they were made from granite – the rough type – and told great tales about their exploits in the ring and brushes with the authorities, usually the boxing authorities, in the shape of English referees.

During that period in my life, being part of the boxing community, even if only a small part, was extremely exciting. It opened my eyes to the world around me, and also led to my questioning of all authority.

The people who take part in professional boxing are the most media-savvy individuals on the planet. The whole of the professional boxing community has an understanding, not just of the skills and supreme fitness needed to take part in the 'pro game', but also of how to promote themselves and the fights they are part of. Being a professional does not just mean taking money to fight, but also being involved in the whole media circus; in some respects, that puts them way ahead of the rest of the sporting world. My father, for example, would spend hours on the phone with numerous members of the local and national British press, giving them 'exclusives' on his fighters' forthcoming bouts. This would often cause hilarity in my household when one of my father's media 'stories' found itself – as happened quite regularly – in the press or featured on television and presented as absolute 'fact'. This made me very sceptical about several aspects of the press, as I had gained a huge insight into how they worked. The 'pro game' – a term my father often used – was about maximizing your earning potential as a professional sportsman; that meant entertaining the crowd and receiving 'nobbins' (money thrown into the ring), sparring, getting sponsors, wearing sponsors' equipment and doing interviews. These duties were all part of professional sport, therefore it was extremely important for a 'pro boxer' to court the press through telling a good boxing tale; my father's fighters excelled at this media manipulation. The number of 'Mac's boys' grew quite quickly over the 1960s and 1970s, and the exploits of this Cardiff stable are a substantial part of Welsh boxing history. Nevertheless, over the years there has been considerable press coverage of 'Mac's boys', but surprisingly very little in the boxing 'history' books, so as a tribute to my late father, his wonderful boxers and the rest of my own family, I have written a small account of this professional boxing stable from Mac's own scrapbooks, my own personal memories and a few other sources.

In the heady days of the 1960s and 1970s, professional boxing was not the money-driven circus that it is today. Yes, obviously they fought for money, but there was not the sort of cash around in boxing that there appears to be nowadays. Most professional boxers, in south Wales anyway, did not earn enough from boxing to make a full-time living and needed to have another job to be able to survive. These fighters worked during the day, and trained during the evenings and early mornings for meagre rewards; most fought and trained for the money, but also for love of the sport, even though, for the south Wales working class anyway, professional sport had been – for years – a ticket out of hard industrial labour. In the 1960s, a fairly prosperous economic period, professional sport was becoming more of a life-style choice and increasingly less about the 'hungry fighter'. Boxing has always, because of its concentration on masculine values and physicality, been a sporting mainstay of working-class Welsh society, and in the 1960s and 1970s this was even more so, as the sport was still very popular. Thus, there were far more professional boxers at that time than today, and they fought all over the UK, but – and particularly in Wales – they fought in small venues, such as the Memorial Hall in Barry, the Drill Hall in Cardiff, the Afan Lido in Aberavon, the Stardust Cabaret Club in Usk, the Double Diamond Club in Caerphilly. If they were lucky, they might get a bout in London, Bristol or Manchester. In those more localized days there was less emphasis on world champions, because they were a rarity – although Howard Winstone was an exception here – and more on English regional, Welsh and British titles. Most of the boxing journey-men and the up-and-coming fighters fought firstly for all those rewards and also prided themselves on their professional attitude to their sport.

In the industrial heartland of south Wales, at the end of the 1950s and beginning of the 1960s, the two main professional boxing stables in south Wales were managed by Benny Jacobs, in Custom House Street in Cardiff, and Eddie Thomas, in his Penydarren gym on the outskirts of Merthyr. These guys often fought mini feuds over the control of professional boxing in Wales, clashing over many issues, not least because Eddie Thomas was a 'Valleys boy' and Benny Jacobs was a 'Cardiff city slicker'. Consequently, even though there were other boxing stables, these two managers carved up most of the boxing action between themselves, and hence had quite a few champions, including Lennie 'the Lion' Williams and Joe Erskine in Benny Jacobs's stable and Howard Winstone, Eddie Avoth and Ken Buchanan in Eddie Thomas's camp. However, as the ex-professional boxer George Evans stated in his book *A Bagful of Monkeys* (2004), these two managers had colourful reputations. For example, he argues that 'Benny sailed close to the wind and was under police scrutiny', and that 'Eddie was in contact with people in London who, on discovering the phenomenal talent of Howard Winstone, swooped on Merthyr Tydfil, smelling rich pickings that were easy to plunder because Eddie Thomas willingly allowed top boxing people to manipulate him'. This created an atmosphere – amongst amateur and professional boxers alike – of distrust, and increasingly around the mid 1960s quite a few looked for other less high-profile south Wales boxing stables, and George Evans along with many south Wales boxers, turned instead to smaller boxing stables for a sense of closeness and support.

Amongst these, in fact the actual stable George joined, was the Cardiff boxing stable run by the larger-than-life manager and my father, Malcolm George Williams, known to the sporting community as Mac Williams. This stable grew from its beginnings in the early 1960s to be by the 1970s one of the biggest boxing stables, not just in Wales, but in the whole of the UK. Mac Williams was a big man in more ways than one: standing 6 ft 4 in. tall and nearly eighteen stone, he towered over his charges, but looked after them as if he was their own father. He loved boxing not only for the monetary rewards, which were meagre compared to those that, thanks mainly to television and commercial contracts, some involved with professional boxing earn today, but for the promotion of the sport itself. Mac started his involvement in boxing during the 1940s and went on to represent Wales and the Royal Navy as an amateur. However, he never turned professional because he did not think he was good enough. The fact was, as he would freely admit to anyone who wished to listen, that the British, Welsh and Cardiff boxing environments were very competitive, with the likes of future British heavyweight champion Joe Erskine – with whom he sparred on several occasions – ABA finalist Trevor Snell and Empire Games bronze medallist Roger Pleace all well ahead of him in the pecking order. Indeed, even though Mac enjoyed boxing as a fighter, being a realist and wanting to stay attached to the boxing environment, he turned his back on fighting and honed his skills in another area of boxing – as a trainer and amateur club organizer.

In his mid twenties Mac began his career as a trainer with one of Cardiff's premier amateur boxing clubs, the Roath Vale club. It was in this setting that he began a long friendship with the famed old Cardiff boxing trainer Billy Mannings, who, after Mac had become a professional boxing manager in the 1960s, would become his number one trainer. In this traditional, small-scale and localized boxing environment Mac began to learn his trade as a trainer and cuts man. His ability as these and as organizer of the club – after taking over the position of secretary – quickly came to the notice of the Welsh Amateur Boxing Association, which offered him the position of trainer to the Welsh team at Aldershot on 17 November 1961, as recognition of his excellent work since becoming a trainer. Mac continued his association with both the Roath Vale amateur boxing club and the Welsh amateur team over the next few years, until another twist in his boxing career changed his life and started him on his professional career as a manager. It was the suspicion and rumours concerning untrustworthy individuals in the professional boxing game that propelled Mac into becoming a professional manager. These rumours added to the poor image of professional boxing, portraying it as a festering pit of 'gangland' characters 'ripping off' naive boxers, leaving them broke and punch-drunk. It was for this reason that two promising amateur boxers, featherweight Billy Thomas from Caerphilly and welterweight Terry Phillips from Cardiff, who both wanted to turn 'pro' but were reluctant, as they needed a 'safe' and reliable manager, eventually turned to Mac Williams for assistance. They persuaded Mac, who had been involved in their amateur training, to apply for a professional manager's licence at the same time as they were applying for professional status, and become their manager. This was rather ironic, considering some of the rumours that hit Mac later in his career, especially his involvement and friendship with some well-renowned East End gangsters, including the Kray twins. Nevertheless, it was his close connection to these two fighters that influenced him for the rest of his boxing career. Mac always took pride in his relationship with his stable and believed that a manager should look after his fighters, and not let money rule over a proper, well thought-out and matched bout. It was this philosophy that often led to him turning down some especially hard fights for his boys, because he didn't want to see them get hurt.

Mac's stable had started, and soon afterwards another Cardiff fighter, bantamweight Terry Gale, joined the clan in the Elm Street Lane gym, Roath, Cardiff (later moving to Arran Street, Roath). Terry Gale became the first in the stable to win a title, but certainly not the last, when he won the Welsh Bantamweight Championship title by beating Merthyr's Gerald Jones in London's National Sporting Club. Only days later welterweight Terry Phillips stopped Ebbw Vale's Geoff Rees with a cut eye, at the same venue, to become the second to win a Welsh title, and the success of this stable had begun. It was at around this time that Mac's stable expanded yet again, when he signed the extremely talented, mercurial young Cardiff amateur boxer Dennis Duffield, known to everyone by his boxing name, Dick Duffy. He had an impressive amateur record, winning the All British Schoolboys' title (1961–3), the Welsh Schoolboys' title, the British Youth championship and the British cadet title; he was also awarded the 1964 'Boxer of the Year' award by the Welsh Games Council. Dick Duffy brought a youthful sense of mischief to the gym because he was the practical joker, always bringing levity and a sense of fun to the hard graft and physical exertion that professional sport needs. Dick was an exceptionally skilful boxer who could sometimes move around a ring in sparring without his opponent laying a glove on him. In his career he would eventually box two final eliminators for British titles at different weights, and once caused the Manchester United and World Cup winner Sir Bobby Charlton to say that Duffy was 'one of the greatest little prospects I've ever seen' after watching Duffy fight and beat Ray Fallone at the Wyvern Sporting Club in Manchester. These Welsh boxers were mixing in the 1960s with elite sportsmen from all around Britain, holding their heads up high and proudly flying the Welsh flag. The gym was boosted again when Malcolm McNeill, the Cardiff teenage flyweight, signed with Mac's boys, and then another Cardiff teenager and future Welsh middleweight champion, Carl Thomas, signed too, as the stable began to absorb lots of young Welsh boxing talent.

One of the central cogs in the smooth running of the stable was the trainer Billy Mannings, known to everyone in the boxing world as Manno. The *South Wales Echo* once called him 'the "cruel" but highly respected task-master of generations of amateur and professional fighters in South Wales'. Manno had a long and distinguished career in amateur and professional sport throughout the south Wales area, as he was also involved, both as a player and a trainer, with baseball in the Grange Albion club, and with Cardiff rugby league. Nevertheless, he was most famous for his legendary serious manner and strict control over his boxing charges. Born in Grangetown and schooled at Grange Council School and St Cuthbert's, Cardiff, Manno displayed an aptitude for sport that helped him spend his whole life playing, training and coaching. He often told anyone who wished to listen that he had had the pleasure of training, as amateurs, Welsh fighters such as Dai Dower; he also trained the 1958 'greatest ever' Welsh Empire Games boxing team, with the likes of gold-medal winner Howard Winstone, Malcolm Collins (silver medal), Ossie Higgins (silver medal), Billy Brown (bronze medal) and Roger Pleace (bronze medal) all in the same team. After teaming up with Mac in the early 1960s his training/coaching skills, allied with Mac's training, management, media and social skills, made them a formidable unit. The most interesting story that helped this stable of boxers connect with Cardiff's glorious boxing past and distinguished it from others was a true one, often told by Manno himself. In 1915, as a young lad, Manno started boxing at the Grangetown YMCA, under the tutelage of Johnny Hayward and Sid Redman. Apparently, these two trainers were 'friends' with the most famous Cardiff boxer of all time, 'Peerless' Jim Driscoll. As part of the Irish-Welsh Cardiff community, the two trainers used to take the young up-and-coming fighters to Jim Driscoll's gym for the great man to impart his knowledge to this new generation of Cardiff boxers. It was on these many occasions that Manno was taught to fight by the great man himself, and it was this connection with 'Peerless' Jim that encouraged the stable to feel a central part of Cardiff's proud boxing tradition. In later years Mac and his stable involved themselves in the renovation and reopening of Jim Driscoll's gym, above the Royal Oak public house at the end of Broadway, Adamsdown, in Cardiff. This link to Cardiff's boxing past was often used by Mac and the boys in their professional marketing and the stable's self-promotion campaigns, as it was felt this connection attracted other fighters to the gym. However, attracting newcomers to the stable was hardly a problem at that time.

The success and expansion of the stable from the early 1960s to the mid 1970s was really quite phenomenal. Mac often referred to his early days in the 1960s, when he argued that there were approaching 1,000 professional boxers in the UK. By the mid 1970s that figure had dropped to under 400. However, counter to that trend, Mac's stable of professional boxers kept growing. His style of management attracted much interest from the rest of the boxing community at the time, and particularly from a number of other Welsh boxers, who all joined the stable either as first-time professionals or as 'pro' boxers moving gyms. These included light-welterweight George Evans, welterweight Dai Harris, light-middleweight Clive Cook, welterweight Glyn Davies, lightweight Bryn Lewis and light-welterweight Peter Hughes. Without a doubt, Mac's prowess as a manager was also moving beyond the bounds of south Wales when he signed Irishman Des Rea, who was then living in Liverpool, and later, from the same city, 'tough-nut' Ronnie Hough. Mac also signed Bristol's top light-weight and ABA finalist, Bobby Fisher, as the stable started to grow outside Wales. Another huge asset to the stable was the capture of Ricky Porter, whose career highlight under Mac's guidance was when he stopped, in five rounds, the future European Welterweight title champion Roger Menetrey. Ricky was the entertainer in the stable and would often sing for the boys; later, after he retired from boxing, he took up singing as a profession. Ricky spent his boxing career moving back and forth from Cardiff to Swindon, and this enabled him to introduce another fighter to Mac who would also become a highly successful member of the team, Swindon heavyweight Eddie Neilson. Neilson's claim to boxing fame was that for years he was known as the 'Swindon Steamroller'; eventually he went on to fight two British heavyweight legends, Joe Bugner and Frank Bruno.

Probably the most successful boxer in Mac's stable was Des Rea. He joined Mac's boys in 1964 and lived in Cardiff during his best fighting years, winning the British title and fighting for the European title in that time. Des became Britain's first junior welterweight champion – and coincidentally Mac's first British title winner – by well outpointing red-hot favourite Vic Andreetti at the York Hall, Bethnal Green, in February 1968. Des went on to fight Italian Bruno Arcari in San Remo for the European title, but unfortunately he lost.

Later the next year, he would also go on to fight American Jose Napolese in a world title eliminator, but regrettably he lost that fight as well. During that period, Mac was often seen in London, fraternizing with the boxing community, as well as the rich and famous, in places like the National Sporting Club in the Café Royal, or eating in leading London restaurants such as Topo Gigio's. Mac made friends and acquaintances quite easily, especially if they were interested in his fighters, and encouraged this type of social networking, believing it would benefit his fighters' public profiles. It was at this time that Mac and Des met Ronnie and Reggie Kray, who were very interested in helping promote Des as a fighter. Ronnie and Reggie were convicted and jailed in 1969 for the murder of fellow East End gangsters George Cornell and Jack McVittie; however, according to Mac, they were not really as powerful in the London area as is sometimes portrayed in the media. They were obviously 'serious businessmen', but they were also very much working-class lads who enjoyed boxing and wanted to become more involved in the promotion of the fight game. They realized that others ran the professional game in the London area and they didn't stand much of a chance in their attempts to move into boxing there. Instead, the Krays thought that they could get into boxing via the back door by showing an interest in the Welsh boxing scene, and openly supported Des in his attempt on the European title. Whether or not any money actually exchanged hands is still unclear today, but there is no doubt that Mac's friendship with such characters was based on one premise, and one premise only: the promotion of his fighters.

By the early 1970s the gym included an even more impressive array of boxing talent. The stable consisted of: three heavyweight boxers, Del Phillips, Eddie Neilson and Rod Parkinson; light-heavyweights Pat Mahoney and Durvan Airey; middleweights Clive Cook, Ronnie Hough and Tony Burnett; welterweights Des Rea, Ricky Porter, Kevin White, Yotham Kunda, Tony Stanton, Peter Quinn and Pat Marshall; and lightweights George Evans, Bryn Lewis and Liam White. It also included the up-and-coming 'star' of the gym for the next decade or so, Cardiff's featherweight – at the time – Billy Waith. Billy would go on to win the Welsh Welterweight title, and fight future world champion Jim Watt and also future European champion Dave 'Boy'

Green in final eliminators for the British title. Waith would eventually – by the end of his boxing career – fight ninety-four professional bouts, which is an impressive amount for modern-day boxing. Nevertheless, as the decade passed Mac continued to sign fighters, such as the Cardiff brothers, middleweight Errol McKenzie, welterweight Horace McKenzie and light-heavyweight Bonnie McKenzie, with Horace and Bonnie winning the Welsh Welterweight and Light-Heavy-weight titles respectively under Mac's guidance. He would also go on to sign Merthyr's Martyn Galleozzie (who became the Welsh Light-weight title-holder in 1976) and Cardiff featherweight Neil Gauci, from the Phil Edwards stable. In the latter part of the 1970s the stable also included featherweights George Sutton, Steve Cleak and Joey Deriu, as well as lightweight Charlie Brown. Mac's high profile and successful style was firmly based on great friendships with his existing fighters, but also on his professional attitude towards the national and local press. Mac kept close friendships with Welsh sports journalists, such as Tommy Lyons, Karl Woodward, John Francis and even his ex-navy shipmate Dan O'Neill, and often gave them stories about his fighters and his brushes with the boxing authorities, which he saw as becoming increasingly distanced from the working-class boxing grass-roots he came from.

Ever the controversial and anti-authority figure, Mac was always challenging the boxing authorities and infamously came into conflict with many a 'homer' referee, often complaining about their poor decisions. However, one of his biggest conflicts with the boxing authorities was due to his views on booth boxing. It was these views that would eventually lead to the Welsh Boxing Board of Control temporarily suspending his licence for a few weeks. Mac was concerned that the boxing booths, that he argued had once produced fighters such as Jim Driscoll and Tommy Farr, were virtually extinct, and he wanted to bring them back. Mac believed that the boxing booth not only created an interest in professional boxing from the fans' perspective; it was also a good way of uncovering hidden talent and an enjoyable carnival for the audience. In fact, in the hot summer of 1976 the BBC2 producers of the *Man Alive* programme, knowing of Mac's interest in booth boxing, asked him if he could supply a 'pro fighter' for a television programme they were making on booth boxing. There was only one travelling boxing booth left in the country, run by Cardiff-born Ron Davies, and in that booth Johnny Williamson, a Gloucester gipsy, claimed himself to be 'King of the Booth'. The producers of the programme wanted to give self-proclaimed 'King of the Booth' Williamson a real challenge, so asked Mac to enter the booth with his fighter and lay claim to the 'King of the Booth' title. Mac chose Caerphilly's Tony Burnett to take part in the show, and they both went to the location in Gloucester where the programme was being filmed. The producers emphasized that they wanted Mac and Tony to turn up at the last boxing booth, accept the challenge and give the boastful Williamson a boxing lesson. This is exactly what Tony and Mac did, and as the BBC crew filmed, Tony stood up in the booth and accepted the challenge from the self-styled 'King'. Even though the Gloucester gipsy was a very gutsy and blatantly 'hard man', Tony proceeded to give Williamson a boxing lesson and knocked the poor 'King' around the ring for a devastating three rounds. Bloodied and battered, Williamson and the booth owner comically declared the fight a draw and shared the title 'King of the Booth' between the two fighters. Tony enjoyed himself so much in the filming of the programme that he spent a few days travelling with the booth, fighting the local 'hard men' all around the south west of England, and living up to his new shared title of 'King of the Booth'. Tony would later be fully involved with Mac as they attempted to re-establish booth boxing in Britain, against the will of the boxing authorities.

The peak of the stable had already passed, and from the end of the 1970s things slowly started to change, as more difficulties arose. The biggest negative on the boxing front had actually happened in 1974, when Eddie Neilson left the stable and signed for London's top manager, Mickey Duff, for an undisclosed large fee. Neilson re-joined Mac in the early 1980s, but his move to the 'big money' Duff stable became the norm amongst young boxers. In fact, competition for up-and-coming young amateur fighters became intense, as 'big money' signing-on fees were being offered to them to turn pro-fessional, and not to just the most promising fighters – as in the past – but to all fighters. It became increasingly more important for most regional managers to encourage 'money men' to enter the game, and themselves to become promoters and sponsors of their fighters, in an attempt to stop local fighters turning pro with the 'big money' stables. This tactic unfortunately did not entirely work, but the money men and increasing commercialization of the sport began to change boxing. Another huge blow to the social cohesion and smooth running of Mac's stable was firstly the retirement in 1977, and then the death in 1978, of Billy Mannings.

Mac's stable of fighters continued through the 1980s and was quite successful, with the likes of British champion Steve 'Sammy' Simms, Welsh cruiserweight champion Abner Blackstock, Newport lightweight Robert Smyth, super-featherweight Miguel Matthews and Cardiff welterweight Peter Ahmed all boxing out of Mac's gym. Nonetheless, the stable never really hit the same heights or, more to the point, had the same sort of impact on the boxing scene that it had made in the late 1960s and early 1970s. However, when you add up this stable's contribution, in fights alone, to the British professional boxing scene, it amounts to well over 1,000 professional fights, no small percentage of that boxing scene, and therefore a little more respect should be given to this fine stable of professional boxers and extremely interesting human beings. Mac's boys won many titles, but unfortunately never one of the prestigious world or European crowns that would probably have given the stable legendary status. Nevertheless, these fighters were the backbone of British and Welsh boxing for over three decades, and displayed every week the guts and determination that make professional boxers a special breed amongst sportsmen – and for a short time in the 1970s they were all part of perhaps the biggest stable in the country.

Mannesmann to Maccarinelli

BOXING IN SWANSEA

HUW RICHARDS

Wales can rarely have had a more extraordinary forty-eight hours of sporting action than the second weekend of March 2008, but it was not entirely to tastes in Swansea and district. Delight was unconfined when the national rugby XV, dominated by players from the Ospreys franchise, sealed the Triple Crown in Dublin on the Saturday afternoon. That triumph, though, was bracketed by two local setbacks. The third longest unbeaten run in Swansea City's ninety-six-year history had been ended on Friday night by a 2–1 loss at home to Millwall, while the early hours of Sunday morning saw cruiserweight Enzo Maccarinelli flattened inside two rounds of their world title fight by David Haye of Bermondsey. It was, as an exultant Haye proclaimed to a doubtless bemused international television audience, a conclusive double for south-east London over south-west Wales. Nor was Cardiff City's qualification on Sunday for the FA Cup semi-final universally popular further west. Maccarinelli v. Haye was reckoned by many sober critics to be the most significant all-British contest since Nigel Benn and Chris Eubank's battles for middleweight hegemony in the early 1990s. It was, though, as former champion Johnny Nelson astutely observed, 'a big trade fight, whereas that was a general public fight'.

The earlier rivalry undoubtedly drew on the cartoonishly contrasting personae of its principals. Yet Maccarinelli v. Haye was not lacking in contrast or resonance. You had Maccarinelli, the family man fighting out of the close-knit stable presided over by Enzo Calzaghe, against Haye, in boxing terms a loner, albeit one whose 'MySpace' page was reported as having '7,000-plus friends . . . most of them are women, many of them scantily clad and some apparently nude. And they all seem to want to be more than just friends.' They were contesting three of the four available cruiserweight belts, making the winner as near to an undisputed world champion as anyone now active. Hence, international interest, and the ludicrous 2.30 a.m. start-time for the benefit of US broadcasters *Showtime*. Boxing, like every other sport, debates whether modern practitioners are less skilful than earlier generations. What is not in question is that, as it has retreated from the networks into the moneyed ghetto of specialist television channels, the moderns have less resonance with the wider public. Yet some still, like Joe Calzaghe and Ricky Hatton, permeate wider public consciousness. Maccarinelli is not yet at this level. Non-aficionado recognition is mostly at the level of 'the other Italian boxer from Wales – not Joe Calzaghe, the other one'. Men who would in other times have been national figures have become essentially local heroes. This is undoubtedly so for Maccarinelli, and one reason why disappointment at his defeat was felt in Swansea well beyond boxing circles. It was not simply that one of our boys had lost to one of theirs, although that certainly mattered. It is also recognition that as well as being a fine boxer, Maccarinelli is a good citizen.

It was not always like this. A decade or so ago, in the latter stages of his schooling at Bishop Vaughan school, he was regarded with rather less local pride and affection. As he told the *Sun*:

> When I was about 15 or 16 I started to do things young kids do. I'd go drinking in the park and wouldn't train properly. I was the height I am now and I used to sneak out and go into town. I was a bit of a nasty kid and looking back I'm pretty embarrassed at the way I acted. I used to walk around with a chip on my shoulder. If they looked at me wrong, I'd think they wanted a scrap and most of the time they did. I'd only do it against someone I thought could fight me back. It was me showing off. I'd been fighting grown men since I was 13 so I was physically strong. And those big doormen don't really know how to fight.

You might see in these brawls an echo of the aspirants of an earlier age challenging the professionals of the travelling boxing booths. What is not in doubt is that he personifies the oft-proclaimed redemptive effects of his trade. If he ever finds himself short of a pair of gloves for a title bout it will be because all have been despatched, complete with signature, to a charitable auction somewhere in south Wales. Where the wealthy, successful, modern sportsman is wont to live apart from his fans, hidden behind minders, security fences and public relations companies, Maccarinelli remains more grounded, prepared to participate in an event as localized, unpretentious, grass-rooted and uncompromisingly tough as the annual Kilvey Hill cement run, climbing the Swansea landmark with a fifty kilo bag of cement on his back in order to raise money for the baby-care unit at Singleton Hospital. He won in 2006, completing the course of nearly one mile in eleven minutes and thirty-six seconds.

It doubtless helps that a staple of the preparation methods used by Enzo Calzaghe at his down-at-heel Newbridge gym is running on the surrounding hills that the trainer describes as the 'most perfect gym in the world'. Before the Haye fight, Maccarinelli trained at night to ensure that his body clock was properly synchronized for the US-friendly start-time. He told one interviewer:

> Running up and down the south Wales valleys in the pitch black isn't much fun. I've been going to bed at around 3 a.m. so I'm in the best condition of my life when I face Haye. When I'm out pounding the mountains most people are tucked up in bed and sound asleep, and it can get pretty spooky. It's so isolated that it's like something out of a horror movie.

The indoors was no more inviting. Maccarinelli said: 'I have to work my ass off in there just to keep warm. It is probably colder in the gym than it is outside.' This was not the only reason for training industriously; as he explained, he was 'more worried about upsetting Enzo by not putting proper graft in, than about Haye in the ring'. The warmth lies elsewhere. The *Observer* writer Kevin Mitchell summoned up echoes of the Liverpool boot-room when he described the Calzaghe gym as 'a house, a talking shop, a cultural gathering place for like-minded fighting men with a common background, common values and a huge respect for their eccentric mentor'.

Maccarinelli's success also, though, speaks to a Swansea boxing tradition that is longer and deeper than is generally realized. Welsh boxers are expected to come from Merthyr, the Rhondda or Cardiff. Yet to look at the Welsh Warriors website (*www.johnnyowen.com*), an invaluable resource for anyone interested in boxing in Wales, is to see another story. The site lists, *inter alia*, every Welsh boxer who has held a British title. There are seven from Swansea – in ascending weight Peter Harris, Floyd Havard, Ronnie James, Brian Curvis, Cliff Curvis,

Colin Jones and Neville Meade – but only five from Cardiff, although Pat Thomas and Jack Petersen won titles at two weights. This is not to attempt to initiate yet another of those much-heat, no-light, 'yah-boo sucks' shouting matches between our two largest cities, which are such a tedious blight on national, and in particular sporting, life in Wales. None of the Swansea men, fine boxers that they were, can match the historic stature of Jim Driscoll or the desperate poignancy of his life story. Cardiff has the edge in European (two to one), Commonwealth (five to three) and world (two to one) champions. Cardiff's tradition of heavies and light-heavies contrasts with Swansea's proliferation of welterweights. What it does show, though, is that Swansea has a highly respectable boxing history. It staged a British title fight as long ago as 17 November 1908, when the ill-fated Tom Thomas retained his middleweight title by knocking out Jack Costello in the sixth. Thomas was trained by the Swansea-based Dai Dolling, who a year earlier had brought British heavyweight champion Gunner Moir to the town to prepare for his world title challenge against Tommy Burns, and who was associated with several other British champions. All the early Welsh giants except Freddie Welsh fought in Swansea. Driscoll drew with one Kid Davies in October 1903. Jimmy Wilde fought in Swansea at least four times. On Boxing Day 1912 Johnny Basham (imagine what a modern tabloid might make of such a conjunction of name and date) was knocked out by Matt Wells.

Swansea has also produced some of the less great names. It does not take a double-entry book-keeper to realize that if one boxer has a 44–0 record, others make up the 44. They also serve who only stand and get hit. Lightweight Marc Smith lost forty-two of his fifty-two fights between 1994 and 2000. He started, more or less, as Ceri Farrell, who fought twenty times as a super-bantamweight, losing sixteen, was finishing. Two of Farrell's three victories were in the space of sixteen days in November 1991 against the same man, Andrew Bloomer of Ynysybwl, who lost all twenty fights in his career but was stopped inside the distance only once, by Naseem Hamed.

The least glittering career can acquire lustre by association. Light-welter Dai Davies lost thirty-five of his forty-six fights in a career lasting a decade from 1972. Towards the end *Boxing News* noted that 'the tattooed Swansea man has now gone 16 fights without a win, but he can never be faulted on effort'. Among those defeats was the second professional outing for a Jamaican-born Londoner named Lloyd Honeyghan, who five years later defeated Don Curry for the World Welterweight title. Light-heavy Kevin Roper won only four of his seventeen fights between 1986 and 1989. Yet his twelve conquerors included one world champion – Nigel Benn – and two challengers, Ray Close and Nicky Piper.

All belong to the tradition of which Maccarinelli is currently the leading representative. He is the sixth genuinely world-class boxer – following Ronnie James, the Curvis brothers, Colin Jones and Floyd Havard – to come from Swansea. Unlike them he has been able to call himself a world champion. Whether this places him above them is another matter. The proliferation of sanctioning bodies and weights has considerably devalued the currency. When Ronnie James fought Ike Williams in September 1946 there were eight champions, one for each of the traditional weights. Maccarinelli has functioned in a world with four sanctioning bodies and seventeen weights, allowing up to sixty-eight champions. This is not his fault. He has to deal with the boxing world as it is, not as one might like it to be. Nor has the World Boxing Organization, whose belt he lost to Haye, always been the most impressive of governing bodies. It famously twice elevated one Darrin Morris in its rankings in 2001, in ignorance of the fact that he was not merely retired, but dead. Yet its current champions include such luminaries as Calzaghe, middleweight Kelly Pavlik, heavyweight Wladimir Klitschko and junior lightweight Ivan Calderon – all rated by *Ring* magazine, the nearest thing to an impartial arbiter, as the best in their divisions. There was no doubting the quality of Maccarinelli performances such as his comprehensive out-pointing of former World Boxing Council champion Wayne Braithwaite, winning almost every round on all three cards, or his demolition of the Argentinian Marcelo Dominguez.

Fighting Haye was his opportunity to become unquestionably the leader in his division. Defeat places him, for the moment at least, in that line of fine Swansea boxers who fell just short of the summit. First among these was Ronnie James, who made his debut at the Mannesmann Hall, Plasmarl as a 15-year-old in January 1933, a time when the boxing press was packed with weekly reports from small hall promotions. *Boxing* reported that: 'Ronnie James emphasized a useful left and proved far too strong for Sid Williams (Pontardawe) and won in the second round.'

James would fight fifty-three times before he was defeated for the first time by Dave Crowley, a world title challenger a few months later. He was still only 18. Those bouts were packed into a quicker-than-once-a-month schedule inconceivable to modern fighters – Maccarinelli has fought thirty times in eight and a half years. His early record is studded with such evocative venues as the Palais de Danse, Pontypridd, the Market Hall, Haverfordwest and Labour Stadium, Merthyr. More than anywhere, though, he fought at the Mannesmann, Swansea's own cockpit. *Boxing Records* website lists eighty-five separate promotions there between 1932 and 1941. It left a vivid impression on Don Finn, who grew up close to it in the 1930s. Its setting on the banks of the River Tawe, just across from the Mannesmann and Baldwin works, was brutally industrial: 'Its frontage faced a massive steel slag tip 30 feet high dumped long ago, to its rear were more smaller Swansea slag tips. To its rear were more smaller slag tips, to its western side old dilapidated industrial buildings.' It was in keeping with these surroundings:

> It was really a very large garden shed, maybe 70ft by 50ft in size. It was of wood, steel and corrugated sheeting with a sloping flat felt roof. It was 100 per cent a fire hazard. At a guess it held maybe 400 to 600. Inside to its west side was a standing area, a very cheap entrance being paid by the local unemployed. It was here I would gain entrance by fair means or foul.

It provided income and exposure for the jobbing pros who prolifer-ated in times of hardship. It was not a rich living – a contract issued to Harold Croaker of Gilfach Goch in 1928 by Jack Fowler, the former Swansea Town centre forward who turned to promoting, to fight Jack Harris, shows that he was paid £1 15s.

Yet names did emerge from the ruck. Don Finn recalls Len Beynon, 'a world-class boxer whose career was ruined by the betting fraternity', and Jim Wilde – not the Tylorstown master, but a namesake heavy 'known to us all as horizontal Jimmy, always getting ko-ed'. Beynon and James figured in the high-points in the Mannesmann's history as opponents when it was graced by former world featherweight champion Freddie Miller in 1938. James floored Miller in the eighth, only to be disqualified for a low blow two rounds later.

Wilde, a well-known local character who owned a café in Alexandra Road near High Street station, was Welsh heavyweight champion until dethroned by Tommy Farr in the second of two ferocious bouts in 1936. The first was drawn, while Wilde prepared for the second by having his own gym built near his home in St Thomas. Earlier in his career he had knocked out two opponents on the same day at Wembley, and he would later be matched with such notables as Buddy Baer, still remembered today for his 'sure I'll beat him next time – if you give me a baseball bat' response to the inevitable question after defeat by Joe Louis.

Both Farr fights were at the Vetch Field, Swansea Town FC's ground, venue for occasional larger promotions in the 1930s. The second Farr fight attracted a crowd of around 15,000. Vetch Field bills invariably featured one of the local favourites, with James on the last three before the war, losing a British title eliminator on disqualification – what the watching Fred Deakin reckoned 'a perfect right-hand punch' was ruled low – to his old nemesis, Dave Crowley.

The Mannesmann was taken over as a Home Guard depot and has never really been replaced as a venue – pre-war plans for a permanent indoor hall in Plymouth Street were never carried through. James, suitably, fought on the final bill in November 1941, knocking out Freddie Simpson of Basingstoke in the sixth round. James had joined the army, and his distinctive skills found a niche training commandos in unarmed combat. He continued to fight when duties permitted, becoming the mainstay of charity promotions held at St Helen's, Swansea's rugby and cricket ground. More than £2,000 was raised for Swansea Hospital when in 1943 he fought Lefty 'Satan' Flynn, an exemplar of the ring propensity for colourful nicknames, maintained in recent years by local heavyweight Darren Morgan, the 'Beast of Bonymaen'.

That exotic nomenclature concealed a British Honduras-born fighter named Selvin Campbell, who won Jamaican titles before moving to

Britain in the 1930s. Flynn beat James twice in 1943. Swansea writer G. G. Lowry speculated that James's military training might be affecting him, writing that he was, 'bigger and better muscled than he was, but his success has always depended on his speed and, in the main, on those short, crisp punches of his'. He argued that James was a better fighter at the lightweight limit of 9 st 9 lb: 'At that weight James is fast and his punching quick and snappy, but over 10 stone he can be slower.'

Lowry's judgement was confirmed in August 1944. James was matched with Eric Boon, champion since 1938, for the British Light-weight title at Cardiff Arms Park. Promoters placed daily adverts in the *Evening Post* for tickets ranging in price from five shillings to five guineas, and at least 30,000 attended a fight held against the back-ground of the Arms Park's bomb-damaged stand, next to the cricket ground on which three minutes' silence earlier that same day had marked news of the death in action of Maurice Turnbull, the first Welsh test cricketer. James triumphed amid 'wild scenes of en-thusiasm', knocking out Boon two minutes and ten seconds into the tenth round as a left to the jaw and right to the body dropped the champion for the ninth and last time. It was, the *Western Mail* reported, 'a sound display of two-fisted boxing', highlighted by body shots which 'not only carried power but were generally delivered with accuracy to vulnerable spots'.

Many of those cheering fans made the same journey in 1946, when promoter Jack Solomons, believing James might have the beating of world lightweight champion Ike Williams, persuaded him to defend his title at Ninian Park. Williams's preparation was hardly trouble-free. He and his entourage demanded fruit juice and oranges, still un-obtainable. He barely made the weight and had to run laps round Ninian Park after the weigh-in to sweat off twenty surplus ounces. It had rained steadily for a fortnight before the bout, with numbers on seats washed away in the deluge.

James, it was reported, had been running in the mountains with his dog for company: 'The dog tired long before him.' The *Western Mail* reported 'thousands of the Swansea boxer's fans from the Welsh valleys pouring into Cardiff all day', with their hero promising to give Williams 'the fight of his life'. Instead, for perhaps the only time in 137 fights, he was truly out of his class – knocked down seven times, more than in the rest of that long career combined, before he was finally counted out for the first time ever in the ninth. He reported that when Williams first hit him with his right uppercut he thought his insides had been crushed, and that 'It was hopeless trying to lead against him because, if you missed, his counter-punch took all the strength out of you.' He had no illusions about any possible rematch: 'It is no good saying that I would like to fight him again. I would never beat him, but if we had met five or six years ago I would have put up a far better show.' There was no disgrace in this. Two years later the *Ring* chose Williams as its 'Fighter of the Year', and in 2002 its experts rated him the twenty-third best boxer at any weight in the last eighty years.

Fighting on the same bill was an 18-year-old Swansea boxer called Cliff Curvis. He gave a tough, experienced Frenchman called German Perez a 'boxing lesson' with 'brilliant ringcraft as usual, carrying the day against a man packing a heavier punch and eight years his senior'. Curvis was the product of a boxing family. His father Dai had been a good amateur and was an even better trainer, his gym in Dyfatty Street one of the centres of Swansea boxing. Brian, Dai's younger son, remembers: 'He was an excellent teacher. He taught the skills of the boxer, to punch and move and not leave yourself in one position for too long.' Sportswriter Mario Risoli records in his biography of footballer John Charles that Dai also had an eye for talent, creating the greatest 'might have been' in Swansea boxing history when he failed to persuade the young Charles – not yet the physical colossus he would become – that he might have a serious future in the ring.

Cliff had his first professional fight at 16, knocking Bryn Collins out in two rounds and progressed fast as a flyweight, a 'smart southpaw who could bang a bit', in the words of Fred Deakin, before losing a title eliminator at 19. Deciding that making the weight was taking too much out of him, he moved up to lightweight. Within a few months, in September 1947, he was matched against James at the Vetch Field. James had been unwell in the week before. Curvis, it was reported, was 'faster throughout' and twice came close to a knockout before James's corner threw in the towel in the seventh. There was a 'warm ovation' for James. Curvis has since told the *Guardian* writer Frank

Keating of being felled by a superb punch: 'I was leaving the ring, elated. I never saw it coming; it was delivered by Mrs Ronnie James.'

This was the passing of the flame. James, stripped of his lightweight title for failing to make the 9 st 9 lb limit for the Curvis fight, did not fight again. Curvis moved up to welterweight and eventually claimed a British title, although not before losing to Eddie Thomas at the Vetch in what Deakin reckoned the best fight of his career, then getting himself disqualified, in the first-ever British title fight between two southpaws, for hitting champion Wally Thom before the referee ordered 'box on'. He took revenge on Thom, reclaiming for Wales the British and Empire titles the Liverpudlian had taken from Thomas, at Liverpool Stadium in August 1952.

The Empire title was short-lived, lost to Gerard Dreyer in South Africa after a 'long count' lasting as long as sixteen seconds when he dropped Dreyer in the sixth. It was a double misfortune – he had broken his left hand, was unable to fight properly for the rest of the fifteen rounds and lost on points.

The British title was never defended. Unimpressed by the purses offered for a compulsory defence, he chose to retire, leaving the ring at 25. Still alive at 80, he is the oldest living British champion.

Younger brother Brian had not planned to follow him: 'What I really wanted to do was play rugby. I was a forward and enjoyed getting stuck in, but I'd love to have been a Cliff Morgan.' He had nevertheless started boxing at eight:

> Dad didn't want me out on the streets playing and made me come to the gym every night. He didn't make me put the gloves on, but it was something to do rather than just hanging around or helping to sweep the gym or something. But looking back it was a silly thing to do. You can't force people into a sport.

It was national service, that two-year penance forced on young men between 1948 and 1960, that pushed him back into the ring: 'I'd won one schools title, but I really hadn't been in the ring for about five years', he recalls. But once talent was spotted, the army refused to take no for an answer. From this came selection for England and an ABA amateur title. He says: 'Aside from any ability I had had a first-class boxing education. I'd spent all that time in the gym watching boxers, learning not only from what they did but from talking to my dad about them.'

Managed by elder brother Cliff, he made his professional debut at 22 – beating Harry Haydock, also a southpaw, inside two rounds. Less than a year later, in his thirteenth professional appearance, he won his first title, taking the Commonwealth Welterweight belt from Australian George Barnes at the Vetch Field. While happy to be boxing at home, he remembers: 'I never liked open-air fights. There was no atmosphere. Inside you could feel the excitement of the crowd in your body. Climb into the ring in the open air and there was none of this.' While the *Evening Post* reported a 'roaring crowd at the Vetch' for a bill also including Howard Winstone, promoter Jack Solomons was unimpressed by the turnout, and said of Swansea's fight fans, 'They just don't deserve a big show like this. The weather held, but the fans were not there.' Solomons, the most powerful figure in British boxing, said he would return to Wales, but only to Cardiff.

But if it was the end for Swansea as a major boxing venue, it was a beginning for Curvis. This was a fine era for British welterweights. Names like Dave Charnley and Wally Swift still echo nearly half a century later, but Curvis was their master. He never lost to a British opponent, and became the first, and so far only, welterweight to win two Lonsdale belts. Curvis, still sharp and lucid, talking from his Middlesbrough home in his seventy-first year recalls both the well-named Swift: 'He could punch and move and you had to be good to catch him – and even if you put him down you couldn't keep him down', and Charnley: 'He was one of those boxers who had "something about him". He could box, had a powerful punch and excited the crowds.'

Only the very best Americans could handle him. Curvis reckoned that Ralph Dupas, later light-middleweight champion, was the best he ever fought, even though when they met at Wembley on 11 September 1962 the American was floored in the first round, was warned several times for holding and ultimately disqualified in the sixth. He remembers: 'He was top class, both a boxer and a fighter and I got lucky'

History accords a higher rating to Emile Griffith, whom Curvis challenged for the World Welterweight title a little over two years later.

189

He was that year's *Ring* 'Fighter of the Year', and thirty-third in its eighty-year poll in 2002. Curvis, with a huge Welsh support following him to Wembley, was beaten on points, and Fred Deakin recalled that he 'seemed strangely subdued . . . he had been known to fight with a lot more fire. The big occasion probably got to him.' Curvis has a different explanation:

> Griffith was good, but not in a different class. I was not fit and should not have been in there, but I had been told that if the fight was postponed I would never get another chance. It was not until afterwards that I found out it could have been postponed.

Curvis went on for another two years, winning his second Lonsdale belt. By the end he was being managed by Arthur Boggis, who also handled Charnley. Negotiations began for a fresh world title challenge, but, he recalls: 'I was no longer motivated. The thrill wasn't there any more.' At 29, he not only left the ring, but as he says, 'divorced myself from boxing. I don't follow it, and have not done so for years.' He left, he says, 'feeling very embittered about boxing and about some of the things that happened to me'. His estrangement from elder brother and former manager Cliff has lasted to this day.

The third in Swansea's trinity of world-class welters was still at primary school when the younger Curvis quit. He was not long out of school before he started exciting fight fans. Colin Jones of Gorseinon – yet another product of a boxing family, with elder brother Ken a Welsh light-heavyweight champion and the younger Peter reaching an ABA final as a bantam – won an ABA title and went to the Montreal Olympics as a 17-year-old.

Many of Jones's big fights were observed from the press benches by novelist Timothy Mo, who described him vividly: 'His blue eyes are like pebbles. He doesn't glower at opponents, but the looks are appraising and utterly cold.' The main criticism of Jones was that while he had immense punching power, he was reluctant to take the initiative in fights. Jones himself said: 'If I hit them clearly they'll go over. You have to pace yourself, wait for them to throw their best shots and then go to work.' This never worked better than in his British title fight in 1980 against Kirkland Laing, who was talented enough to later beat Roberto Duran, but generally seen as an under-achiever. *Boxing News* reported that after eight rounds of 'patient but unrewarded pursuit, Jones saw his chance and took it brilliantly', stopping Laing in the ninth. The Londoner later asked, 'How could I lose to a guy so far behind in boxing ability?', but Jones proved it was no fluke by winning the rematch, also in the ninth.

Jones came closer to a world title than any previous Swansea boxer in two epic contests in 1983 with Milton McCrory, a product of the legendary Kronk gym in Detroit, for the World Boxing Association Welterweight title. The first was a draw. Mo hailed 'one of the best British performances in America ever . . . a neat reversal of the usual pattern of a skilful British fighter meeting an American puncher and being overwhelmed after a bright start'.

The rematch five months later led *Boxing News* editor Harry Mullan to bemoan 'I have never been surer of a result than I was at ringside in the 105-degree heat of the Dunes Hotel open-air stadium as we awaited the judges' verdict . . . Jones did everything but knock him down'. Jones asked 'How can he call himself a champion when he ran like a bloody thief?', but the split decision went McCrory's way.

Jones's third challenge, against Don Curry in January 1985, ended in the fourth round. Mullan observed him afterwards: 'On impulse he bent forward and kissed the belt. It was as though he was kissing goodbye to the dream which had driven him on through the years, through the ABA and Olympic Games and on to the British, European and Commonwealth professional titles.' Not yet 26, he said he would only fight again if it was for a world title. The opportunity did not recur.

Two more Swansea men made an impact on boxing's wider con-sciousness in the 1980s. Heavyweight Neville Meade, Jamaican-born and a 1974 Commonwealth Games gold medallist for England, came late to the British title, winning it at 33 with a one-round demolition of Gordon Ferris and holding it for two years until defeated by Newport's David Pearce. *Boxing News* described him affectionately as a 'most unlikely hero in a division that traditionally spawns comic-strip champions'. At the end of the decade Floyd Havard was good enough to take the British Super-Featherweight from Pat Cowdell, a former Olympic medalist, Lonsdale belt winner and world title challenger. Havard went on to challenge the Puerto Rican John John Molina for the world crown, losing in the sixth. He went out still near the top as British champion, his last defence being at Swansea's Brangwyn Hall, winning his last seven fights and losing only two out of thirty-six in all. In 2008 he was reported as planning to move to the Ukraine. Kevin Mitchell remembers:

> Floyd was a compact, stylish boxer who never quite made the most of his gifts. Unlike most fighters, he quit the business when on a winning run, but, although he'd won back the British title, he was taking low-key fights he should have put behind him at that stage. He was good enough to win a version of the world super-featherweight title, but cuts did for him against Molina in his one shot at the big time. Havard was a former amateur champion who took quickly to the demands of the professional game. His sharp punching drained rather than devastated opponents. You always got the impression he was on the verge of something special. He was a joy to watch.

Enzo Maccarinelli represents the continuation of a fine tradition. Some might argue that it is a tradition of failure, of falling just short of the very highest standards. This is true only if you also believe that the Swansea City teams who rose three divisions in four seasons or the Cardiff City team thwarted by a missed penalty in their last match were failures because they did not become Football League champions.

He may yet transcend that history of near-misses. That might enable him to use the power wielded by champions to mend another gap in Swansea history by return big boxing to his home city – he has said that one of his ambitions is a title fight at the Liberty Stadium. If not, there is promise in the successor generation represented by his nephew Tobias Webb, an ABA champion. What is certainly to be hoped is that he, Webb and all that follow also emulate an unquestionably positive Swansea boxing tradition – that of getting out of the ring with faculties unimpaired while fans still ask why he has retired, rather than fighting on until they ask why he has not.

On the Cusp

INTO THE CALZAGHE ERA

MARTIN JOHNES

In April 1993 the Colombian boxer Ruben Palacio failed an HIV test. This personal tragedy was overshadowed by the fact that he was due to defend his WBO world featherweight belt that very week. He was promptly stripped of his title, and that left a hall already booked for a world title fight, a challenger ready, tickets sold, a television slot secured, a championship sanctioning fee paid, but no champion. The promoters thus desperately searched for someone prepared to fight with less than a week's notice. With only two days to go, they found Steve Robinson, a 25-year-old journeyman boxer from Ely in Cardiff. He was not in any boxing organization's top ten but the WBO, perhaps unwilling to lose its sanctioning fee, agreed that the fight could be a title decider.

Robinson's professional record was an unimpressive thirteen wins, nine defeats and one draw. Many of those defeats had been against house boxers who had the crowd on their side, but there was still nothing in Robinson's record to suggest he deserved a world title shot. His income from boxing was so meagre that he had been supplementing it with a £52-a-week job as a storeman. Apparently unable to afford his own telephone, the story went that he had to be called at his mother-in-law's, where he received the news over a plate of pie and chips. The surprise of the opportunity meant he accepted without even asking about the money. The fight was held in the erstwhile challenger's home territory at Newcastle, but John Davison was shaken by Palacio's withdrawal and had possibly overtrained. Robinson, in contrast, 'boxed with the freedom perhaps of a man with nothing to lose' and kept going with a 'bombardment of fast, accurate combinations' that was enough to win the fight in a split decision from the judges. He had earned £13,000 and become Wales's first world champion since Howard Winstone. No one could quite believe it, and for Robinson the nickname the 'Cinderella Man', the name once bestowed on former world heavyweight champion James J. Braddock, was promptly resurrected.

The WBO was probably the least prestigious of the four world governing bodies, but, with his fitness and skills boosted by being able to train full-time, Robinson showed in his first defence that he deserved both to be where he was and the new earning power that gave him a £250,000 purse. He gave a flawless performance against a fancied challenger, who himself was a former world title-holder. The *Boxing News* headline simply declared 'Robbo is for Real'. That was perhaps his best fight, but six subsequent successful defences confirmed his status amongst the world's best. Robinson was, however, a cagey fighter, relying on hard work rather than spectacular skills or an explosive punch, and that meant he never won the acclaim his position might have given him. One boxing writer noted:

> All he does is stick to well-schooled basics, allied to outstanding fitness and an absolute belief in himself which his astonishing run of victories has fuelled, but the end result is a formidable opponent who could at the very least hold his own with any of the three other world title claimants, and on home ground maybe even beat them.

This was perhaps grudging praise, and Robinson felt that the London media were just waiting for him to lose. He complained,

> Even when I win, I can't really win respect. They prefer a guy like Frank Bruno. He's more their style, living in London, going on the telly, a big funny guy doing the pantomimes and stuff. That ain't my style. So where's the story for these reporters, where's the flash they need?

They found that flash in the rising star of British boxing, Prince Naseem Hamed. He was everything that Robinson was not: explosive, arrogant and a big, big hitter. This combination did not always make Hamed likeable, but it did make him highly commercial, and his backers decided that Robinson's WBO belt was the best bet to give the 'prince' a world title. Hamed had made his name at the lighter flyweight, but the WBO saw pound signs and made him their number one challenger, despite the fact that he had not even boxed at featherweight before. The governing body consequently demanded in 1995 that Robinson defend his title against Hamed within sixty days. The controversy of this decision was added to because Frank Warren, whose influence with the boxing organizations was significant, promoted both Hamed and Robinson. He protested that he could do nothing about the situation, but Robinson's fans felt that their man had been let down. Robinson, not long back from honeymoon, was thus left with a fight that he did not yet want, for a sum that was less than his challenger's and half what he thought he deserved. His humour could not have been helped by publicity for the bout that invited the public to 'See the Prince become King'.

The majority of the 16,000 crowd at Cardiff Arms Park had certainly not paid to see such a thing, and they stood on their chairs and sang 'Hamed, Hamed, who the fuck is Hamed?' Robinson, however, looked distinctly uncomfortable from the moment of his fanfare entrance, which involved a neon red dragon, the Royal Regiment of Wales's goat and much smoke. It got worse when the fight actually started, as Hamed, unorthodox in his style and his leopard-skin loincloth, taunted and totally outboxed Robinson. The Welshman was tough and courageous, and went out like a champion, but he was, as *Boxing News* put it, 'gulping for air as he was sent from post to post, each blow knocking lumps of blood from his mouth. It was a ruthless, sinister demonstration of domination.' The fight was stopped in the eighth, after a swift vicious left hook from Hamed knocked Robinson over. The referee did not even count.

Boxing is a cruel sport for losers. Afterwards, Robinson told the *Sun*, 'Before I lost my title to Naz my phone never stopped ringing. But all those friends I thought I had disappeared along with my championship belt.' His career did pick up again in 1997, when he took a European title and went eleven fights unbeaten. But he then lost a succession of title fights and retired in 2002, after six successive defeats. He was 33 and acknowledged the decline in his physical condition. 'I haven't got the fire any more', he concluded.

The intricacies of boxing politics that had helped take away Robinson's title prematurely also denied one of his sparring partners a title shot when he was at the peak of his prowess in 1993. Whereas few predicted Robinson's rise, flyweight Robbie Regan of Blackwood had always been tipped as a possible world champion. He was an aggressive boxer who wore down opponents and kept them on the defensive. But reaching an agreement for a title fight was proving elusive, and it was 1995 before he got the chance. Outside Wales, the

WBO champion Alberto Jimenez was regarded as the hot favourite for their clash, but *Boxing News* did note that 'after years of waiting Robbie's probably in the mood to ignore pain, blood and anything that comes his way in the quest for the championship'. Jimenez dominated, and Regan's corner retired the badly bleeding challenger in the ninth. He had defended well, but was outclassed and outpunched by a fighter superior to anyone else he had come up against. Regan was left in tears at the end, and *Boxing News* concluded that a world title was maybe beyond him.

Six months later Regan did win an IBF interim championship put together because the holder was injured, but there were only 750 people at Sophia Gardens to witness it and the title held little credibility, with even the awarding body fluctuating over whether it was valid. By his next fight some were saying Regan was past his peak. Weight problems meant that he had moved up two divisions to bantamweight, but he managed to secure a title shot in 1996, despite not being in the WBO's top ten. It was a gamble, but he exceeded all predictions, briefly floored the champion and won a unanimous decision from the judges. 'What a boyo!' declared the front-page headline of *Boxing News*.

A kidney virus then left Regan unable to defend that title for two years and thus unable to earn a living, either. As he put it, 'my body simply fell apart'. Then in 1998, in the week before he was due to enter the ring once more, an MRI scan showed a scar on the surface of his brain and the British Board of Boxing Control refused to allow him to fight again. Through a flood of tears, he told the Cardiff audience there to watch him defend his title that he had to retire from boxing. His trainer Dai Gardiner, fearing a repeat of what had happened to one of his other boxers, Johnny Owen, said it was a 'blessing' that the problem had been detected before it was too late. As the understanding of what precisely had been found sunk in, Regan was less impressed. He complained,

> These MRI scans are taking away our livelihoods. The way it's going at the moment there will be no boxers left. It's killing the sport. The scans are picking up on minor faults that many people in the street might have. If rugby and soccer players had to take the same tests they'd be failing them all over the place.

The British Board of Boxing Control stood firm, maintaining there had to be 'health before wealth'. Regan was left to begin a new life as an electrician.

As Regan was entering that profession, leaving it was his friend Barry Jones from Ely. In December 1997 he beat Wilson Palacio to take the WBO Super-Featherweight World title and told the press, 'Up to now I have earned peanuts from boxing. I have had to carry on as an electrician, but stopped working seven weeks ago to devote all my time preparing properly for the fight of my life.' He was well aware of the risks of the sport, but also determined to become financially secure from it, saying 'If I can earn £500,000 in the ring you won't see me fighting again. I want to get out with all my marbles, while I can still speak properly.' Four months later a brain scan showed two membranes in his brain had separated by 0.2 mm, and he lost his licence to box. He had a title defence lined up that should have earned him nearly £70,000, which he had planned to use as deposit for a house. Initially, Jones was philosophical, saying 'I don't know if that is a good thing or a bad thing. It would have been my biggest pay night but I might've sustained serious brain damage.' He knew boxers his own age who were 'shot to bits. I don't want to take that kind of punishment for love or money.'

But money matters more than anything else in boxing. Jones found himself signing on, and finances forced him back into the ring. He appealed against the decision and was eventually able to produce medical evidence, which he had had to obtain at his own expense, that any damage would not affect his vital functions. The BBBC accepted this, despite some criticism from other doctors. As he was about to fight again, after an eighteen-month absence, Jones told the press, 'the risk of damage is so slight as to be negligible. There's more danger of me being struck by lightning or run over by a car. I'm not stupid or foolhardy, but believe I've been something of a fall guy for the board.' Yet he also admitted, 'I could end up slurring my words more than I should – I knew that when I started. But professional boxing is my choice.'

In 2000, in his second bout back, Jones suffered the first defeat of his career when he lost to the Brazilian Acelino Freitas, the new WBO world super-featherweight champion. Jones put the champion on the floor in the first round but was comprehensively beaten in what was only his second fight in two years. He never boxed professionally again, and ended up managing a bar in London. Money again led to some discussion in 2005 of his returning to the ring, but Jones was at least luckier than some of his contemporaries. In 2004, Regan was sentenced to eighteen months in prison for causing actual bodily harm after breaking into a house and attacking a couple with whom two of his friends had a feud.

Yet another Cardiff boxer, a contemporary of this trio, was to experience a very different career. Nicky Piper lost three world title bids, but in 1995 he did win a Commonwealth Light-Heavyweight title. Moreover, perhaps to a greater extent than any other Welsh fighter, even Jack Petersen, he was able to make a public career outside the ring. A tall, good-looking, athlete who sustained few facial injuries and who could boast of being a member of Mensa, Piper moved on to a career as a media pundit and after-dinner speaker. His work for charity, the Sports Council for Wales and the British Boxing Board of Control earned him an MBE in 2006.

Robinson, Regan and Jones had all won world titles, but none was particularly famous outside their sport, and only Robinson held a title long enough to be able to derive much financial reward from it. All three were a long, long way from the millionaire's game that came to Cardiff when Frank Bruno met Lennox Lewis at the National Stadium in 1993, for the WBC World Heavyweight title. Twenty-eight thousand were there to witness what was rather oddly hyped as the 'greatest event in the history of Welsh sport'. It was a poor fight that brought the sport yet more criticism. The general feeling was that the beating handed out to Bruno should have led to an earlier termination of the bout. But it did at least add to Cardiff's growing credibility as a venue for major fights.

With most of the fans still in the pub, the stadium was virtually empty for the bottom of the undercard, but making his professional debut there was one Joe Calzaghe. He had been born in London but raised in Newbridge by a Welsh mother and Italian father. Enzo Calzaghe had been a part-time musician on the fringes of the national pop scene, but he increasingly turned his attention to training his son, who began to show considerable potential as a teenage boxer. Joe did not turn professional until he was 21, a rather late age in an era where the status of the amateur boxing scene had fast faded. For making that switch he received a £3,000 loan and a £300 weekly wage that was deducted from his purse, although it appears that he sometimes found it difficult to pin his management down on what the exact figures were.

The life of the new professional was a hard one, and Calzaghe struggled financially in the subsequent three years, but he was proving himself a boxer of real talent. He won twenty of his first twenty-one fights with knockouts, ten of which were in the first round, all the while revealing devastating speed and powerful combinations. But he was rarely on television, and consequently few knew who he was. A world title thus seemed a world away. It might have been different had he exhibited the kind of extrovert showmanship that Naseem Hamed was then both electrifying and annoying the world with. Things might also have been different had Calzaghe been selected for the 1992 Olympics. The Welsh Amateur Boxing Association, however, had seen fit not to select Calzaghe as Wales's representative at the UK qualifiers because he had pulled out of some past international contests with injuries. It was an experience that left Calzaghe very critical of the amateur set-up in Wales, and feeling that boxing out of his home nation was a real handicap. It had denied him the chance of winning the widespread profile that the Olympics could have given him. But then again, early fame and fortune could also have denied him the hunger that would later help make his career.

Disillusioned with his progress, Calzaghe switched promoters to Frank Warren in 1997 (until June 2008) and saw his purses immediately rise high enough to buy a £43,000 BMW. New doors also opened, and his fourth fight with Warren was for a world title. He was due to meet Steve Collins, but two weeks before the fight the Irishman decided to give up his WBO belt. Collins claimed that he did not have the motivation to carry on, but he probably knew that he would lose. In stepped the belt's former holder, Chris Eubank, very famous, very talented, but never the same ruthless fighter after a bout where he had left Michael Watson in a coma. It was a wild, spectacular fight that went the distance, despite Eubank being knocked down in the first round. Calzaghe was left bruised and battered, but he had won a world title. The new champion, Eubank told the press, was an 'exceptional fighter'.

In the next nine years Calzaghe's power and speed meant he defended his title seventeen times and held his position as world champion for longer than any other British or Welsh boxer before him. It was a remarkable record, especially since injuries had stopped him sparring before some fights. Yet Calzaghe could walk down the street and rarely be recognized. Nor was his record given much credence in the USA, the financial capital of world boxing. Too many of his defences had been against modest fighters, and not every performance he had given was electrifying. His failure to fight in the States also restricted his profile and reputation, and Americans argued that he had never met anyone with a tough chin and two good hands. This naturally held back Calzaghe's earning potential. In 2002 *Wales on Sunday* estimated he was worth £1.5m, which did not make him even one of the twenty-five richest sportspeople in Wales. Still, the *Financial Times* noted in 2004,

> Calzaghe will never have to run a pub, rely on after-dinner speaking or studio appearances on Sky to pay the mortgage. He has the money that Britain's most famous world champions lack but they have what he craves and that, as the advert says, can't be bought. Respect is priceless and Joe Calzaghe knows it.

In failing to win that respect Calzaghe was a victim of both boxing politics and the general state of the sport. Boxers did not want to lose, and with four governing bodies offering world titles there were much easier routes to claiming to be world champion than facing Joe Calzaghe. During the first nine years of his reign as champion the other super-middleweight titles were to be held by nineteen different fighters. Amidst such a merry-go-round, he could only beat those who were willing to face him. Boxing's confusing set-up meant that there were 136 world boxing titles at the different weights, and thus, even in Wales, few sports fans who did not follow boxing closely were sure quite how good Calzaghe was or whether his title meant very much. Calzaghe himself remarked that, 'The politics makes boxing a shit sport and it can be horribly cruel.' *Boxing News* had declared in 1995, 'Is it any wonder that the fans are turning away from a sport which becomes more chaotic and anarchistic by the day?' Meanwhile, the

Guardian was warning that the 'sport will die of natural causes if people are disenchanted with its major champions. Boxing always used to have dignity, if nothing else, but it has lost that and probably lost its way.' Calzaghe was further hindered by boxing largely deserting terrestrial television in search of the greater bucks offered by satellite stations. Whereas football was popular enough to take its fans with it when it made the same move, the switch of Britain's best boxers to Sky in 1995 simply made boxing less popular. In the early and mid 1990s Chris Eubank, Nigel Benn, Steve Collins and Michael Watson, all super-middleweights like Calzaghe, had been watched by an ITV audience of ten million. Calzaghe could boast of nothing like their fame and status. Had he been born a few years earlier he would have been part of their very popular and lucrative scene. He would have made a lot of money, but he might also not have held a world title for very long.

How the boxing world thought of Joe Calzaghe changed in 2006, when he faced Jeff Lacy to add the IBF belt to his WBO title. Lacy was unbeaten, and widely regarded in the United States as the next Mike Tyson. The fight had already been postponed once after Calzaghe broke his hand, and he had wanted to pull out again because of a hand injury. His father and others persuaded him that to withdraw would destroy his credibility. His place in boxing history was on the line, and the fight programme's title of 'Judgement Day' was for once more than the normal exaggerated hype of the boxing promoter. No one watching on television or in the Manchester arena would have believed that Calzaghe was either carrying an injury or considered an outsider. His fast punching simply destroyed Lacy, to earn a forty-first straight win while the 12,000 crowd chanted 'Easy! Easy!' The widely respected boxing writer Hugh McIlvanney wrote,

> All who watched Calzaghe outspeed, out-think and punishingly out-box the American through every one of 12 rounds had no option but to recognise what they were seeing as one of the greatest displays of superb technique, confidence and fighting intelligence a British boxer has delivered in a major contest.

Suddenly, Calzaghe's stature was completely transformed. He was taken seriously by the American boxing scene and became more widely famous in the UK, even being invited to take part in the BBC's *Strictly Come Dancing*. The importance of the American market was evident in the selection of his next opponent. Peter Manfredo had become known through an American boxing reality television contest. He pulled in the American viewers, while Calzaghe's stature in the UK was now such that the fight took place at Cardiff's Millennium Stadium before 35,000 people. Calzaghe remarked, 'I couldn't have dreamed that it would all work out like this, star billing in your national stadium before a global audience. It's what it's all about, all those years of hard work and frustration.' He outclassed Manfredo in three rounds. If there were any remaining doubts about Calzaghe's stature they were banished in 2007, when he defeated the unbeaten and very talented Mikkel Kessler to take the WBC and WBA titles. Calzaghe was finally the undisputed super-middleweight champion of the world. Then, in April 2008, he showed he could move up a weight and still beat the best when he outpointed the great Bernard Hopkins in a messy fight in Las Vegas. It was the first time Calzaghe had fought in the States, but his professional and determined perform-ance after being knocked down in the first round further cemented the international recognition that he was the real thing.

The Kessler fight had taken place at the Millennium Stadium before 50,000 fans, but to meet the demands of American television it did not begin until 1 a.m. To sit anywhere near the ring cost £500, while even the cheapest tickets were £40 plus booking fees for a very minimal and distant view, unless you watched on the stadium's big screens. Given that many modern boxing fans knew little about the intricacies of the sport, that probably did not matter so much. They appreciated more the kind of wild fight Calzaghe had given against Byron Mitchell, where the fists were flying in a fast aggressive exchange, than the subtle artistry that was obvious only if you were close up and looked for it. Even if modern boxing provided few frantic fights in the mould of Calzaghe v. Mitchell, it did provide a hostile and hyped sense of occasion, as was clearly evident against Kessler. After the playing of the Danish and Welsh national anthems, the first of which was loudly booed, the MC announced a fight between two undefeated champions for the undisputed middleweight championship of the world – but he preceded this tantalizing promise with a list of corporate sponsors.

Such was the contemporary world of boxing: the same old world of fighting buried somewhere beneath a veneer of sponsorship, money and politics, a veneer that had meant that Calzaghe had been a world title-holder for ten years before he could call himself undisputed champion.

Calazaghe himself was also at odds with the razzmatazz of modern boxing. He did not seek the limelight or hang out in celebrity night-clubs. Outside the ring he could be shy and moody, which meant he did not like engaging in the kind of self-publicity and commercial work that could have raised his profile and his fortune. As the *Daily Telegraph* put it, 'Like Clark Kent, he conceals his gifts beneath a veneer of civilian quiet.' Calzaghe himself conceded,

> I'm not a flash bloke. I'm prudent and some might say tight! I'm not a first-class traveller who hangs out with millionaires on a private island. I drive a normal car . . . I still live in Newbridge and still drink at the same pub. All that makes me different is that I'm a world-class boxer, that's all.

In this ordinariness and despite his CBE (April 2008) Calzaghe was more reminiscent of the Welsh boxers that had gone before him than many of his millionaire contemporaries. Like Driscoll or Petersen, Winstone or Owen, Calzaghe was a man still firmly rooted in the community from which he came.

The communities of industrial south Wales had, however, changed significantly between the eras of Calzaghe and his predecessors. Gone was the hard industrial climate that made men value so much the physical toughness that boxers embodied. This meant that fewer and fewer people were taking up boxing. Indeed, the sport was becoming a symbol of that passing traditional industrial world of south Wales. This was clear in Merthyr, where public statues of three different boxers were erected in the town in the early 2000s and the celebration of dead pugilists seemed to sum up a town more comfortable looking backwards than forwards. Indeed, at the unveiling of Johnny Owen's statue, a local minister explicitly spoke of the town needing the 'disciplines of the ring, the dedication and drive that gave Owen heroic status to counter the scourges of modern culture'. Calzaghe's victory in the popular vote for the 2007 BBC Sports Personality of the Year showed that contemporary boxers could still win some popular acclaim, but it could not disguise the long-term problems of the sport. Being entertained by real fighting made many feel uncomfortable, even though the sheer power and pain of punching is never remotely as apparent on television as it is ringside. There were only five professional tournaments held in Wales between July 2005 and July 2006. In the same period there were just forty professional boxers based in Wales, most of whom were part-time. Taking part as an amateur was also less popular in a Wales where office- and shop-workers outnumbered those who worked with their hands. In 2001 there were just 1,829 members of the eighty-nine clubs that made up the Welsh Amateur Boxing Association. In 2008 there were eighty-seven clubs, forty-six of them in Glamorgan alone.

Yet, for all the long-term decline in boxing, Wales could now claim to be at the centre of British boxing and enjoying one of its most successful professional periods ever. In Calzaghe, Wales could boast one of the finest British boxers since the Second World War, whilst across the divisions there always seemed to be either Welsh champions or contenders. The Swansea fighter Enzo Maccarinelli was part of 'Team Calzaghe', a group of fighters based at Enzo Calzaghe's Newbridge gym. Remarkably, in 2007 the gym could boast four world champions. As well as Calzaghe and Maccarinelli, it was also the base for Gavin Rees, the WBA Light-Welterweight holder, and Gary Lockett, the WBU middleweight champion. This made Enzo Calzaghe, who had never boxed professionally himself, one of the most successful trainers in the world and one of the best in Britain, ever. Moreover, as well as being home to four world champions Wales was now also the base of the British Boxing Board of Control, after it relocated to Cardiff in 2002. It had had to sell its London headquarters after Michael Watson was awarded £400,000 in compensation because failures in the Board's safety precautions had contributed to the long-term injuries he suffered whilst fighting Eubank. Cardiff had actively courted the Board by offering a £20,000 grant and a peppercorn rent. Some of the London media thought the move 'bizarre', but the local authority hoped to attract lucrative fights to the Millennium Stadium and use boxing to boost the profile of the Welsh capital.

Plans to host a fight between Mike Tyson and Lennox Lewis in Cardiff, or indeed any other major card that did not involve a Welsh fighter, never reached fruition, but the city did at least show signs that boxing was growing in popularity amongst a few women and middle-class men eager to prove their worth or just find a new way to keep fit. Those who trained in Cardiff could find themselves under the tutelage of Steve Robinson, who had opened his own gym. He argued, 'With white collar boxing people can get a buzz from fighting. They can get rid of all the stress that builds up in their day jobs. They can forget about everything.' A female dentist from Radyr found that boxing training was 'a great antidote to a demanding job. Boxing isn't about slugging away at someone – you've got to think about what you are doing. It develops mental toughness and confidence which helps in everyday life.' Claiming utilitarian functions for boxing was, of course, nothing new, although more common had been to root these in an understanding of the sport as one for the underprivileged. Typical was Barry Jones, who remarked in 1997 that because of boxing, 'I've never been in trouble with the police. It's an individual sort of sport but it's kept me off the streets and out of trouble.'

Keeping 'boys off the street' is the explicitly stated aim of Swansea's famed Gwent Boxing Club, which has developed over fifty years into one of the formative influences in the communities of Town Hill and Mayhill. Just like the Newbridge club, first visited by Joe Calzaghe when he was 10, and the Penyrheol club that recruited the nine-year-old Colin Jones, all the Welsh clubs, from Aberaman ABC to Ynysybwl and Glyncoch ABC, recruit young boys and girls, hoping to turn them into prizewinners, ABA champions and quite possibly professionals. At the peak of the amateur world is the Welsh team, which trains at army camps under a national coach whose ambition is to produce Olympic and Commonwealth medal-winners.

Nevertheless, the dangers of the sport inevitably attract criticism. No boxer is unaware of the dangers, but to dwell on them is to misread boxing. As Calzaghe put it,

> I look on boxing as an art. People who are ignorant only see the brutality, but if they were to sit down and watch proper boxing, they'd begin to appreciate the skill of being able to hit and not be hit. I'm proud that

I've managed to keep my features intact. I'm proud that my face hasn't been smashed and that there's no scar tissue around my eyes. Why is that? Am I really that lucky? I don't believe so. I'm just good at what I do. When I spar I always let the other fighter come to me and I get pleasure from making him miss, being slick and moving like a snake, out-thinking him and making the right moves and having the nerve to execute all that in the ring against a live opponent. That's boxing and that's the art.

By the start of the twenty-first century, fewer and fewer people fully appreciate the subtleties of that art because they have not boxed themselves, while the banishment of the sport's best practitioners to pay-per-view television means that few have the opportunity to see that art at work. And yet the rewards for those practitioners who make it to the top are higher than ever, especially if they indulge in outlandish behaviour and spectacular punching, and their personality feeds a wider craving for celebrity. But whether those rewards are sustainable, and whether the sport itself can survive in an age that is increasingly regulated and safety-conscious, is questionable. In sum, Wales may never produce another fighter of Calazaghe's calibre again because his sport may fade as its art becomes less relevant, less valued and less seen.

Afterword: Fighting On

PETER STEAD, GARETH WILLIAMS AND DAI SMITH

The year 2008 was Calzaghe's. Those reporters and pundits analysing either the sport of boxing or, more generally, the Welsh cultural scene, continuously cranked up the rhetoric as they attempted to decide just how great and significant was this boxer from Newbridge whose image featured so regularly on our screens and on both front and back pages. As the prospect of a bout at New York's Madison Square Garden emerged, the *Western Mail*'s Delme Parfitt slipped in his verdict that Joe Calzaghe was 'Wales's greatest ever sportsman'. Earlier in the year Wales's leading boxing authority, Lord Brooks of Tremorfa, President of the British Boxing Board of Control, had more thoughtfully moved towards a less strident conclusion. He saw Joe as 'the best Welsh fighter since World War Two, if not the best British fighter', but then added: 'Even more than that, he has to be considered one of the best of all time after going undefeated for nineteen years'.

As Joe Calzaghe reflected on his very personal sporting achievements he was left in no doubt that not only was he fighting for the Welsh nation, he was in the process of defining a new era for his country. It is a characteristic of Wales that it willingly embraces celebrity and allows its mood to be determined by the reported successes of a whole range of showbiz and sporting personalities. By way of defence Wales can claim that it is well able to distinguish between ephemeral fame and true excellence. In sport in particular, the cognoscenti pride themselves that only the truly great and internationally-acclaimed stars are awarded the status of performers whose individual genius confirms a general national identity. In 2008 a whole nation basked in Calzaghe's hard- and newly-won American fame.

Older fans recalled the fame of Winstone, Dower or Farr, but in truth there had been nothing like this media promotion of boxing since the halcyon days of Driscoll, Welsh and Wilde. The ubiquity and persistence of today's mass media gave Calzaghe a glamour that was probably unprecedented, but in many respects the careers of all the Welsh fighters of 2008 (and for a while in the middle of the year it seemed as if every week saw a Welsh fighter either defending or challenging for a title) reminded us that little had changed as far as the fundamentals of the sport were concerned. The *Daily Mail* printed a photo of the ringside seats at Calzaghe's Las Vegas fight against Bernard Hopkins. There in close and rapt proximity were Catherine Zeta Jones, Tom Jones, Sylvester Stallone, Bruce Willis and Arnold Schwarzenegger. In boxing it was ever thus: the nobility patronized the prizefighters, Hollywood always sustained the Los Angeles fights and in New York no fight crowd was complete without its film stars and politicians. Calzaghe had brought back the glamour to his sport, but how many of his new-found friends could imagine the conditions in which he had prepared for his fight?

In general we can conceive of the familiar route taken by rising rugby and soccer stars. Boxers make their way into the public eye after emerging from a different world. It is a world known only to the small boxing fraternity and to enthusiasts of American popular culture. Writers like Budd Schulberg and Leonard Gardner have accustomed their readers to the stale pungent smells and rhythmic sounds of seedy boxing gyms that seem to be the same in whichever unfashionable neighbourhood they are to be found. In recent years the leading boxers of Wales have had their new followers taking out the map to check on the location of Bonymaen, Cwmbran and Blackwood. The Cardigan-shire farmer and successful middleweight Alan Jones does twelve hours' work with his herd before training in his own Llan-non cowshed. Meanwhile in the valleys and towns Welsh boxers pound the roads and hills on their own before returning to concrete and corrugated iron gyms that seem more suited to demolition than to visits by London reporters and photographers. Joe Calzaghe has never romanticized his sport. Boxing for him is 'just a job' and one that he first trained for on the edge of town in a tin shack perched precariously over the river Ebbw.

That town, Newbridge, is situated halfway between Abercarn and Crumlin going north, and between Blackwood to the west and Cwmbran to the east, and was created in order to accommodate workers from the North and South Celynen collieries whose miners' lodges were militant off-shoots of the South Wales Miners' Federation. But as well as being a coal township it is historically, as its quarry cliffs remind us, a town of stone. Nearly all valleys buildings, from community halls to terraced houses, are to a greater or lesser extent constructed of the Pennant sandstone

212

which was quarried on an enormous scale in this locality. 'Its texture is hard, making it impossible to cut to a smooth face,' notes the Gwent/ Monmouthshire volume in *The Buildings of Wales* (2000). It could be talking about Joe Calzaghe. And just as, from Blaenavon to Blackwood, the county's workmen's institutes are among its most striking architectural features, so they are all, including the one at Newbridge, stylistically hybrid, combining classical, Gothic, and rough-hewn elements: that's Calzaghe, too.

Newbridge's sloping, winding High Street is lined by chapels, a church, the Workmen's Institute (opened in 1908), with the huge, near-derelict Memorial Hall (1924) behind it, hostelries, and a betting shop (where Calzaghe, father and son, are still regularly to be seen), all institutions of the kind that have repeatedly featured in the lives of the fighters in this book. It is difficult not to see in the large burial ground of nearby Beulah Baptist Chapel, with its unusually regular array of headstones, a symbolic representation of Joe Calzaghe's unbroken sequence of defeated opponents over the last nineteen years. The very names of Newbridge's first architects – Gasenius Lewis, Swash and Bain, Abbs and Wippell – are aptly descriptive of the local hero who has swashed, bained and wippelled his way to the world's top flight.

'I'm a boxer, a guy from the Welsh valleys,' he tells us. The industrial valleys of Gwent, as we saw in our opening essay, produced prize-fighters tempered by the heat of the forges and furnaces where the labour was hard and physical. The 'Butcher Boy', 'Stitcher Bach' and Daniel Desmond never lived to see their legacy taken up by later fighting Gwentians like Johnny Basham, Dick Richardson, David Pearce and Joe Calzaghe, nor would they perhaps have appreciated the cultural shift masked by that chronological leap whereby 'prizefighting', as the county newspaper put it in 1868, was 'no longer looked on as a test of courage, but as brutal work'. Joe Calzaghe never knew that earlier phase; he was courageous, but never brutal.

Calzaghe's *No Ordinary Joe* (2007), written 'with Brian Doogan', is unlikely to be the last ghost-written sports autobiography (the 1816 *Memoirs* of Daniel Mendoza were the first) but Joe's Newbridge could indeed be the last of the boxing nurseries to produce Welsh world title holders. The Cwmcarn gymnasium where he and his fellow champions

Enzo Maccarinelli, Gavin Rees, Gary Lockett and Bradley Price work out under the watchful eye of Calzaghe senior is a crumbling bastion of a once-defining valleys' masculinity in the face of imposed economic decline, unwelcome social change and maybe an impending cultural anonymity. Is the essence of Calzaghe's appeal that he puts emotionally restrained modern men and women in touch with their ancestral selves and a more barbaric past? 'Boxing,' to quote Joyce Carol Oates who provided the epigraph that prefaces this book, 'at its moments of greatest intensity . . . seems to contain so complete and powerful an image of life – in its beauty, vulnerability, despair, incalculable and often destructive courage – that [it] *is* life, and hardly a mere game.' Exactly. Joe Calzaghe played football at Pentwyn-mawr Juniors; he has never 'played' boxing. But at the same time he embodies the paradox that is at its heart, that its essentially primitive nature makes it the most complex of sports, offering savagery, skill, courage and vivid ritual in equal measure.

Joe Calzaghe's long career has encompassed all of these, and it is closing in an explosive climax that has eclipsed the frustration of his early fighting years. Its end might yet come to overshadow all of the great Welsh boxers who preceded him. He has already had his 'career-defining' fight, the perfect storm of speed and percussion against the bewildered American Jeff Lacy in 2006 – 'Everything came together . . . it was better than knocking him out' – but, in 2008, with Bernard Hopkins's brand of mental thuggery and physical intimidation dismantled on American soil, you sense that Joe knows an American Trilogy will seal the deal and finally silence any malign critics still lingering, on either side of the Atlantic, who had once written the Newbridge boxer down as a strictly home-turf warrior.

The tension between that America where reputations are made as fact and where Calzaghe was actually made culturally – in 'American Wales', a shorthand for our industrial past whose meaning still reverberates within this sport – resonates through his whole career as it did for Driscoll, Welsh, Wilde, and Farr. In his autobiography he dances around and between the possibilities as gracefully and as tantalizingly as he moves, in and out and out of reach and back again, in a whirring blur of gloves to deceive and punish his opponents. Hopkins? Wright? Taylor? Roy Jones? He would, at one time, have fought them all, he says. But then again, why should he bother? 'I never really had the urge to go to America to fight . . . This is where I live and my attitude was . . . that they could come over . . . here to fight me . . . I've never felt like I had to go there for the history . . . and I don't think my career could ever be classed . . . as a disappointment if I never fought in America'. Yet, and without drawing breath, even before Hopkins and Las Vegas in the spring of 2008, he switch hits: 'My future, I hope, will be in America . . . cementing my legacy . . . I'd like to fight in America . . . even once . . . just to show them that there's been a great fighter in the Welsh Valleys all these years'.

Even once is already enough. Even twice could be better than enough. The sense of a need for completion is palpable in all he now says and does. How could it be otherwise for a driven sportsman whose boyhood idolatry, now wonderfully reciprocated, was reserved for Sugar Ray Leonard, a ringman as athletic and as handsome, unmarked and photogenic, as Calzaghe himself? And besides, Joe's one true begetter as a master craftsman is his feisty Sardinian father Enzo, a character study for a Philly Italian cornerman misplaced in Gwent and worshipper at the dazzling feet and hands of Muhammad Ali and Marvin Hagler. Style is the common theme, a compound of pace and power and, stunningly, of the unteachable gift of the will-to-win, of heart itself. The mix, for Joe Calzaghe, seems to have been as aesthetic ('I see boxing as an art. Hit and not to be hit') as it was genetic ('I have the heart of a fighter . . . this is what I was born to do'). And, maybe, too, it really is cultural – '. . . sometimes it seems like it was all mapped out for me' – and Sardinia needed to find Wales for it to happen.

An individual journey has almost come to its conclusion. What it lit up in the hearts and minds of his ever growing band of fans cannot now ever be dimmed. Enzo and Joe seem to have always known how it could end, and perhaps how, for the son, it should end. In any case this boxer has booked a rightful place in any pantheon of Welsh greats, their legacy now his. A wider inheritance from Joe Calzaghe to those who will fight on must – in a Wales as long gone as the closed Celynen collieries which once created Newbridge and as distant as the triumphant Miners' Strike in his birth year of 1972 – be a moot point. And yet, what is without doubt is that the ferocious pride and intelligent skills of this truly remarkable winner, outstanding even in a long line of

215

Welsh champions, has shown us again how fighting traditions can be upheld and values translated from generation to generation. One way or the other, sons also rise.

INDEX

Monmouthshire 10
Montgomeryshire 6
Montreal 36, 190
Moody, Frank 58, 95, 103
Moody, Glen 58, 95
Moody brothers 58
Moore, Pal 67–8
Moran, Owen 27, 29
Morgan, Cliff 188
Morgan, Dan 114
Morgan, Darren (the 'Beast of Bonymaen') 185
Morgan, Griffith (Guto Nyth Brân) 5
Morgan, John 7–8
Morris, Darrin 183
Morris, John 7
Morriston 121, 122
Moses, Glyn 53
Mountain Ash 15, 28
Mullan, Harry 191
Muller, Heine 73–4, 80, 82, 84
Murray, Al 'Battling' 63
Mussolini, Benito 151
Myfyr Wyn, *see* Williams, William

Napolese, Jose 173
Nash, John 8
National Police Gazette 39
National Sporting Club (NSC) 23, 24, 25, 26, 28, 30, 37, 45, 60, 61, 63, 64, 65, 66, 68, 170, 173
National Stadium (Cardiff) 200
Naval colliery (Penygraig) 89
Nazareth House (Cardiff) 25, 29, 30
Neate, Bill 6
Neath 4
Neilson, Eddie 172, 173, 175
Nelson, Johnny 179
Neusel, Walter 84, 94, 95–6
New Orleans 15
New York 24, 36, 42, 48–9, 50, 52, 68, 69, 76, 81, 97, 98, 100, 137, 212
New Yorker 5
Newbridge 181, 200, 205, 206, 207, 211, 212–13, 214, 215
Newcastle 195
Newman, Paul 106
Newport 8, 11, 137, 143, 144, 176, 191
Newport Pagnell 10

Newtown (Cardiff) 20, 25, 28, 30
Ninian Park (Cardiff) 73, 74, 75, 76, 80, 81, 82, 107, 137, 154, 186
Nipper, Matt Wells's 62
Niro, Robert de 106
No Ordinary Joe 213, 214–15
Nolan, Joe 11
Norris, Leslie 130–1
North Wales Gazette 6
Northey, Jack 11–12, 15
Nottingham Ice Rink 106
Nurse, Herbie 119
Nutter, Kid 62

Oates, Joyce Carol 68, 119, 214
O'Brien, Donald 39
Observer 181
Occupation: Prizefighter: The Freddie Welsh Story 53
Octoroon, The 126
Odd, Gilbert 147
O'Leary, Paul 127
Olson, Carl 'Bobo' 106
Olympia (London) 38, 43–4, 80
Olympic Auditorium (Los Angeles) 156
On the Waterfront 105
O'Neill, Dan 86, 146, 147, 174
Out-fighting or Long-range Boxing 27
Owen, Daniel 124–5
Owen, Dick 157, 160
Owen, Dickie 47
Owen, Johnny 109, 155–61, 198, 205
Owen family 159, 160–1
Owens, Tom 6

Padden, Billy 60
Palacio, Ruben 195
Palacio, Wilson 199
Palais de Danse (Pontypridd) 184
Palermo, Michele 108
Palmer, Pedlar 63, 112
Papke, Billy 114
Parfitt, Delme 211
Parkinson, Rod 173
Partridge, Bill 79
Pastrano, Willie 142
Paterson, Jackie 105
Patterson, Floyd 142
Pavilion (Ferndale) 57